The Phoenix Picturehouse:
100 Years of Oxford Cinema Memories

A selection of brochures collected by Mary Elphic and Jan Hagerty.
Photograph by Rob Hardy.

THE
PHOENIX
PICTUREHOUSE

100 YEARS OF
OXFORD CINEMA MEMORIES

Deborah Allison, Hiu M. Chan and Daniela Treveri Gennari

London

First published 2013

Picturehouse Publications, London
A division of Picturehouse Cinemas Ltd.
www.picturehouses.co.uk

A CIP catalogue record for this book is available from the British Library.

ISBN 978-0-9926461-0-3

Designed by Paul Stapleton, www.psstudio.co.uk
Printed in England by Aquatint BSC

This book is printed on acid-free paper

Front cover photograph: The Phoenix (formerly known as The Scala) re-opens as Studio 1 & 2 on 28 December 1970. Courtesy of Oxford Mail/The Oxford Times (Newsquest Oxfordshire).

Back cover photograph: The Phoenix Picturehouse in 2013. Courtesy of Picturehouse Cinemas.

This book was researched and compiled with assistance from **Oxford Mail**

Contents

For those in love with *Cinema Paradiso*, *The Purple Rose of Cairo* and *The Smallest Show on Earth*, this is the real thing. Just set in Oxford...

Jeremy Smith
Group Features Editor, The Oxford Times and Oxford Mail

Acknowledgements

This history of The Phoenix has been a truly collaborative effort, with an enormous number of people contributing in various ways. We are particularly grateful to contributor and consultant David Parkinson and to our historical consultant Ian Meyrick for sharing their wealth of knowledge, expertise, and memorabilia. The support received from staff and students of the Film Studies department at Oxford Brookes University has also proved invaluable; we would particularly like to thank reminiscence group leader Colin Clarke and research volunteers Sean Kelly, Caitlin Quigley, and Leyla Richardson.

The story of the cinema is really a patchwork of personal stories—those of its proprietors, staff, and customers—and we are delighted that so many have shared their tales. In describing the cinema's earliest days, the passing years might have left us with little in the way of first-hand accounts had we not had the fortune to meet former employee Martin Selwood (a lively and active playwright, novelist, and songwriter, who is approaching his own centenary) and the family of the late Syd Taylor. Mr. Taylor was, by all accounts, an exceptional man for whom cinema represented just one of his passionate interests and wide fields of knowledge. A childhood patron and later employee, he recorded detailed accounts of his experiences at The Phoenix (then trading as The Scala). Some have provided material for news articles and for Paul Marriott's 1978 pamphlet, *Early Oxford Picture Palaces*; by courtesy of Syd's son and daughter-in-law Ken and Irene Taylor, and granddaughter Lisa, we believe others appear here for the first time.

In researching the early days, we have also been greatly assisted by Linn Harmer, Peter and Christine Jay, David and Julie Parker, and Genevieve Poole, all of whom have shared memories and photographs of family members who played their part in the cinema's development. We are also indebted to *The Oxford Times* and *Oxford Mail* for allowing us to reproduce so many items from their archive, and would like to acknowledge the help and support of features editor Jeremy Smith and librarian Chris McDowell. We extend further thanks to Michael Riordan, archivist at St. John's College, Oxford; Chris Gilliam, archivist at the Oxfordshire History Centre; Jonny Davies, co-ordinator (special collections) at the BFI National Archive; and Martin Humphries, director of The Cinema Museum, for rooting out materials from their collections, and to those institutions for permitting their reproduction.

When compiling our account of later years, we were spoilt for choice of material, thanks to the quantity and quality of reminiscences and materials shared with us. The recollections of interviewees Kitty Cooper, Lyn Goleby, John Hughes, Tony Jones, Alastair Oatey, Bob Ord, David Powell, Mike Vickers, and Jim Wright are particularly prominent in these pages, but we are no less grateful to our other interviewees and reminiscence group members: Marc Allenby, Alison Bentley, Clare Binns, Judy Brown, Ann Cole, Jonathan Flint, Timothy Gee, June Parker, Michael Robinson, Jim Tallett, Mike Warner, and Steve Wiener. We would also like to thank Christopher Bird, Elaine Blerkom, Bernie Burgess, Alison Gomm, Anthony 'Grim' Hall, Catherine Hounslow, Ian Hunter, Winifred Jones, James Leheny, Patricia Marshall, Patrick Moles, Claire Monk, Kyna Morgan, Ron Nicholson, Alan North, Philip Pullman, Sylvia Saunders, Peter Schofield, Martin Tapsell, Julia Woods, and Sharon Woodward for their letters and emails.

Many customers (and several past and present staff members) were kind enough to complete one of our centenary questionnaires. We are as indebted to the many anonymous and pseudonymous respondents as we are to Karin André, Sue Bateman, Peter Bicknell, Jeannie Bincliffe, Anton Bitel, G. R. Bowman, Anne Brau, Diana Brown, Jane Lavender Brown, Margaret and Harry Charlton, Seonaid Danziger, H. Dell, Scott Ellis, JoJo Goodfellow, William Goodfellow, Christopher Gowers, Michael Gross, Ronald Hammond, Helen Hawan, J. Hibbs and D. Payne, Catherine Hilliard, Clem Houston, Glyn Humphreys, Theodora Hunter, Robin Jacoby, Martin Jennings, Jesse Jones, Denis Kane, KJ Keating Doyle, Roy Kennedy, Paul Lenz, Frankie McGowan, A. Mackrell, F. Marks, Dianna Marsh, Jeffrey Miller, St. John O'Rorke, Monica Payne, Diane Pearson, Rosemary Pountney, Susanna Pressel and James Fry, Jan Rae, Rita Reale, Philippa Redman, Steve Rolfe, Elisabeth Salisbury, Angela Stack, Harry Steedman, Tim Treacher, Patricia White, and Arthur Wickson. Some cinemagoers completed the questionnaire orally, and we apologise if any names have been misspelled. To anyone who believes they've been missed out: you may have opted not to share your full name, or we may have messed up. Whatever the circumstance, please do get in touch if you would like to see your credit added or corrected in any future edition.

Further thanks go to Pat Church, Sam Clements, Mary Elphic, Jan Hagerty, Rob Hardy, Stuart Jarvis, Martin Jennings-Wright, Ric Mellis, Matt Taylor, James Webster, Liz Woolley, and Ollie Wright for sharing photographs and memorabilia—some of which is reproduced in this volume, with the balance providing an invaluable research resource.

For their contributions to the production of this volume, our especial thanks go to designer Paul Stapleton and cover designer Hassen Rasool. We would also like to acknowledge the advice and support of Jane Kelly and Brian Kinsey from our printers Aquatint BSC, Mark Wealthy from Picturehouse Cinemas, and James Harrison from Oxfordfolio.

Others who have assisted the Phoenix Centenary Project in divers ways include Nicky Beaumont, Peter Bestwick, Catherine Bray, Tim Brown, Alisdair Cairns, Ciara Cecil, Steve Chance, Steve Chibnall, Michael Cordner, Helen Davies, David Fisher, Sara Frain, John Fleming, Neil Gardhouse, Kenny Gold, Debbie Granville, Paul Homer, Katherine Hughes, Reg James, Darren Jones, Eric Liknaitzky, Henry K. Miller, Max Moonlight, Emma Mortimore, Martin Myers, Stephen Pill, Rhianne Pope, Harry Rigby, Tim Rogerson, George Sawer, Suzy Sheriff, Richard Sills, Charlotte Spain, Peter Stalker, Jonny Tull, Kiri Walden, Sophie Wilson, Melissa Woodley, and Simon Woplin. The size and nature of their contributions are various, but all have been of benefit and are gratefully received. Last, but by no means least, we wish to express our gratitude to all staff at The Phoenix Picturehouse.

Photographic credits:

These are given with each picture. Every effort has been made to trace the copyright holders of images. If, inadvertently, any copyright holder has not been acknowledged, they are asked to forward details so that a correction can be included in any future edition.

Foreword

It came as something of a shock while I was reading the manuscript of Deborah Allison, Hiu M. Chan and Daniela Treveri Gennari's wonderful history of my favourite cinema to hear that Mel Smith had died. I saw his directorial debut, *The Tall Guy*, at The Phoenix back in 1989 and still remember the laughter that rang out during the hilariously torrid sex scene between Jeff Goldblum and Emma Thompson. Smith had read experimental psychology at New College in the 1970s and I found myself wondering how often he found time between his studies and his involvement with the Oxford University Dramatic Society to pop down to Walton Street to watch a film. What did he see? Did he go alone or with friends? And did he have a preferred seat?

But, of course, Mel Smith is just one of the dozens of Oxford residents and graduates who have made their name in films and it is tempting to speculate how many of them were regular patrons of a venue that is now celebrating its centenary. Donald Crisp had already left Oxford and become an established screen actor in the United States by the time the North Oxford Kinema opened its doors on 15 March 1913, but it is likely that he is the first university alumnus to have appeared on a silver Oxford screen. Maybe a young Laurence Olivier saw Crisp in the 1920s when he was a pupil at St Edward's School in Summertown? Perhaps, in later years Maggie Smith, Ronnie Barker, Hugh Laurie and Emma Watson also took a break from their homework to catch a matinee at what was variously known as The Scala, Studio 1 & 2 and The Phoenix?

The University authorities put The Scala out of bounds to students in

1927 because of their excessive rowdiness at evening screenings. But the ban proved short-lived and one would like to think that writers of the calibre of Graham Greene, Alan Bennett, Dennis Potter, Richard Curtis and Armando Iannucci spent hours in a cocoon of Jericho darkness, along with such directors as Anthony Asquith, Charles Crichton, Roger Corman, Ken Loach and Terrence Malick, and such acting luminaries as Ivor Novello, Richard Burton, Dudley Moore, Terry Jones, Michael Palin, Kris Kristofferson, Michael York, Rowan Atkinson, Hugh Grant, Kate Beckinsale, Emily Mortimer and Rosamund Pike.

Yet, perhaps the most important former patrons of The Scala were those behind *Sequence*, the magazine of the Oxford Film Society, whose first editor was future critic Penelope Houston and whose key contributors were Lindsay Anderson, Tony Richardson, G'vin Lambert and Cambridge import Karel Reisz. This cabal was fortunate enough to have had on its doorstep in the late 1940s a cinema committed to showing foreign-language, as well as the latest mainstream British and American releases and a wide range of repertory titles and revivals. Indeed, this imaginative programming inspired Anderson, Richardson, Reisz and John Schlesinger to start making their own films, many of which were shown in the Free Cinema selections at the National Film Theatre in London, which gave rise in the late 1950s to the social realist style that still dominates much independent British production.

But, while The Phoenix has played its part in shaping of filmmaking in this country, it is even more valuable as a window on the wider world. Although it is a community cinema in the very best sense of the term, this bijou venue has been treating Oxford audiences to the best films ever made since before the Great War. One only has to leaf through Hiu M. Chan's magnificent tome *100 Years at The Phoenix: Archive of an Oxford Cinema 1913-2013* to see how many masterpieces, classics, favourites, sleepers and curios have been shown here. The odd turkey has slipped through along the way, but audiences have come to trust the programming and that is why The Phoenix is held in such esteem by so many. It's also a landmark in its own right, hence, Studio 2 proving pivotal to the Inspector Morse mystery, *The Silent World of Nicolas Quinn*, a v the time it was filmed for television in 1987, the picture the susp had changed from the fictitious skinflick, *The Nymphomaniac*, to the more sophisticated, if still contentious *Last Tango in Paris* (Bernardo Bertolucci, 1972).

My own first visit to The Phoenix came when I was an 18-year-old undergraduate in October 1979. I saw Robert Altman's scathing social comedy, *A Wedding* (1978), with fellow Mertonian Chris Chambers, whose knowledge and judgement led me to discover that Oxford was actually the City of Dreaming Screens, as The Phoenix, The Penultimate Picture Palace, Not the Moulin Rouge and, what were then, The ABCs on George Street and Magdalen Street gave me a cinematic education that later enabled me to become a critic. I still remember the excitement of attending press shows in the early 1980s, when I started reviewing for Kate Lock at *The Oxford Star*. Nor shall I ever forget the friendly welcome invariably extended by such staff stalwarts as John Hughes, Martin Jennings-Wright, Kathy Mace, Michael Cordner, Katrina Stokes and Matt Taylor.

As I read about the changing regimes and the various renovations that have made The Phoenix what it is today, I realised it has been my local cinema for over a third of its lifetime. During that period, it has come to seem like a home from home and the majority of those who took the trouble to answer the questionnaire about their Phoenix experience clearly felt the same. Indeed, it was deeply satisfying to discover that so many people shared my love of the old place, with the charming contribution of Winifred Jones (née Goodwin; see page 65) encapsulating its significance to both Oxford and its permanent and passing populations.

When I first set foot in the foyer 34 years ago, video was in its infancy and the only places to see classic films were on television and in cinemas like The Phoenix. Nowadays, the ever-expanding range of home entertainment formats means it is easier than ever before to see pictures from all times and places. But there is something reassuring about the fact that people from Oxford and the surrounding county still prefer to see these gems on a big screen in like-minded company. One would like to think that digital technology will help independents revisit their glory days by making a wide range of new and repertory titles available at affordable prices, as cinema will only survive as an art form if new talents are inspired to make the classics of tomorrow. The Phoenix has been doing its bit for a century. Let's hope it continues to do so for many years

David Parkinson
Oxford, July 2013

Preface

Recently, a gentleman came in to buy a movie ticket. I recognised him immediately, as he is a regular. He said to me, "I have been coming to this cinema for decades, you know. I only come here to watch a picture, nowhere else. The kiosk used to be over there, and the movie tickets used to be handwritten…" And there, he began to tell me the whole story of the cinema. It was then I realised that this historic building holds special memories for a lot of our customers.

Many customers treat The Phoenix like a second home. They know about all the films we show, and know each of us behind the kiosk. I recognise most of the regulars; each has their own style, and talks about films in their own tones. If anyone were to shoot a documentary of The Phoenix, the range of dynamic characters coming through its doors would amaze you. In the meantime, we hope our book will play its part in conveying the essence of this very special place.

Hiu M. Chan
Oxford, August 2013

Dear Phoenix Picturehouse staff

I'm writing this on my return from yet another visit to The Phoenix, having been reminded that I'd forgotten to complete the Phoenix memories questionnaire Ben gave me at the Jericho Street Fair.

I say forgotten; more accurately, I'd put it aside on the grounds that I couldn't come up with a gem of an experience to contribute to your centenary celebrations. But, sitting in Screen 1 this evening, I realised that that's the whole point: for me The Phoenix isn't a special occasion/unique experience kind of place—it's part of the backdrop of my life, and has been ever since I moved to Jericho as a student eighteen years ago.

First I visited with gaggles of friends, tumbling in from a backstreet pub (late-night screenings were the order of the day). Then came visits with my folks, after they retired and moved in up the road. (My darling dad was moved to burst into spontaneous applause during Jane Austen's Emma, at the moment when gallant Mr. Knightley steps in to dance with wallflower Harriet Smith). Next came visits with my boyfriend (the landscapes in Mongol as wide as my in-love smile). Then Kids' Club with my little girl (sticky from glueing with Hiu and Natalie, and stuffed with popcorn—always salty once she'd realised I wouldn't want to share if it wasn't sugary). Then heartbreak, and the medicine of solitary, delicious matinees on days off work. And now I love them best, my solitary visits: I can lose myself in the film, come to in my own time rather than feel wrenched back by a companion eager to know my verdict as the credits rise. New releases, classics and, live from the National Theatre, the piercing sad sweetness of Benedict Cumberbatch's monster in Frankenstein—there's so much to be relished.

Nor is The Phoenix just about film, for me. The first piece of art I ever bought came from the Phoenix bar: a collage created from discarded OUP fly covers, which spoke to me as I sat with a drink and a friend. On my sitting room wall, it speaks to me still.

Your cinema is full of memories for me. It also holds the promise of more in the making. Thank you to you all for the warm welcome I always receive.

Kindest regards,

Julia Woods
November 2012

Introduction

The Phoenix Picturehouse has always been far more than just a building equipped with seats, a screen, and a couple of projectors. As the memories and experiences so many customers have shared with us make clear, it is also a site of pleasure, learning, social interaction, and escape: in the words of Rita Reale, "a place of necessary sanctuary."[1] Time and again, such comments underscore the extent to which this cinema, and the films and facilities it has offered over the years, stands both typical and unique among its fellows.

The history of The Phoenix (formerly the North Oxford Kinema, The Scala, and Studio 1 & 2) illustrates two very different but interconnected things. On the one hand, The Phoenix can be seen as representative of 100 years of British cinema and cinemagoing history, which has followed broader social, artistic, and technological trends. On the other, it is an absolute one-off, belonging solely to its North Oxford environment: an institution shaped by the specific input of a sequence of individual operators in synergy with the loyal and active participation of local residents and film enthusiasts.

The Phoenix is one of only a handful of British cinemas that can lay claim to having been continuously open for 100 years (bar a few fleeting intermissions for refurbishment and such like). Its longevity means it has stood its ground through a string of notable phases and landmarks in local, national, and cinematic history. In the process of researching this book, we have learned far more than we ever anticipated, and have come to view The Phoenix as a gateway into a broader understanding and appreciation of its place and times.

Cinema and social history

When we started our research in 2011, we did so with a relatively narrow focus in mind: to collect and share information about the operation of this particular cinema and the ways people have experienced it. As we went along, it became increasingly obvious that this activity paralleled far wider fields of research, in which we hope our account will come to play its part.

We learned, in particular, just how far the history of The Phoenix can be viewed as a case study of British society across the past 100 years. Historical variations in the films it has shown, changes to the building as a physical and liminal space, and the ways customers have engaged with it (what, when, why, and with whom they have attended, and to what effect) all contribute to a broader portrait of the era.

We can, of course, learn much about British (and international) society from films themselves. In recent decades, screen studies have spread widely across further and higher education. As well as examining film forms and techniques, and the industrial structures underlying their production, distribution, and exhibition, film scholarship has, from the very start, looked on movies as offering insights into current and historical attitudes to events occurring off screen. Examples range from wartime propaganda to contemporary representations of class conflict and urban decay. Indeed, long before film studies began to gain acceptance as an academic discipline, the more insightful critics often highlighted what they saw as the implicit import of popular movies—perhaps none more famously than Balliol alumnus Graham Greene, whose comments about the licentious appeal of child actress Shirley Temple landed his publisher on the losing end of a lawsuit.[2]

Running parallel with this area of study (and taking place largely outside the academy) has been a fascination with the history of cinema architecture. In Britain, the Cinema Theatre Association (which has supported the production of many books, as well as publishing *Picture House* magazine, building up an archive, and organising cinema tours) has been a focal point for learning in this area. Changing architectural models (from the motion picture palaces of the silent era to the more utilitarian venues of later years, and from the multiplexes that first arrived in the mid-1980s to the 'boutique' single- and multi-screen cinemas popular today) are intimately connected to the different kinds of viewing experiences sought and gained by cinema patrons. Such changes in fashion have informed the successive structural and decorative alterations The Phoenix has undergone.

In recent years, film studies has broadened its scope to include audience experience as a major area of interest—as Daniela Treveri Gennari elaborates in her essay, 'A Place Like Home.' Although we have endeavoured to chart the history of The Phoenix from a variety of perspectives (including material about its programming, architecture, technical facilities, and business operation), this, and the attempts of the cinema's various operators to respond to and improve on audience experience, has always remained at the heart of the story we set out to tell. The memories woven throughout this book are more than frills and frippery; they are its very fabric.

The Phoenix: one of many, and yet one of a kind

The Phoenix has had a rich and colourful history. In many ways, it embodies the changing norms of the British cinema sector. At the same time, the innovations introduced by its various operators in their attempts to gain competitive advantage in the local marketplace have ensured it has always been looked upon as a site of unique experience.

The range of film product shown has always been, to some degree, typical of the times, as David Parkinson demonstrates in his sprightly survey, 'The Phoenix History of World Cinema.' We can find examples in the programmes of short fiction and 'topical' films screened in its earliest days; in the continental art films so fashionable for students in the 1950s and 1960s; and in the low-budget sex films of the 1970s. (Those readers interested in learning more may also wish to download *100 Years at The Phoenix*, Hiu M. Chan's near-complete archive of its 21,000-odd films, from phoenixcentenary.wordpress.com.) Nevertheless, the cinema's longevity as a dominantly art-house venue sets it apart from the crowd. Its reputation in this field has been closely aligned with a sequence of individual operators, which is one reason we have allotted substantial space to them in our history.

During the past decade, technological development has had an enormous impact on cinema programming, both at The Phoenix and else-where. The spiralling number of platforms through which films can be accessed (cinemas; free-to-air and subscription television; DVD and BluRay; digital download) has contributed to changes in viewing habits, which have in turn influenced the range and balance of what cinemas show. At the same time, the emergence of live satellite broadcasts has broadened the types of entertainment on offer, as operas, ballets, and other cultural forms have come to sit alongside 'traditional' film shows.

The various ways in which attending The Phoenix has fitted into the social activities of generations of viewers also partake of more wide-spread historical patterns. Some of these have remained the same for almost a century—children have always tried to sneak into films the censors have decreed them too young to watch, while courting couples have always enjoyed getting close in the dark. Others have changed over the years, in parallel with wider cultural shifts. For instance, attend-ance was far more regular in the days before the prevalence of television ownership, when there were far fewer forms of low-cost entertainment on offer. In those years, household budgets and the relative pricing of different commodities meant that many looked on going to the pictures not merely as a leisure activity but also as a relatively cheap way to keep warm during wintertime.

While the accounts of cinemagoing experience related to us by Phoe-nix customers are often indicative of their various generations, many also share a sense of what it means to attend the cinema within a particular lo-cale. This goes beyond the particularities of the venue itself, and extends to the Jericho area and to Oxford as a city. Such comments impart some fascinating details about the changing nature of this wider environment.

An anecdote related by Sylvia Saunders is a case in point. Her brief paragraph combines description of an unidentified film (of the type that probably wouldn't be made anymore) with an account of the social at-titudes displayed by a 1940s audience, an oblique reference to Oxford's famous boat racing traditions, and a titbit of specific local history of which none of this book's authors were previously aware.

This is a story from my late sister-in-law, who was nursing at the old Rad-cliffe at the end of the war, so 1945-47 or thereabouts. Probably now a politi-cally incorrect remark, but at the time she saw Sanders of the River *[Zoltan*

Korda, UK, 1935] *or some such title. A dugout canoe was paddled vigorously down river by a boatload of rather bare and very well-muscled Africans, and a languid upmarket voice cried out, "Oh, well rowed, Balliol." At the time, Balliol was one of the few colleges that had an intake of black students. No comment!*

True enough, such behaviour would be deemed inappropriate these days, but this was Oxford in the 1940s. It was a different time and, indeed, the fact the anecdote has seemed worth retelling three times (to a family member, to us, and finally to you) is indicative of just how effectively reminiscences of attending The Phoenix give insight into a particular social milieu.

Telling the story

In researching this history, our main resource has been the generosity of past and present staff and customers, who have shared experiences of The Phoenix across a period of more than eighty years. In helping us to learn about the cinema's early days, we are also grateful for the help so kindly given by friends and families of staff members who have since passed on. The *Oxford Mail* has been a staunch supporter throughout, helping to publicise our project, and opening its archive to us. A host of other individuals and organisations have found due recognition, we hope, within the acknowledgements.

We were adamant from the start that the history of the cinema should be told in as many different voices as possible. It has, therefore, been drawn primarily from a combination of interviews (conducted in person and by telephone), letters, emails, questionnaire responses, and reminiscence group discussion. These accounts have been supplemented and contextualised by Hiu M. Chan's painstaking assembly of a century of film schedules (drawn mainly from listings in *The Oxford Times*), alongside other oddments of archival and scholarly research. Photographs and documents lent by customers, staff, and cinema historians have also proved an enormous asset; through them we were able to access a great deal of material not previously in the public domain, and are delighted to be able to share much of it with you here.

In endeavouring to present a range of different voices, we have chosen to quote extensively (in preference to paraphrase), with the longer passages of first-hand recollection appearing in italic type. In editing the material, we have striven to preserve the varying cadences of the original speech or written form; while we have made occasional concessions to standardising punctuation, we have generally left syntax alone. When drawing excerpts from longer sources, we have not always highlighted elisions. Moreover, some passages are presented out of their original chronology, but (we trust) never out of context. We hope our correspondents and interviewees will forgive us these few tweaks, which were rooted solely in our desire to promote ease of reading and to minimise areas of duplication.

We have divided the book into two parts: a chronological account of the cinema's changing fortunes; and a collection of commentaries on its significance as a window on the world from what many regulars think of as a home from home.

Part One, compiled by Deborah Allison, begins with the story of the early, silent years, during which the cinema changed hands frequently, as successive owners struggled to find a successful business model. Later chapters focus on four operators of longer tenure, each of whom brought their own changes to the cinema. In each case, we have sought to tell the story from a combination of business and customer perspectives. Staff members describe what successive managements endeavoured to achieve, and, quite often, the gaps between their ambitions and the economic possibilities, while customers recall the pros and cons of those realities.

Opening Part Two, David Parkinson's condensed history of a century of movies is both informative and nostalgic, as he takes us on a whirlwind tour of the cornucopia of films that have brightened Walton Street. Next, Daniela Treveri Gennari draws on well over a hundred questionnaire responses to present an illuminating account of what The Phoenix has meant, and continues to mean, to those it serves. We end with a celebration of The Phoenix by those best placed to comment: its customers. We hope you will enjoy their reminiscences as much as we have done.

Part One
History

Chapter One

Early Years: 1913–1930

The age of silent film was a difficult and highly unstable one for The Phoenix (known variously in this period as the North Oxford Kinema, The Scala, and The New Scala). The kind of programming with which later customers would come to associate the venue didn't begin to take hold until the 1930s. Before that, during its first seventeen years of existence, no less than seven proprietors tried their hand, each bringing their own particular style of operation. We open this chapter with a brief account of how The Phoenix came into being, after which we trace some of the many innovations introduced by successive owners in their struggle to make this patently challenging business flourish.

Pre-cinema history

Located on Walton Street, in the Parish of St Giles, in the Jericho area of Oxford, The Phoenix Picturehouse stands on ground belonging to St John's College, which remains its landlord to the present day. Founded by Sir Thomas White in 1555, St John's owns a great deal of property within Oxford, and the college played an important role in the development of the city's suburbs during the second half of the nineteenth century.[1] In the early 1860s, the college took the decision to augment its existing building programme by developing a sizeable piece of land that was leased, at that time, to a local nurseryman for twenty-six pounds per year. In 1863, surveyor John Fisher laid out the Jericho Gardens estate, creating new roads and splitting the land into plots to be auctioned off on ninety-nine year leases.[2]

Development of the Jericho Gardens estate centred primarily on the creation of upmarket residences, and the pro forma leasehold agreements printed by the college contained a clause prohibiting any commercial use.[3] Walton Street proved an exception to the rule, however, and was developed as a hub for local businesses serving the new community springing up around it.[4] Thus, the lease for Lot no. 4 (on which the cinema now stands) includes several handwritten amendments. These prohibit "manufacture, trade, or business" only if conducted in a "noisy, noisome, or offensive" manner, or if it "in the judgement of the lessors shall be injurious to the health or comfort of the neighbourhood." A final clause appended to this section of the lease insists that the lessee must not "suffer the said premises to be used as a chapel school or place of Public Worship" without prior written permission from the college.[5] Worshippers at the temple of the seventh art can give praise that this clause has been upheld literally but never figuratively!

Lot no. 4 was a long, thin strip of ground measuring 118ft 9in by 17ft 6in, whose narrow side abutted on Walton Street to the east, and which stretched all the way back to the newly built Cranham Terrace. Its south side adjoined the premises of Jericho House, and its north side a plot leased to one Mr. Crapper. On 15 January 1869, Lot no. 4 was leased to Joseph Higgins of the City of Oxford Brewery (the owners of Jericho House) for the princely sum of three pounds per year.[6]

The leasehold on the property saw several changes of ownership through succeeding decades until, in September 1907, it passed to William Abraham Soden, who traded as a chimney sweep from a property next door to the current cinema premises.[7] This family business, established in 1803, and now in its sixth generation, still tends to Oxford's chimneys from its base in Forest Hill.[8]

Richard Henry John Bartlett

Plans to convert the premises to a cinema were established during Mr.

Soden's tenure, and were approved on 27 November 1912 before, on 7 December, he was granted license to assign the lease to Richard Henry John Bartlett, of 229 Banbury Road—an assignment that took place on 6 January 1913.[9] So began Lot no. 4's new incarnation as a motion picture palace.

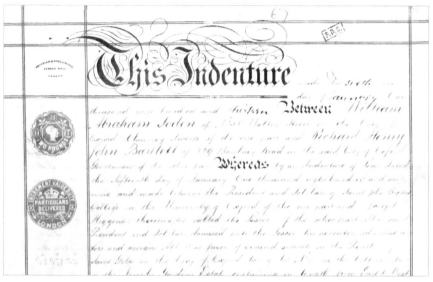

Extract from the 6 January 1913 lease agreement. Reproduced with the permission of the President and Fellows of St John's College, Oxford.

Some months before the property was signed over to Mr. Bartlett as sole lessee, he had already tasked local architect Gilbert T. Gardner (1880-1955) with drawing up plans for what would become known as the North Oxford Kinema.[10] One of Mr. Gardner's biggest challenges was to fit the cinema around a house that remained standing on the plot. This necessitated a relatively narrow entrance and foyer area, before the premises widened to accommodate the auditorium at the rear of the building.

Not a great deal is known about Mr. Bartlett. The lease ledger held in the St John's College archive describes him first as a 'Gentleman' and later (in 1920) as an 'Oxford Land Agent' belonging to Lloyds Bank Chambers, Carfax.[11] Records show that he practised as a law clerk at least as far back as 1882, when he acted as a trustee in a bankruptcy case,

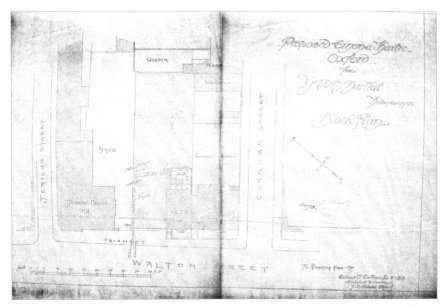

Block Plan of Proposed Cinema Theatre, Oxford, prepared by Gilbert Gardener for R. H. J. Bartlett, November 1912. From Syd Taylor's collection.

and that he remained in this profession as late as 1929.[12] Alongside bankruptcies, his duties ranged from being an executor of wills to Justice of the Peace, and a registrar of births and deaths.[13] He even did a stint as deputy coroner, which saw him embroiled in a court case concerning a labourer crushed to death in a quarry.[14]

The late local historian Paul J. Marriott reports that a Mr. Green became Bartlett's business partner at an early stage.[15] Even less is known about Charles Green, who is not referenced in the lease ledger until July 1920, when he is described as a "secretary to a building society" who resided at 185 Divinity Road. By this stage, Mr. Bartlett had already sold the cinema business to another operator, who promptly took out a mortgage with Bartlett and Green![16]

A 1917 letterhead lists a W. Beeson as their third partner. We have been unable to identify Beeson with certainty, but speculate that he may well have been Walter Thomas Beeson (1862-1947), father of the noted entomologist Cyril Beeson. His lengthy tenure as the St John's College surveyor means he is a person with whom Bartlett and Green would certainly have been professionally acquainted.[17] An obituary in the college magazine notes that Beeson "at the age of 85 was still, at his own insistence, in the employ of the College which he had served faithfully for seventy-one years. It is perhaps not widely known that Mr. Beeson was largely responsible for the modern form of St Giles' Fair, of which he was the manager for many years."[18] If the cinema were indeed an extracurricular activity of this particular Beeson, then his skills and position would have made a good complement to those of Mssrs. Bartlett and Green.

A 1917 letterhead names the proprietors. Courtesy of the Oxfordshire History Centre (catalogue ref. P150/X/2).

Although Mr. Bartlett seems a somewhat unlikely character to be dabbling in the newfangled cinema business, he was undoubtedly the driving force behind this venture. As well as holding the lease on the property, it was Bartlett who commissioned the design and building of the cinema, and it was he to whom prospective employees were directed to apply.[19] Despite being the cinema's proprietor for only a few years, he would retain an association with the business until 1925 (the last few years in the sole capacity of its mortgagee). His departure did not mark the end of his cinema career, however; five months later he would become mortgagee of another Oxford picture house: the now long-gone Electra Palace in Queen Street.[20]

Far more is known about architect Gilbert Gardner, who was responsible for the design of several notable buildings in the area. His great niece, Linn Harmer, has supplied a brief biography along with some personal recollections.

Gilbert Gardner was born in 1880 in the Oxfordshire village of Northmoor. His father was a footman at Barton Abbey and his grandfather a basket maker. They lived in Church Street. Soon after his birth, the family moved to Cambridge Street in St Ebbe's. When he was only two years old, his mother died and the four small boys were brought up in Oxford by their grandmother and unmarried Aunt Rachel, who had been a schoolteacher.

Gilbert Gardner (right) aged twenty, pictured with his family in 1901. Courtesy of Linn Harmer.

He must have shown some promise at the Holy Trinity School, but he is not mentioned in the headmaster's logbook. When he was about seven years old, he became a chorister at Holywell Church, where the Reverend A. Tollit took an interest in him.

The fact that Gilbert could sing was very fortunate for him, as the vicar's father was the county surveyor H. J. Tollit. He took the young Gilbert under his wing and, in 1894, he was articled as a trainee at the practice at 7 St. Aldate's in Oxford. He remained there for the rest of his working life. In due course, he became a partner and a fellow of the Royal Institute of British Architects.

All his academic qualifications (first class honours in building construction and quantity surveying) were gained at the local technical college. In due course, he married Ada and moved to 152 Divinity Road. They had one daughter: Jose-

phine, my godmother. He lived in Divinity Road until the end of his life in 1955.

I remember visiting him there in about 1947. We visited the family every Christmas morning. The grown-ups, including my grandmother and aunt, had a small glass of sherry. My uncle was in his seventies by then, and I remember him as a kindly old gentleman. There were many small ornaments on the mantelpiece, which I, as a small child, longed to touch. However, in the 1940s, children were expected to sit quietly and not be the centre of attention.

Gilbert Gardner is remembered for the design of many Oxford buildings: The Wesley Memorial Hall in New Inn Hall Street, Headington Girls School, The Phoenix Cinema, The Morris Oxford Garage in Long Wall Street, and Greyfriars on Iffley Road. The house where I grew up on Eynsham Road was designed by him as a wedding present for my parents, Gilbert and Grace Gardner, in 1935.[21]

Gilbert Gardner. Courtesy of Linn Harmer.

The new cinema was constructed at impressive speed. On 12 February 1913, *Oxford Journal Illustrated* published a detailed description of 'Oxford's Latest Picture Palace,' which highlighted the care being taken in the provision of safety and comfort to its customers. Fire safety precautions were paramount in an era when films were printed on nitrate stock (a highly flammable substance of a similar chemical composition to nitroglycerine—the active component of gunpowder and dynamite). If a film stuck in the projector gate, the heat generated by the powerful lamp could easily ignite it.

A perturbing number of fatal cinema fires had prompted the introduction of new legislation in 1909, when the Cinematograph Act laid out new safety laws, and played a significant role in shifting film shows from itinerant fairground booths to licensed, permanent premises. It prompted a wave of cinema building across the UK, and spawned five new purpose-built cinemas in Oxford.

The North Oxford Kinema followed hot on the heels of The Electric Palace in Castle Street (opened November 1910; closed 1923; demolished 1968), The Picture Palace in Jeune Street (opened February 1911; closed circa 1918-20, reopened as The Penultimate Picture Palace 1976, later trading briefly as the Section 6 cinema; closed again 1994; re-launched as The Ultimate Picture Palace 1998), The Electra Palace in Queen Street (opened March 1911; closed 1958; demolished 1978), and The Cinematograph in George Street (opened March 1912; closed March 1935).[22]

The puff piece ran:

The latest addition to Oxford's places of amusement is now rapidly approaching completion, and is to be known as the North Oxford Kinema. Situate in Walton-street, in the heart of a thickly populated district, the new theatre will no doubt prove a great convenience both to the residents in the immediate neighbourhood and those farther north. Everything is being done to make the building as up-to-date and convenient as possible. Fire-resisting construction is employed throughout, the upper floors and flats being of re-inforced concrete, and the lantern-room will be fitted with an automatically self-closing fire-proof armoured door. The ceiling of the auditorium will contain no woodwork whatever, the plastering being done on hy-rib metal lathing fixed to steel joists. The roof is covered with 'eternit' fire-proof slates. Consequently the public may rest assured that all danger from fire has, as far as possible, been eliminated.

Special attention is being paid to providing adequate ventilation and comfortable heating. Ample and convenient emergency exits have been arranged. With regard to the seating, comfort has been studied in preference to the usual method adopted of crowding in as many as possible. As to the pictures, the management are making careful preparations for throwing on the screen the most up-to-date films, and no expense is being spared in order to make the pictures the clearest and best to be seen in the provinces.

The steel-work for the building has been supplied by Messrs. Homan and Rodgers, of London. The electric lighting and heating is being carried out by Messrs. Isons, Kidman and Watts, of Oxford, and the building is being erected by Messrs. E. Organ and Son, of 205, Cowley-road, from the designs and under the supervision of Mr. Gilbert T. Gardner, licentiate R.I.B.A.[23]

The emergence of this new building made a big impression on local resident Syd Taylor, who went on to document the following childhood memory:

[I was] born in Juxon St. (just off Walton St.) in May 1909, and it was three years later that, at the age of barely four years old, I was going to be introduced to the first cinema. My grandfather in those days used to take me for walks in the Walton St. area and, one day, I distinctly recall him calling at Burbank's chemist's shop. Coming out of said shop, I remember seeing men working on a building across the road. I asked my grandpa, "What were the men doing there?" He told me he would take me into that building one day to see moving pictures. This completely baffled my very young mind, and I remember saying, "Pictures can't move," whereupon he tried to explain moving pictures. Granddad failed to make me understand just how pictures could move. It was to be another two years before I saw my first moving pictures in that new cinema, or Kinema, as this picture house was called. It was, in fact, named the North Oxford Kinema.[24]

Syd would become a regular customer and, later, the venue's chief projectionist. His lifelong enthusiasm for recording its history in the form of photographs, letters, and interviews, is the basis for much of our knowledge about this cinema's earliest years.

On 15 February, an advertisement appeared in The Oxford Times, advising cinemagoers that the North Oxford Kinema would open in early March, "for the Exhibition of the Newest Pictures."

Four weeks later, and pretty much on schedule, a further newspaper advertisement announced that the North Oxford Kinema would open to the public on Saturday 15 March at 2.30 p.m. This communication

IMES. SATURDAY. FEI

Entertainments.

THE

North Oxford Kinema,

WALTON STREET, Oxford

(Adjoining Jericho House).

WILL BE

Opened for the Exhibition of

the Newest Pictures

EARLY IN MARCH. 1913.

Courtesy of Oxford Mail / The Oxford Times (Newsquest Oxfordshire).

proclaimed that the new venue "will be found to be one of the most comfortable and up-to-date picture palaces in Oxford." In the same edition, an advertisement for the cinema's screening schedule provided further details of opening hours and prices.

NORTH OXFORD KINEMA,
Walton Street.

DAILY at 2.30 (except Good Friday),
CONTINUOUS PERFORMANCES NIGHTLY,
From 6 o'clock till 10.30 p.m.

Special Pictures on Easter Monday,
When there will be continuous Performances
from 1 o'clock till 10.30 p.m.

Prices : 3d., 6d. and 1s.

Courtesy of Oxford Mail / The Oxford Times (Newsquest Oxfordshire).

An anonymous Oxford Times reviewer described the inaugural offering of the North Oxford Kinema as an "attractive programme," further noting that the venue was "comfortably furnished."[25] (Each weekly issue of *The Oxford Times* included a section called 'The Picture Palaces,' featuring reviews of the film programmes running at the city's various cinemas.)

Under the management of William Bex (previously of Flint Picture Hall, North Wales), the North Oxford Kinema boasted continuous performances from Monday to Saturday, with twice-weekly programme changes on Mondays and Thursdays.[26] This practice accorded with the conventions of the time and the venue would adhere to it, by and large, for many years to come.

The North Oxford Kinema, Walton-street, was opened informally on Saturday, and an attractive programme is being shown this week. The building is comfortably furnished with tip-up seats on a sloping floor, and there is accommodation for 500 persons. At the entrance is a vestibule, which is to be transformed into a comfortable lounge. There are two emergency exits, and two wide gangways. The latest type of machine has been installed in a fire-proof operating chamber. The building is well ventilated, fitted with electric light throughout, and heated by gas radiators. The films, which were shown during the first part of this week, included "The Wood Violet," an excellent descriptive Vitagraph drama; "The Trail of Cards," a story of the abduction of a ranch-owner's daughter and her rescue by her lover; and "The Red Cross Nurse," an exciting drama, depicting the robbery of a courier, and the capture of the delinquents through the aid of a nurse. There are also two good scenic films, one depicting a Scandinavian city, and the other the Highlands of Scotland. The comic element is represented by "Friscot and Tweedledum fight a duel," "When hearts are trumps," and "Love-sick maidens." The theatre, which is under the management of Mr. W. Bex, will be closed on Good Friday, but will re-open, as usual, on Saturday. The programme is changed on Mondays and Thursdays, and continuous performances are being given from 2 until 10.30. On Easter Monday a strong programme will commence at one o'clock, and will continue until the usual closing hour.

Courtesy of Oxford Mail/The Oxford Times (Newsquest Oxfordshire).

The Scala in May 1913. From Syd Taylor's collection.

The first extant photograph of Oxford's newest picture palace was taken two months later, on 31 May 1913, by an unknown photographer sited in an upstairs room of the chemist shop over the road. (The black cloth that invariably cloaked cameras of that era has sneaked in to the top of the picture).[27] The photograph shows a uniformed commissionaire waiting outside for the rush of Jericho locals. Headlining the bill, in large letters above the cinema entrance, is *The Spider*.

We presume *The Spider* to be a lost film, as we have been unable to find information about it in modern databases (although at least three other films with the same name were in circulation at around this time). However, a review published in *The Oxford Times* summarises its appeal (and describes other highlights of the supporting programme):

A splendid programme is provided for the weekend at the North Oxford Kine-ma. By special request the management have obtained a thrilling drama by Am-brosia, entitled The Spider. *It tells how the Gold King, who has fallen in love with a Countess, draws the man she loves into his net, and threatens her lover with ruin if she will not marry him. She sacrifices herself for her lover's sake, but dies in her lover's arms soon after the wedding.*

A Perilous Cargo *[Harold M. Shaw, US, 1913] shows how a brave girl rescues her lover from a burning ship, which has a quantity of gunpowder on board. There is also a fine Mexican drama [*The Mexican Spy *(Wilbert Mel-ville, US, 1913)] by Lubin [Manufacturing Company]. Some special films are promised next week.*[28]

Other films on the bill that weekend included *A Desperate Chance* (Ke-nean Buel, US, 1913), the Francis X. Bushman drama *The Cat's Paw* (US, 1912), an Italian *Foolshead* short starring the pioneering slapstick clown André Deed under his alias Cretinetti, and *Dick and the Potion* and *Turin*, neither of whose details are known.[29] This was a time when film programmes still consisted of a series of short films, rather than the feature-length productions we are familiar with today.

Syd Taylor: *When the Walton St. Cinema was built, it was very rare to see a film over 16 minutes in running time. There were many complete story films that were only 8 to 10 minutes 'long'. The programme would last approx. 2 hours! British and Continental films were far superior to the Americans. The 1914-18 War gave the Americans the chance to catch up.*[30]

The programmes consisted of single reel (approx. 1000ft.) complete stories. There were also half reel (known as 'split-reel') films—usually travelogues, etc. The newsreels were of approx. 5 min. duration. Big annual events like the Grand National, Derby, Boat Race, etc., were longer, and shown the same night as the event.[31]

Mr. Taylor recalls the thrill of his first visit to the North Oxford Kinema, made in 1915, at the tender age of six.

A little friend of mine came to the door on a Saturday afternoon and said his mum had given him a penny to go to the 'pictures' and could I come with him. My grandma (I was living with my grandma, as my father was in the army in France) gave me the necessary penny, after some consideration, and I and my friend scuttled off to the N.O.K. We joined the crowd of kids waiting for the gates to open. A chap with a cricked neck appeared from inside and, saying to an invisible (to us) lady in the cash desk, which was on the left-hand side of the vestibule, "READY?" and acting on the answer, "YES," proceeded to slide the iron gates back and let about half a dozen kids in at a time. At the cash desk, no ticket was issued for the penny admission charge; a square metal check was issued. After passing thro' swing doors, we found ourselves in an inner vestibule, where the metal check was taken from us by a pageboy.[32]

This ticketing arrangement was common practice at the time, and The Cinema Museum in London has an example of a similar token dispenser in its collection. Syd Taylor noted elsewhere that the chap with the cricked neck was a Mr. Bull, who would later work as a projectionist at the Jeune Street cinema (now the UPP).[33]

I first knew him as the man who opened the sliding gates to let us kids rush to the cash desk at the Saturday matinees, and we kids also knew him as the man 'who showed the pictures.' A few years later, I met him again at the Red, White and Blue pub, when he was the licensee. I think his wife was cashier when he was a projectionist.[34]

The price of admission in those days was 1½d, 2½d, 4d, and 6d. Sat. matinees were 1d, except when on certain days during the First World War, the Oxford Co-Op in co-operation with headquarters, which I believe in those days was at Walsall, used to have a tie-up with the management, which was the showing of a five-minute advert plus paying half the cost of admission, which meant us kids paying only ½d at some Saturday matinees.

I do clearly recall the first picture I saw on the screen, on that first Sat matinee. It was a picture of a crowing cockerel and, I have since reasoned, they must have kicked off with the Pathé Animated Gazette. I don't recall a great deal about the rest of that first film show, except the name of the serial was The

Scarlet Runner *[William P.S. Earle and Wally Van, US, 1916]. When the title came on I thought we were going to see something about kidney beans. It proved to be an exciting film about motorcar racing, The Scarlet Runner being the name of the hero's car. The only other film in that programme that I recall was a comic film about a couple of comic looking geezers pushing a railway train along the lines. Little did I realise I would be operating the projectors in ten or so years time.*[35]

At those kids' matinees, the lady pianist (a Mrs. Boone), played a most delightful and tuneful march to the 'topical.' It must have been a favourite of hers—it was a march she played more frequently than others. The tune stuck in my memory over the years and I searched for recordings of it with no avail.[36] *A few years ago, I was amazed and delighted to hear it, at St Giles' Fair—and then, it was only necessary to ask the showman the name of the piece that had just been played; the answer, 'The Winning Fight.'*[37]

Mrs. Boone stands out much more than the other pianists. She played at the old North Oxford Kinema and later, in 1923-4-5, at the same cinema (now The Scala), as a relief pianist. She later became cashier at the same cinema, remaining as such for some years. Mrs. Boone told me she had played at all the Oxford cinemas at some time or other.[38]

Although some have claimed the North Oxford Kinema was not among the most impressive of its local fellows (the boasts of its proprietors notwithstanding), it featured a level of opulence quite alien to twenty-first century cinemagoers, which Mr. Taylor never ceased to champion. He describes how the cinema was decorated on his first visit in 1915, and how it remained by the time he began work as a projectionist ten years later.

In my opinion, and indeed of many others who are old enough to remember, the North Oxford Kinema (later The Scala) was, until its alteration in the 1930s, the finest and best decorated cinema in Oxford.[39] *This cinema was, in my opinion, the prettiest and finest bijou picture house for miles around.*[40] *It also had the best projection room and was known as the picture palace with the clearest pictures in Oxford.*

In comparison with the size of the auditorium, it had two spacious vestibules. The outer one had a full-size sweet shop on the left-hand side.[41] *It was quite a large shop and had two big windows: one facing the street, the other facing inside the vestibule. The shop sold as big a variety of sweets and chocolates as one would wish and, just inside the door, was a machine for dispensing aerated mineral waters and known as a 'soda fountain'—a new and up-to-date machine in those days. The outer vestibule was decorated with moulded panels and had a decorative ceiling, a feature of which was dome shaped skylights.[42]*

Next to the shop on the left of the vestibule was the cash desk. At the back and facing the street were three sets of double doors, through which one passed into the second vestibule, which was then, and all the time I worked there, furnished with a lounge suite: a settee and two chairs all in wickerwork, which were cushioned. On the right-hand side were large windows of leaded glass, decorated with long, deep red curtains. The windows were in a recess, which also boasted a couple of large decorative plants in huge pots on decorative pedestals.

On the left-hand side of this inner vestibule were two doors. One, the first on the left, opened up to the cash desk way in the manger's office, and, if one ignored the cash desk come manager's office, and went straight ahead, one went up a longish flight of stone steps, which curved round, leading to the projection suite, which comprised a large workroom, the projection room and rewind room. The projection room (or operating box) had five portholes, two for the projectors and three for observation. There was also a large circular porthole in the workroom so that one could watch the show from there.

The auditorium, which seated just under 500, was, to me, the prettiest hall I have ever been in. Going back to that first visit as a small boy I remember very well how I was somewhat overawed at the beauty of this place. I suppose you might say, "Well, it was because it impressed you as a boy, and it was so new, and the electric light a change from your comparatively drab home," but this is not so; this cinema has always left me with that impression—whenever I went there, and all the time I worked there.

Going through the second set of doors, one came to the wide gangway across the back of the auditorium—the back gangway being screened off by a dark red velvet curtain hung with large brass rings on a long brass curtain rail. There was a centre row of seats and two side rows of seats with gangways on each side, separating the side rows from the main central block. The ceiling was curved; the walls were wood panelled from the floor to about 4 feet high. Let into this panelling at intervals down each side were gas radiators for winter heating. Above the panelling the walls were decorated with shaped plaster panels typical of the period.

About five feet in front of the front rows, a red curtain similar to the one at the back of the hall screened off the orchestra pit. The curtain was, of course, curved at each end to completely mask off the pit. The screen was of specially prepared canvas, stretched into a frame—bevelled, like an enormous picture frame, covered in black velvet. An unusual feature was that the screen was slightly curved across the top. Each side of the screen was a pillar. The screen being set between these two pillars greatly enhanced the decorative effect. Also, on each side of the orchestra pit was a decorative pillar with a flourishing palmlike plant of large proportions.[43]

The main lighting consisted of six pendants—each one consisting of a large central glass bowl (with a 100-watt bulb) with three outer glass shades (with amber bulb). Five minutes before the programme commenced, the central bulb lights were dimmed down and the amber lights created a golden glow in the auditorium. This effect was pleasing and a novelty in those days.[44]

The mechanics of film projection impressed the young Syd Taylor as much as the viewing environment and the films themselves.

I remember it was 'magic.' I was enthralled and went every Saturday afternoon afterwards.[45] I went not only to be entertained; I was beginning to wonder how it was all done. I looked back to see the beam of light emanating from the portholes, and it was not long before I realised two projectors were being used.

Syd Taylor (bottom right) in 'Gaffer' Dent's Class, 1922. From Syd Taylor's collection.

*Soon, I was amazing my friends, because I could tell them exactly when the light
from the porthole would change to the next. I had noticed that this phenomenon
occurred about once every 15 minutes, but the change could be pinpointed, because the picture on the screen became spotty, and I would say to my pals, "Look
round now and you will see the beam change from one hole to another."*[46] *I was
disappointed when it closed for several months due to the war and consequential
staff shortage.*[47]

Although war closed the North Oxford Kinema in March 1916, by
June of the same year it was up and running again.[48] It would remain
under the proprietorship of Bartlett, Beeson, and Green for a further
twelve months until, in June 1917, they sublet the premises to a new
proprietor: Hubert Thomas Lambert.

Hubert Thomas Lambert

H. T. Lambert was born on 26 July 1896 in Horspath, an historic village
lying a mile to the east of the Oxford City boundary. He began his cinema career as a projectionist in Jeune Street, and would go on to work
in most of Oxford's cinemas, including The Regal (in Cowley Road),
The Ritz (in George Street), The Electra Palace (in Queen Street), and
The Palace Picture House (in Cowley Road). At The Palace, he was
reportedly the first Oxford film projectionist to screen talking pictures,
although that wouldn't be until around ten years after his time as the
proprietor of the North Oxford Kinema. He died in Headington on 20
February 1970.

During the First World War, Mr. Lambert saw active service in
France with the 3rd Worcestershire Regiment. Visiting Oxford on 48-
hour leave, he married Maud Louise Lewis in St Paul's Church on Walton Street on 30 April 1916.[49] Their marriage lasted for more than half
a century. A wedding day photograph taken on the roof of the North
Oxford Kinema during its brief period of closure suggests he was already
an employee before he took over the management of the business the
following year.

H. T. Lambert was invalided out of the war in early 1917. Taking
over the operation of the North Oxford Kinema shortly after his re-

Hubert and Maud Lambert pictured on the roof of the North Oxford Kinema in 1916. Courtesy of David and Julie Parker.

turn, he went into business with a Mr. Lewis, whom his granddaughter believes to be Maud's brother Benjamin. Other family members also worked at this cinema in its early days. They included Hubert's brother, Cecil; Cecil's wife, Kate, who was employed as an usherette; and Kate's sister, Agnes, who ran the box office.[50]

Hubert's youngest daughter, Sheila, reports that Maud also worked there as a cashier (a fact confirmed on their wedding certificate), until she left in 1918 to have her first child, William Hubert Thomas Lambert. Two daughters came along later: Margaret Helen Elizabeth Lambert in 1922, and Sheila Betty Lambert in 1934, both of whom are still alive.[51]

Relatively little is known about the way the cinema operated under Mr. Lambert, as he didn't advertise his weekly programme in *The Oxford Times* (which was the practice of his predecessors and successors alike). However, Syd Taylor records that "Lambert and Lewis first supplemented the pianist who accompanied the films with a banjoist [and later] considerably raised the tone by instituting a three-piece orchestra under the direction of Mr. Kempster, a well-known local musician. The film programmes were also three hours long."[52] H. T. Lambert ran the North Oxford Kinema for just under three years, until the leasehold was transferred from Mr. Bartlett to a new owner. Whether this sale was a cause or effect of the end of Mr. Lambert's tenure as proprietor remains unknown.

*Hubert and Maud Lambert celebrate their Golden
Wedding in 1966. Courtesy of David and Julie Parker.*

NORTH OXFORD KINEMA.

H. T. LAMBERT,
    Proprietor.

WALTON STREET,
OXFORD,

April 19th. 1920.   *192*

" To Whom it may concern,"

.This is to Certify that William Arnatt has been engaged by me

for the past three years as Operator. I have found him in every way

reliable and trustworthy. able to repair films and work the machines

and to whoever he applies for similar work I can confidently

recommend him,

Signed,

H J Lambert

*1920 letter of reference for projectionist William Arnatt. Courtesy of the Oxfordshire
History Centre (catalogue ref. P150/X/2).*

Poole's Entertainments

The next owners (as described by the lease ledger) were "John Reginald Poole, of 146 Westgate, Gloucester, Amusement Caterer, and Elizabeth Francis Poole of Wotton Lawn, London Road in the City of Gloucester, Widow, trading as 'The C. W. Poole's Entertainments.'"[53] After purchasing the lease in 1920, they changed the name of the cinema to The Scala, upgraded the auditorium décor, and introduced a new style of film programming.

Portrait of John Reginald Poole. Courtesy of Genevieve Poole.

The Poole family was a large clan with a long-standing show business career and reputation. A centenary pamphlet written by John R. Poole (1882-1950) puts the business as starting in 1837 (although this may not be its precise year of registration). The Pooles' pre-cinema claim to fame was their celebrated 'Myriorama'—a panorama and diorama show. Named from the ancient Greek words, *myrio* (many) and *horama* (views), these educational and entertaining displays often took the form of 'A Trip Round the World,' with other shows being based on contemporary and historic events, such as 'Loss of the Titanic' and the 'Bombardment of Alexandria.'

Presentations centred on a series of enormous painted canvases, which were moved across the full width of the stage using a complex system of rollers. A lecturer brandishing a long pointer would describe the places and events depicted, with a clown sometimes interrupting him to lighten the mood. A musical trio accompanied in the early days, being later upgraded to a ten-piece orchestra. Elaborate (and sometimes risky) pyrotechnic effects added to the dramatic impact at appropriate moments. These lavish performances required a crew of around forty to fifty, and large theatres to house the extensive stage gear, the performers, and the huge crowds they attracted.[54]

John's youngest granddaughter Genevieve describes the wonder of these presentations, which attracted an enormous following:

The Myriorama shows must really have been something, as they brought other cultures and countries, travel adventures, and major national and world events to local people at a time when long-distance travel was rare, and film and television not yet invented. The scenes were planned, sketched, and often painted in miniature first, then were painstakingly painted with great detail on to the huge canvases. The special effects used were daring and atmospheric. These spectacular and enterprising performances were attended by literally thousands in each venue around the country, all queuing up in eager anticipation. Poole's Myrioramas provided a feast for the eyes and the ears, an exciting treat for the whole family, and were quite unique in their presentation.[55]

In the early years of the twentieth century, the Poole family expanded their business to include cinema operation. In 1910, Joseph Wolseley Poole began to exhibit films on a regular basis at the Corn Exchange in Chichester and the Victoria Hall in Cowes. That same year, Charles W. Poole III (known as 'Young Charlie,' or 'Charles Junior') opened the Empire Electric Theatre and Music Hall in Taunton and, by 1914, was running other cinemas in Torquay, Teignmouth, Plymouth, and Newton Abbot.[56] As the heyday of panoramas passed (soon to be eclipsed by this modern form of entertainment), other members of the Poole family would also look to cinema as the future for their business.

The C. W. Poole who gave his name to the company running Oxford's Walton Street cinema was the second of three Charles W. Pooles. After his death in 1918, his widow and his eldest son continued to operate the business under his name. The company's renown as a purveyor of spectacular entertainment was often promoted in its newspaper announcements; in the listings for The Scala's second week, the new proprietors assured Oxford's cinemagoers that they did indeed belong to the family "of Myriorama fame."[57] Later advertisements continued to trade on this eminent name, entreating cinemagoers to "Go to Poole's Scala" or simply exclaiming, "It's Poole's!"[58]

Although we have no first-hand memories of Elizabeth or John, Genevieve reports:

I do know from family that John Poole was a big man, both in stature and personality! He smoked large cigars, and was proud to be part of a showmen family business. He became a Baillie (a dignitary in the City of Edinburgh Council) and was in line for becoming the Lord Provost (the Scottish equivalent of Mayor).

The Scala was managed by one of John's two younger brothers: Vivian George Poole (1893-1929), a war veteran who had suffered severe injuries during his service.

Genevieve: *My father spoke about Vivian Poole often; he was a bit of a hero to him, and he spoke of his uncle with great fondness. Vivian lost both legs in the war and was a wheelchair user, so it was pretty impressive that he managed The Scala, especially in the days before accessibility. One of the reasons my father admired him was the way he dealt with his war disability. He was determinedly active, using strong arms to move himself around on the ground/floor, and having a prototype wheelchair made, which was well ahead of its time. His wife was apparently an amazing woman who made sure his life was as 'normal' as possible, and took him all over the place. The family would have been intent upon including him in the business, and it sounds from my dad's description like Vivian wouldn't have been fobbed off with a desk job!*

Films were booked at the Gloucester-based head office. Although records in the Kinematograph Year Books list the booker as E. A. Rogers, this is probably a typographic error, with the likelihood being that programming duties fell to Ernest C. Rogers.[59] Ernest (who would later become the company's general manager) had joined the business as a boy, following in the footsteps of his father, Arthur, who spent more than half a century with Poole's as a "marine artist, engineer, architect, producer, theatre and cinema manager."[60]

Seeking to improve the experience on offer to cinema patrons, Poole's invested in a programme of refurbishment before reopening the doors. Works included the installation of a new ventilation system—an improvement that must have been especially welcome in the days when 500 patrons regularly squeezed into an auditorium space far smaller

than the current layout (which seats just 292). *The Oxford Times* also
praised Poole's choice of décor, which featured "a dainty silvery grey
and white" colour scheme.[61] As ever, the changes didn't meet with universal approval; Syd Taylor felt they "completely spoilt the screen area
by painting the pillars, the surrounding wall, and part of the ceiling
matt black," although one might equally argue that blacking out the area
around the screen was a sensible move that would reduce distractions
from the film show.[62]

grammes. A Metro drama of social life is announced for Thursday next.

NORTH OXFORD SCALA.

The North Oxford Cinema re-opened on Monday
under its new name—The Scala—and under the
experienced management of Mr. J. R. and Mrs. C.
W. Poole. well known entertainers at Gloucester,
Stourbridge, Ipswich, Edinburgh, Bristol and
other places. The palace has been re-decorated,
and the new colour scheme is a dainty silvery grey
and white. The ventilation has already been improved, but even better things in this way may be
looked for in the future, as the alterations are not
quite completed. One new ventilating machine
has already been put in, and another is to be fixed
shortly. The performance is continuous from 5.30
to 10.30 p.m. (Saturdays from 2.30), the first programme finishing at 8. An attractive programme
was arranged for the re-opening. For the week-end
Sessue Hayakawa is to be seen in "The Debt."
This great emotional Japanese actor always provides an interpretation of drama that is intensely
vivid. "The Debt" is said to show him at his
best. Another feature is a Vitagraph serial
called "The Iron Test," and there are two
or three comedies to give a lighter touch.
For Saturday a continuous entertainment from
2.30 p.m. till 10.30 p.m. is announced, but there
will be no children's matinee.

CATHEDRAL SERVICES

Courtesy of Oxford Mail/The Oxford Times (Newsquest Oxfordshire).

The newly named Scala launched on 19 April 1920. It was, Poole's proclaimed, an "Instantaneous Success!! Everyone greatly delighted."[63] The main attraction in the inaugural programme was *Virtuous Wives* (George Loane Tucker, US, 1918), an upmarket society drama produced by Louis B. Mayer, and featuring his newly contracted star Anita Stewart.[64] At the film's New York premiere, the accompanying printed programme had announced, "Mr. Louis Mayer presents Miss Anita Stewart in a series of new productions designed for the better theatres. Miss Anita Stewart and her company will interpret only famous plays or widely read stories by well-known contemporary authors. Each subject's title will have a box-office appeal at the better theatres second only to that of the star's name."[65]

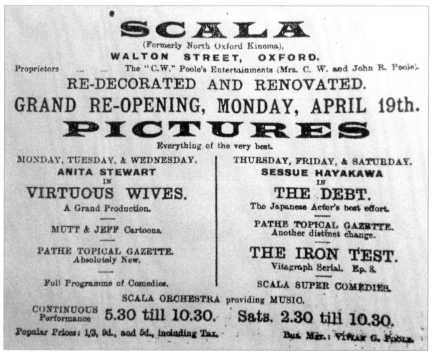

Courtesy of Oxford Mail / The Oxford Times (Newsquest Oxfordshire).

Poole's clearly intended to position The Scala as a 'better theatre,' and prices were raised accordingly—now ranging from 5d for the cheap seats to 1s 3d for the premium seats. In their business strategy to attract an affluent and sophisticated audience, the traditional Saturday children's show and the weekday matinee performances were dropped in favour of concentrating on the evening's entertainment. A reduction of the programme length from three hours to two doubtless came as a disappointment to some, while creating a more select night out for others. In the early days of Poole's ownership, the Scala Orchestra provided live musical accompaniment (although the company would later revert to a less costly pianist).[66] Advertisements show that, for those who could afford it, Poole's even introduced a service for booking seats by telephone. In an era when there was only one telephone for every forty-seven people in the UK, this facility was doubtless designed to signal both the cinema's modernity and its high-end appeal.[67]

John R Poole speaking at the 23rd Reunion of Cinema Veterans (19 April 1950, at The Trocadero in London). Beside him sit Arthur Warrs (President of the Cinema Exhibitors' Association) and Sir Henry L French (Director General of the British Film Producers Association). Courtesy of Genevieve Poole.

May 2–8. 1921

SCALA

WALTON STREET, OXFORD.

All Films Entirely New to Oxford.

CONTINUOUS 5-30 TO 10-30.

Matinee— Saturday at 3 p.m.

WEEK OF MAY 2nd.

1921 MONDAY, TUESDAY and WEDNESDAY,

From the wide-read Novel by A. S. M. HUTCHINSON.

A GREAT BRITISH PRODUCTION by the Hepworth Company

Once Aboard the Lugger

Featuring

Eileen Dennis & E. Holman Clark

THE INVISIBLE HAND

Episode 7. Featuring Antonio Moreno and Pauline Curley

TOPICAL BUDGET, Your Daily Paper Picturised.

A Strong Programme of other Subjects support the above.

THURSDAY, FRIDAY and SATURDAY,

1921 LEW CODY

IN

The BELOVED CHEATER

A fascinating romance of Hearts and Sweethearts A production of unusually gorgeous settings elaborately staged.

" Take them in your arms, Breathe pretty words in their ears,
Look lovingly in their eyes, And they'll all Kiss,
From Babies to Grandmothers.

JACK DEMPSEY

The World's Heavyweight Champion in the greatest Serial of all times,

"DARE-DEVIL JACK"

Episode No. 3. Don't Miss It!

TOPICAL BUDGET, Animated Press Par Photography.

The above Features supported by Full Programme of other items.

Popular Prices: 1/3; 9d. & 5d. Including Tax.

SEATS BOOKED at 1/6 (Tax included) Phone No. 867

BOOKING OFFICE HOURS—10-30 a.m. to 12-30 p.m. 2 p.m. to 4 p.m.
5-30 p.m. to 9 p.m. DAILY.

Scala handbill, May 1921. Courtesy of James Webster.

Scala advertisement in The Oxford Times (9 February 1923, while operated by The C. W. Poole's Entertainements). Courtesy of Oxford Mail / The Oxford Times (Newsquest Oxfordshire).

Walshaw Enterprises

In the summer of 1923, The Scala passed to new operators once again, and Vivian Poole returned to work with the family's touring myriorama shows.[68] Walshaw Enterprises, a company that took its name from owner George Walker and manager W. Shaw, subleased the venue from Poole's. Like Poole's, they had links with Gloucester, where they ran the King's Kinema on Westgate Street, so a prior business relationship seems likely.[69]

We know very little about Mssrs. Walker and Shaw, although newspaper listings offer some insight into the way they ran The Scala. They brought back the Saturday matinees for a while, but their subsequent decision to drop them again suggests that these shows attracted limited trade. Syd Taylor also credits them with reinstating the orchestra, although, as most of the advertisements make no mention of this costly attraction, it was probably not a long-term regular feature.[70] The most interesting innovation noted by Mr. Taylor is their purchase of a cine-camera, with which they produced their own weekly newsreel, the *Scala Local Topical*—"a very expensive thing [that] ran for a year or two."[71]

Unfortunately, the business failed financially and, by April 1925, Walshaw Enterprises was unable to meet its debts.[72] The cinema closed down with immediate effect; its screen would remain dark for several months, until another businessman decided to try his hand at finding a model to make the venue pay.

Scala advertisement in The Oxford Times (28 November 1924, while operated by Walshaw Enterprises). Courtesy of Oxford Mail / The Oxford Times (Newsquest Oxfordshire).

Ben Jay

In September 1925, Ben Jay became The Scala's fifth proprietor (sub-leasing from Poole's once again).[73] Often described as a colourful 'Cockney showman,' Ben also ran cinemas across East London, with venues in Dalston, Shoreditch, Hackney, and Tottenham.[74] His grandson, Peter Jay, offers the following account (extracted, with kind permission, from a draft copy of his forthcoming autobiography, *Jaywalking*):

The earliest pictures of Ben Jay show him standing outside a tailor's shop in the East End of London, tailor's tapes proudly round his neck, and no one really knows how he progressed so quickly to owning the leases of several cinemas in London and the Home Counties, and then at the seaside. But he was a character, a king of stunts, a real showman. He and his wife, Martha, would project a fantastic image of success, bedecked in fedoras and furs, with their big black American cars— gangster style Buicks dripping with chrome. Legend has it that at the height of the 'Ben Jay' circuit it numbered forty cinemas, with two even in the heart of London's Tottenham Court Road. Ben had a specially drawn side view caricature of himself that he had printed Alfred Hitchcock-style on his personal notepaper that was just headed simply 'From the Gov-

Ben and Martha Jay. Courtesy of Peter and Christine Jay.

ernor's Chair.' In another dusty photo, Ben and Martha are seen hanging out with Hollywood legend 'Snozzle' Durante, looking every bit part of Tinseltown set in London.

Another family legend told many times by Grandma Martha Jay was that Ben was the first person in Britain to actually sell ice cream in a British cinema. He would buy it in the street from the 'Hokey Pokey' man ice cream seller and cut it into wafer size chunks, separated by paper, and sell it inside the theatre to the audience's great delight.

Martha always told fantastic stories of their Oxford cinema, when the undergrads would throw out the little old lady who played the piano for the film and take over with the then outrageous beats of the latest ragtime music to the cheers of the fellow students. Bartering was commonplace, with chickens, eggs, and fruit and veg being easily and gratefully substituted for the price of a cinema admission. Martha was often the ticket seller.[75]

Ben's son Jack offers further insight into the way that he conducted business, recalling what would now be considered some rather irregular dealings in obtaining films to show:

Portrait of Ben Jay. Courtesy of Peter and Christine Jay.

My father, when he first started with the moving pictures, I can remember used to go to London, and go to Wardour Street and say, "What have you got to offer?" and on the pavement were all the films in sacks. You used to take your operator with you and you'd say, "What have you got there?" and the feller said, "I've got Charlie Chaplin films," so he said, "Well don't take it back to the distributors, we'll show it for two days," and he used to give the fellow a drink and take the film in the sack and go back to the cinema. And he used to write outside the cinema, "Tonight—Charlie Chaplin in so and so," and he'd put it on without a license or anything, just for the sake of what in those days was half a crown or something, and this trading used to go on, on the pavement in Wardour Street.[76]

When Ben took on ownership of The Scala in Oxford, he immediately set about reinventing it in his own inimitable style. Peter Jay describes the thrill of discovering a relic of those very first days:

The old film flickered and fluttered into life on the makeshift screen that had been created on an old sheet draped between two chairs in the Norfolk Manor House's dining room. Speeded up rainy sepia images of the main street of a bygone Oxford flashed by, until, seconds before the end, the final shots revealed a young boy in school uniform standing on the steps of an old-fashioned cinema. A cheeky, toothy smile flashed at the camera beneath an old school cap and it was ended. The mystery of the dangerous, explosive, nitrate 35mm film that had lan-

*guished in its rusty protective steel tin for all those years was solved. The young
people in the room cheered and applauded; the young boy who stood on the steps
was their granddad Jack Jay, and beside him his father Ben Jay. Ben Jay was the
man who created this film of Oxford to lure customers to see themselves on the Big
Screen of his Oxford cinema in the 1920s. There was scarcely one minute of film
in the can, but the van with the tripodded camera on top had toured the town
for over a week, all day, every day with the cameraman cranking the camera,
working hard to capture the images. An early Ben Jay stunt that characterised
his style and the buccaneering feel of Britain's pioneering early cinemas, to see
yourself on a big screen years before the advent of home movies and videos was a
guaranteed cinema filler, and thousands who had seen the van and the camera
packed the cinema expecting to see themselves—in vain! There was no film in
the camera—most of the time.*[77]

On Monday 14 September 1925, the cinema was re-launched as 'The
New Scala,' featuring a twice-weekly change of feature double bills, as
part of a continuous programme beginning at 2.00 p.m. Ben Jay's first
programme advertisement heralded "An Innovation to Oxford—RE-
DUCED PRICES in the Afternoon up to 4 o'clock."[78]

Despite also operating cinemas elsewhere, Ben based himself at The
New Scala, where he became a familiar face to regular customers, alongside his brother Manny, the cinema manager.

Martin Selwood recalls attending The New Scala as a child in the
mid-1920s:

*I was born in the middle of Oxford, in Union Street, which doesn't exist now.
It's called Hart Street, and it's next to the University Press if it's still there. I
used to deliver newspapers for my mother all round Jericho. That was the Oxford Mail. And of course I see it as it was, in my mind. I can see the shops opposite The Scala Cinema; opposite was Burbank's, the chemist, and to the right of
that was the greengrocer, and to the left of that was a sweet shop—two little old
ladies used to serve in it. Next to that, to the left, was a cake shop (a high-class
cake shop), and so on.*

*There were two brothers—they were Jews: the Brothers Jay. I remember them
well. They tried all sorts of things to get more people in: tea and biscuits in the afternoon, and balloons all over the place. They were showmen, but they never really
made it go.*

One thing that I used to love, that used to frighten me to death, was Doctor Fu Manchu by Sax Rohmer. As a boy I used to dream about him, but I still liked it. Miss Stroud was the pianist. She used to watch the pictures and play the tune according to what was going on. If it was [cowboy hero] Tom Mix it would be going like mad, and so on. And then they had a small orchestra, but I think it was too expensive.[79]

New Scala advertisement in The Oxford Times (30 October 1925, while operated by Ben Jay). Courtesy of Oxford Mail / The Oxford Times (Newsquest Oxfordshire).

There were often musical performances between films. "I can't remember the name of the fellow now," says Mr. Selwood, "but I can remember his face. It was made-up, like powdered, and he used to sing."

In a series of letters and interviews, Syd Taylor described his own experiences of the cinema under Ben Jay's proprietorship. Not long after the new owner's arrival, the teenaged Syd was standing outside the cinema when Mr. Jay emerged, and asked:

"Would you like a job as a projectionist, son?" When I explained I already had a job [at Acott's music shop in the High Street] he offered to take me on in the evenings. We never discussed wages. At the end of my first week he asked: "How much do I owe you?," thrust his hand in his waistcoat pocket and pulled out 17s 6d. It was more than I was earning for working all day at Acott's and as you can imagine it wasn't long before I joined him full-time. The following year I became his chief projectionist.

SCALA.

Phon: 867.   **WALTON ST., OXFORD.**   Proprietor and Manager: BEN JAY.

CONTINUOUS PERFORMANCE DAILY, 2—10.30 P.M.

SEATS CAN BE RESERVED AT 1/10, EXCEPT SATURDAYS.

MONDAY, NOV. 15,
FOR
SIX DAYS.

FIRST TIME IN OXFORD.

CHARLES R. ROGERS PRESENTS

"The UNKNOWN SOLDIER"

DIRECTED & PRODUCED BY
RENAUD HOFFMAN

A **RENAUD HOFFMAN**
PICTURIZATION
WITH **CHARLES EMMETT MACK**
MARGUERITE DE LA MOTTE
& **HENRY B. WALTHALL**
ADAPTATION BY JAMES J. TYNAN
BASED UPON THEME SUGGESTED
BY DOROTHY FARNUM.

THE MANAGEMENT ARE SHOWING, IN ADDITION:

Monday, Tuesday & Wednesday,	Thursday, Friday & Saturday,
TOM RICKETTS & DOROTHY DEVIER IN	JANE NOVAK & LIGHTNING, THE DOG, IN
When Husbands Flirt.	**Lure of the Wild.**

PRICES ARE REDUCED AT MATINEES, AND AFTERNOON TEA SERVED GRATIS.

New Scala advertisement in The Oxford Times (12 November 1926, while operated by Ben Jay). Courtesy of Oxford Mail / The Oxford Times (Newsquest Oxfordshire).

Ben Jay was a magnificent showman. He rechristened the cinema The New Scala—although he dropped the New after a couple of years.[80] *Programmes consisted of two features, comedies, serial, cartoon interest, news, etc.*[81] *"If there was only one child in the front row I'd give him the full show," he used to say. "Queues outside are a good advertisement." [He] introduced fourpence and eight-pence only with free tea and biscuits at matinees. That was very popular particularly in the wintertime with the poor people of Jericho, who could keep warm, get a free tea and see the programme twice round for fourpence.*[82]

Crowds outside The Scala in 1926. From Syd Taylor's collection.

When I worked there in the twenties, I have known customers, usually university chaps, to be sent up to watch the show from [the] port in the workroom, when the place was full. In fact, on such occasions, I have known the inner vestibule packed with students all standing on soap boxes, crates, [and] chairs supplied by the management, with the inner swing doors opened, so that they could see the screen.[83]

In the summer months, in Ben Jay's time, if the business dropped due to hot weather, he would advertise special carnival nights. He would purchase crates of the market trader's merchandise: penknives, biscuit barrels, cruets and the like.

NEW SCALA

Walton St.] **CINEMA** [Oxford

Prop.: BEN JAY.   Man : MANNY JAY

Continuous Performance · 2 to 10.30 p.m.

MONDAY, JANUARY 17th
For Three Days.

Enormous Attraction !

BETTY BLYTHE
IN
CHU CHIN CHOW

A Gorgeous Oriental Spectacle with
a romantic and thrilling story

BETTY BALFOUR
(of 'Queen of Sheba' fame) as
ZAHRAT, the beautiful slave

HERBERT LANGLEY
as 'CHU CHIN CHOW'

Also

HIS PAL'S WIFE
Starring **GLENN HUNTER**

Usual Prices.

Seats can be Booked   -   'Phone 2967

TEA SUPPLIED FREE at MATINEES

New Scala handbill, January 1927. Courtesy of The Cinema Museum, London.

These would be given as free gifts to individual patrons as they entered the inner vestibule. The carnival nights also featured a longer musical interlude and sing-songs and, indeed, a longer programme.[84] In Ben Jay's day we even sold Easter eggs at Easter time.[85]

He was keen on getting good musicians. The orchestra he had at The Scala in the '20s was brought down from London—under the direction of a Mr. George Tugwood. There were 9 musicians—George on the piano, 3 violins, sax., trombone, trumpet, drums and organ; the latter being a glorified type of the then popular American organ—not a bad instrument tho', the bellows being motorised. This combination was ideal for the musical interludes, when the audience joined in the choruses of the popular '20s numbers (words on the screen), but for certain film scenes, the brass had to be dropped sometimes. How the patrons enjoyed the music in those days.[86] Songs of the day, 'If You Knew Susie,' 'Margie,' 'Don't Bring Lulu' and 'Ma He's Making Eyes at Me' were most popular.[87] He augmented [the orchestra] some evenings with bandsmen from Morris Motors.[88]

When Ben Jay installed his larger orchestra, he had a huge decorative mirror installed at the back of the auditorium, the main purpose of which was to assist the orchestra. The orchestra leader, who was the pianist, had a mirror fixed on the piano front, which took the reflection of the picture on the screen from the large mirror at the back of the auditorium.[89] A singer at The New Scala used to hold a mirror and reflect the spotlight on young girls in the audience. During the silent film accompaniment George Tugwood had an electric foot switch, which controlled small dim lights. Each music stand contained one, so every musician would have immediate indication of the next music change to accompany the different moods of the film when George Tugwood pressed the button with his foot.[90]

Community singing was as popular with the university chaps as it was with the locals and, occasionally, when we had got into the first ten minutes or so of the last feature film, the boss would come into the projection room and say, "They don't want any more films—get ready to sort out some song slides; the band is going to play." So, with the porthole glasses out, I would listen to the strains of the verse and feverishly search through a pile of song slides, hoping to find the words of the right song in time for the chorus. They were hectic days. We worked long hours—eleven to twelve a day and occasionally longer than that.[91]

Although Ben Jay catered to a mixed crowd, the student audience was particularly lucrative—although sometimes troublesome. Syd Taylor explains:

Normal prices were 4d, 8d, 1s 3d and 1s 10d but members of the university were only allowed in the best seats and a merry dance they used to lead us. In the middle of the main picture Ben would come into the box and say: "Cut the camera and put the lights up. They want a comedy." So we'd dig out an old one-reeler to keep them happy, then we'd go back to the main feature again where we left off. Another favourite trick of theirs was unscrewing the seats. Ben employed a second commissionaire in term-time to

Syd Taylor (left) outside The Scala in July 1927. The other man is currently unidentified, but the boy is thought to be Ben Jay's son, Jack. From Syd Taylor's collection.

keep them in order, but it was a thankless task. If he spotted anyone he'd move in to throw them out. Then the cry would go up: "Rescue St. John's" or "Rescue Balliol," and more often than not the poor commissionaire would end up being chucked out himself.[92]

Oxford University authorities did not look upon such rowdy conduct with approval. In 1927, the cinema lost its 'university license,' which effectively placed the cinema out of bounds to undergraduates— alongside local pubs. However disruptive their behaviour may have been, the top-rank admission prices paid by students made an important contribution to the cinema's revenue stream, and this ban caused a serious dent in business levels. After losing student patronage, Ben Jay gave up The New Scala and focused his attention on his other venues.[93] It marked the closure of a colourful era, but luckily not the end for the Walton Street cinema.

J. N. O. Bailiff

Little is known about The Scala's next owner, J. Bailiff, except that he also ran the Palace Cinema in Henley on Thames, which he listed as his main business address.[94] He reportedly ran a third cinema in High Wycombe, although details about this are very hazy.[95] The cinema manager at this time was Harry Malpass, who would retain his position after Bailiff's departure.[96]

Syd Taylor continued to work at The Scala during Mr. Bailiff's tenure, while the young Martin Selwood continued to attend. The fact that neither has volunteered any particular recollections of this time suggests the cinema ticked along without any great drama or innovation. The free tea for weekday matinee patrons (one of the most popular features Ben Jay had introduced) remained on offer.[97]

Several photographs taken by Syd at this time show the cinema looking very much as it had done in his descriptions of earlier years, although the frontage appears to have sprouted some new lights to either side of the entrance.

The Scala auditorium in 1928. From Syd Taylor's collection.

The Scala façade in August 1928. Both pictures from Syd Taylor's collection.

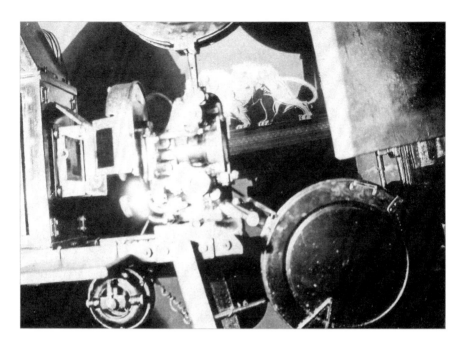

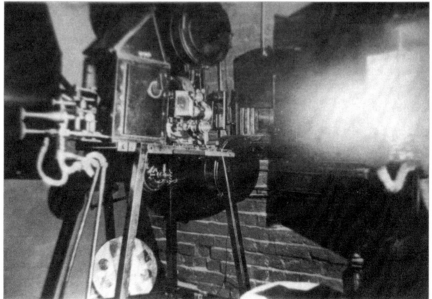

The Scala projection booth circa 1925-1930. Both pictures from Syd Taylor's collection.

Edward Alfred Roberts

After little more than a year, Mr. Bailiff also departed and, on 31 December 1928, the lease was finally transferred from Poole's to Edward Alfred Roberts, whose occupation is described in the St John's College lease ledger as 'Gentleman.'[98] Mr. Bailiff's exit appears to have been as smooth as his arrival, without any interim period of closure.

At the age of fourteen, long-time juvenile customer Martin Selwood followed in the footsteps of Syd Taylor and made the transition to a member of the Scala projection team. Starting out as a 'box boy,' he later moved up to become an 'assistant operator' (a job we would describe as a projectionist these days). He recalls the cinema's operation at that time:

> When I joined there in 1930 on Easter Monday (I left school on the Friday and started work), I think I got ten shillings a week (which is fifty pence). I was lucky to get a job at all, as it was the great 1929 Depression. When I started, Mr. Roberts owned the business. He was a gentlemanly sort of person, a very nice man. Harry Malpass was the manager. He owned a Raleigh motorbike and sidecar. The second operator was Jack Walford, who was not all that healthy. He always looked a bit pasty. He was a decorator really. His father was a decorator. The chief operator was Syd Taylor, who was a showman type of person. Everything connected with shows, fairgrounds, he was interested in. I used to correspond with Syd Taylor until he died. He used to send me pictures of showman's roundabouts and things. He was the only connection I had with the cinema afterwards—right up until he was in his eighties.

One of Mr. Roberts' innovations was to install a new system of amplified music to replace the live musicians. Mr. Selwood recalls:

> They bought a Panatrope, which was a big blue metal box with two turntables, and a switch to switch from one to the other. The operator (who was quite a posh fellow) used to sit behind curtains, watch the screen, and put different records on according to the film. On the records, he painted different sections. Until they changed to talkies, that was the music that they used.

The proprietorship of Mr. Roberts (the seventh in just thirteen years) turned out to be as transitory as that of his predecessors. In June 1930, The Scala changed hands once again. The arrival of John Edward Poyntz marked the beginning of a new chapter for the cinema. Finding a recipe for success at long last, the Poyntz family would run it for the next forty years.

Chapter Two

The Poyntz Family: 1930-1970

The era in which the Poyntz family ran The Scala is remembered fondly by many customers who still attend The Phoenix today. It was during these years that the cinema developed a reputation for showing the kinds of foreign-language and art-house movies that, in 1966, led the *International Film Guide* to describe it as "one of the two or three best cinemas outside London in terms of programme quality."[1] A great many staff and customers have spoken or written to us about their memories of these years, and we're grateful to be able to share a selection of those memories here.

The beginnings of an era

The recollections of former Scala employee Martin Selwood offer an unparalleled insight into the ways in which John Poyntz first developed the programming and business model that so many cinemagoers remember. At the same time, the more personal elements of his story paint a picture of what life was like for a working-class boy in Jericho in the early 1930s, and what going to the cinema meant to his generation.

The Poyntz came from Llanelli in Wales. I don't know why they wanted to move. Perhaps it was a better proposition. They were rich, and they went to

America on the Queen Mary *and came back on the* Normandy. *They'd go for the long weekend to the South of France. Mr. Poyntz was a big man: very, very strong—could lift the front of a car up. I was afraid of him! He had a big Rover car, Mr. Poyntz did, and he bought a new Austin 12, which he didn't like (it wasn't powerful enough) so he bought a big MG. You think of MGs as small sports cars, but this was a big MG, and I think it was about £575, which was quite a bit of money. He would often stand there and say 'hello' to people that came in. He used to stand on the steps smoking a cigar until about nine o'clock in the evening. Then he'd go into the Jericho House next door, and he'd stay there until closing time at ten thirty.*[2]

Ann Cole: *My parents kept a pub right next door to the University Press— The Clarendon Arms. The [Scala] owners used to come along and have drinks; they used to be our customers. He used to bring the two daughters as well. I can see him now. I always saw him in his overcoat, and he always wore a trilby. I don't remember him ever taking his trilby off.*[3]

Martin Selwood: *They had three daughters, but Alison (the eldest one) was married, and they had a cinema at Olney in Buckinghamshire. And then there was Daphne, the next eldest, and Maisie was four years older than me. [On a typical day] there was Daphne in the box, issuing the tickets, there was Maisie showing people down to the seats with one other girl and a man, and sometimes I would as well. There was a commissionaire, Reg, dressed in uniform. We used to get there at half past nine in the morning until half past ten at night. It was fairly easy going, and then perhaps they'd come home to dinner, and they'd start at two o'clock letting people in. And it was continuous until ten thirty.*

The auditorium was comfortable.

Martin Selwood aged fourteen. Courtesy of Martin Selwood.

It wasn't as plush as some of the Regals and Odeons, and so on. It was a cheaper sort of cinema. I can see it in my mind as clean as any. When you went through the double doors, on the left-hand side were the ladies' toilets. And there were two rows between the seats—so there were the rows on the left, and the main body of seats, and the rows on the right. Down at the bottom on the left were the exit doors for emergency. And the screen had loud speakers on stands (one on each side: six-inch British Thompson-Houston speakers), and the panels were painted in different pictures. They weren't pictures as you know them as photographs; it was just scrawls of whatever the artist painted. And then hanging from the ceiling was a bare 300-watt bulb, which they used to light up the whole cinema at the end of the show when the patrons were leaving. On the right-hand side, just inside the door, was the switch for louder or softer, to go up to the operating box. And on the right was a gas radiator; sometimes we used to jump up and sit on it to keep warm! And curtains all along.

On a wet day, when they had more patrons than normal, they used to stand at the back by the curtains (quite a crowd of them) to watch the film. In fact, a very funny thing happened: I was always a sweetie boy, and on this particular day I bought two-penny worth of eucalyptus gums. It was a big crowd at the back watching, and Mrs. Poyntz was there. They used to have friends come and visit them, so I saw these people talking to Mrs. Poyntz and, assuming they were friends, I offered the woman a sweet. I thought the man looked daggers at me, and Mrs. Poyntz said, "Not a sweet, you fool, a seat! Find them a seat!" I felt a bit of a fool!

Outside the entrance they had great big posters, one on each side (very tall, I suppose about twelve feet by four), and there was another big one on the top of the cinema. I don't know who used to change it. I think George, one of the assistants, used to do it. But that wasn't anything to do with me or my interest. My interest was behind the scenes, upstairs in the box.

By the time Mr. Poyntz took over The Scala, most other Oxford cinemas had already installed synchronised sound. This was a shortcoming he was quick to remedy. On 6 October 1930, The Scala presented its first talking picture: the Hollywood musical revue, *Happy Days* (Benjamin Stoloff, US, 1929). Advertised by its studio as an "all-star... all-talking... musical romance," *Happy Days* boasted "100 entertainers," including Janet Gaynor, Victor McLaglen, and Marjorie White. Three days later, McLaglen could be seen again in another nautical musical from the Fox studio: *Hot for Paris* (Raoul Walsh, US, 1929).

The ability to show talking pictures was crucial to the development of his business, especially when it came to catering to university students (whose ban had evidently been overturned by this point).

Martin Selwood: *When they changed to talkies the sound was very good (the BTH was as good as anybody's) and they were on a level with the other cinemas. It had two six-inch speakers, one on each side of the screen, and in the box the nine-inch monitor, which was mounted on slate. And two ma-*

SCALA CINEMA

WALTON STREET.   'Phone 2967.

**Continuous Performances Daily,
2 till 10.30.**

OPENING ON MONDAY NEXT with newly-installed BRITISH THOMPSON-HOUSTON "TALKIE" SYSTEM with

"HAPPY DAYS"

Showing Next Monday, Tuesday and
Wednesday at 3.25, 6.5 and 8.45.
Also on

THURSDAY, FRIDAY & SATURDAY,

"HOT FOR PARIS."

Both star films, supported by the usual
full programme.
Prices 6d. to 1/10.

*Courtesy of Oxford Mail / The Oxford Times
(Newsquest Oxfordshire).*

chines, of course, for talkies, with a photoelectric cell in the front of the box down below, and the exciter lamps on a switch so you could switch if one went faulty. Every so often Eric Searle used to come down from Rugby (the headquarters of BTH) to see if everything was alright.

Mr. Poyntz was very cute. He used to use foreign films for undergraduates because, of course, it helped them with the language. The top price in the cinema was one and ten pence and, by law or otherwise, they were only allowed in if they paid the one and ten pence. So he got every undergraduate at one and ten pence, instead of the sixpence, nine-pence, or one and tuppence that we commoners paid, you see. I think that's how he made it pay. Don't forget that students then were not from poor families like they are now; they were from rich people, so they could afford that. He seemed to know just what to do to get the money in. It was a different kettle of fish altogether.

It was the only cinema that showed foreign films, so during term time it was always packed with undergraduates. They would behave in the cinema—totally different to November the fifth in Cornmarket, where they'd all go mad and

throw fireworks everywhere and set everything alight! They behaved in the cine-
ma, because they were there to learn the language—German, especially. There
was one film that I've seen so many times I was sick of seeing it: Mädchen in
Uniform *[Leontine Sagan, 1931]. And French films, of course. There was no*
hanky-panky, no fooling about.

Talkies were very popular because, you see, after silent films—with the si-
lent films, when somebody spoke, the words came up on the screen, and then the
people came back again. But with talkies you could see them talking, hear them.
H. B. Warner was one of the QCs in a film, and you could see him gesticulating
and talking, which was wonderful after seeing words come up. And, of course, Al
Jolson and that sort of thing was popular.

Other people from the town weren't interested in the foreign films. There were
out of season films for them. In vacation they had two films—Felix the Cat,
Mickey Mouse, that sort of thing, which was still very popular. All the comedies
were very popular. Harold Lloyd, Laurel and Hardy, Charlie Chaplin, Ches-
ter Conklin, and all those. It was adults that came, and children on Saturday
morning. Children would shout out and scream at what the cowboys were doing:
"Don't do that, Mister!" and so on.

I think it was sixpence on a Saturday morning for children. But other times it
was sixpence, nine-pence, one and two, and one and ten. It was well distributed.
The cheap seats were two rows of sixpennies. Now when people talk about poverty
they don't know what poverty is. If we had a hole in our shoe, we didn't go and
send it to be repaired. You got a piece of cardboard and stuck it in the shoe. And
if that wore out, you'd stick another piece in, or repair the shoe yourself. My son
was asking me about workhouses in Oxford, and I said, "Oh, there was one up the
Cowley Road; I remember it well." People used to say, "The way you're going on
you'll soon be up the workhouse." They had beautiful gardens in front of them,
tended by the inmates; I can see it in my mind as clear as anything.

A lot of people would go for the one and twos, and the one and tenpence for
the people that could afford it. Because after all, most people were earning thirty
shillings to three pounds a week, so that one and tenpence—it seems nothing
now, but it was quite a bit then. They had two seats in one, by the way, in the
one and tens, with no armrest for courting couples.

Generally it was a change twice a week (Monday and Thursday) because
they wanted the money twice a week, not once a week. People came twice-weekly
almost all the time. You see, there was no television, and there was nothing like
there is now, so there were two things: the radio, and the pictures. "It's rain-

BRITISH PICTORIAL PRODUCTIONS LTD.

PRODUCERS OF THE

EMPIRE NEWS BULLETIN

AND

UNIVERSAL TALKING NEWS.

TELEPHONES:-
REGENT 2418-9.
TELEGRAMS:-
"FILMOLITAN, WESTCENT, LONDON."
CABLES:-
"FILMOLITAN, LONDON."

EDITORIAL OFFICES:-

90, WARDOUR STREET,

LONDON, W.1. 2nd Sept. 1930.

S.Taylor, Esq.,
The Scala Cinema,
OXFORD.

Dear Sir,

    We are extremely obliged to you for your letter of August 30th, addressed to Universal Pictures Ltd.

    It seems to us that the St.Giles Fair should make quite an interesting subject for our news-reel.

    You may therefore take it that we shall be very glad to send an Operator down on Monday next to film same.

    If there is anything you can do in the way of assisting us to obtain good pictures, we shall be more than obliged to you.

           We beg to remain, Dear Sir,

              Yours faithfully,
              EMPIRE NEWS BULLETIN &
              UNIVERSAL TALKING NEWS

Can you please say at what time the Fair opens?

                        Editor.

Letter to Syd Taylor in response to his suggestion for a filmed news bulletin featuring St Giles' Fair. From Syd Taylor's collection.

ing—let's go to the pictures." It was always the pictures. You could have radio at any old time, but a new picture was a big attraction.

Although talking pictures were a great advantage to The Scala, the new projection system brought problems of its own, as Mr. Selwood explains:

There were two forms of sound: the sound on film and the sound on disc. The discs were sixteen-inch diameter, and you put the pickup on the inside, not the outside. The turntables weighed about a hundredweight or more; they were tremendously strong. Right at the beginning of the film there was a cross, and you got that into the gate, and you got the pickup on the inside of the record. When you started, with the two position handles, they both went together in synchronisation. The problem was, if the film broke, you had a hell of a job to get it back in synchronisation. You'd see the chap pull out the gun, put it back in, and then it would go "bang!" And there would be old Syd [Taylor] trying to manipulate the pickup!

Another funny thing, of course, is when the film broke, if you were stupid, you could join it inside out, so that when you saw it going through on the screen not only would it twist when it went through the gate, and make a hell of a noise, but the [actors] would suddenly go one way and then start going the other way. So if I ever did that—ooh, a terrible row! But it's quite easy to do, because you see when you're splicing them you could easily get it backwards (although one side was shiny and the other was matt).

In the talkies, if there was only one person operating you had to be able to operate both machines together. So you had a piece of string with hooks on, and you hooked these up when you knew the spool was coming towards the end, and you'd stand in the middle of the two at the rear stat, because you've got to swap the sound and swap in two machines. So you'd get your hand on the top lever, and then when you saw the second mark on screen you'd push that and swap it over quickly. And then, of course, take the old one out and get it ready for the next one.

In the days of highly flammable nitrate film, difficulties in the projection booth could lead to far more serious problems. Indeed, in May 1930, one-time Scala proprietor Ben Jay ended up before the judge and was fined five pounds at Enfield Police Court, for "failing to keep films not in use in a closed metal box of substantial construction."[4]

Martin Selwood: *They used carbon arc lamps, which were brilliantly white and gave off nasty sulphur fumes. It was a rather unhealthy job. I was on my own once when both operators were ill, and I had a fire when the film stuck in the gate and caught light immediately. That was Fredric March and Norma Shearer in* Smilin' Through *[Sidney Franklin, US, 1932]. Of course, I broke the top and bottom immediately and did all the things I was instructed to do, and Mr. Poyntz came running up. I got it all going again, and it was back to normal. You see, when I was young, I was extremely quick. I was very, very strong, but I was very, very quick. If anything went wrong, and you had to knock the shutter in to cut out the light I was always the first. Things went wrong quite a lot, because the films were joined up. If something went wrong and you had to cut it and splice it, it would perhaps not be spliced very well and it would click in the gate and break.*

There were twenty minutes per reel, and we had a big tin trunk that we used to put them in for safety. So you put the one that came off the machine on the right, and put the one on the left to replace it. 'Inspector Goodenough' used to call occasionally, and we'd get a telephone call preceding his visit, saying "Goodenough's about." So you'd rush around and pick up any old bits that he might not think much of, and look at the sand bucket to see that it was clean and clear. We had a great big heavy door, which swung to if there was a fire, and had to make sure it would swing to—so you did all this before he came.

The manifold difficulties of cinema projection in those days never dampened the artistry of chief operator Syd Taylor, who often used tex-tured glass slides and gels to create memorable colour effects when projecting short black-and-white films. "He used an empty spool, and he stuck on there different colours," Martin Selwood explains. "So at the beginning of the film he'd have that on the other machine and gradually rotate it. You'd get a kaleidoscope effect on the screen."

A selection of Mr. Taylor's textured glass slides. From Syd Taylor's collection.

Syd Taylor on the cinema roof in 1930.
From Syd Taylor's collection.

Syd Taylor outside the cinema in 1930.
From Syd Taylor's collection.

When not projecting, the operators would sometimes take on other duties:

Sometimes we worked through the night painting the screen white. I used to keep the arc lamps going so they could see the screen clearly, and a couple of chaps would be there with their ladders doing it white for several hours, because, of course, it got dusty and a little bit yellowy. We never got paid anything extra for it (there was no overtime or anything like that), but it was fascinating.

Installing sound, and showing foreign-language films for a primarily undergraduate audience were not the only changes John Poyntz made when he took over the running of The Scala. He also closed the sweet shop in the foyer. Syd Taylor recalls him saying, "No more chocolates, sweets or ice-creams. People should be able to sit and watch a picture in peace. Besides, I don't want to upset the old lady who runs the sweet shop across the road."[5] Martin Selwood's recollections show that an outright ban was not immediate, although smelly takeaways were definitely against the rules.

They sold chocolates, ice cream, and sweets from a tray that the girl went round with—more or less all the time, she'd go round, with a little torch and some change (a young girl; I've forgotten her name now). I don't think the shop was ever what you'd call a flourishing shop. Most of the time it was just used for advertising the programmes. I think, if it had been me, I'd have used the shop a lot more, as a lot of the time it was filled with just rubbish.

I remember the musical director of the Panatrope said to me, "Could you get me some fish and chips?" Well, Del Nevo's were just up the road (tuppence for a piece of fish, and a penny for the chips). I got them, and they said, "Don't let Mr. Poyntz know you've taken fish and chips into the auditorium!" So I sort of smuggled them down to him.

Mr. Selwood ceased regular work at The Scala in August 1931.

I went to an electrical firm, as I've always been keen on electricity, and I was a bit worried about these fumes, which were quite dangerous. I still kept in touch, helping about twice a week showing customers to their seats, mainly because I was in love with Maisie, Mr. Poyntz's youngest daughter. I thought she was fantastic, I really did. I mean, to me she was a film star. We went out secretly for five or six years. From the operating box you could step out on to the roof of the ticket office, and, from there, there was a wooden ladder down into the Jericho House gravelled path. To the right of there was the window of the ladies' toilets. Maisie used to open and shut the window if she wanted to give me a note, and on the note was, "See you nine o'clock at The Horse and Jockey," or something like that. Very romantic! She must have liked me, because on my sixteenth birthday she bought me some nine-carat gold cufflinks, with a little note, but I knew nothing could ever come of it anyway because they were rich and I was very, very poor. I wouldn't say we

*Martin Selwood aged ninety-three.
Courtesy of Martin Selwood.*

lived in the slums, but sort of one step up. Then came the shocking time when I went into the cinema and sat down, and she said, "I've got something to tell you. I've secretly married Eric." I really didn't know what to think—how anybody who'd been going out with me secretly in the evenings (going for a walk, cuddling me, kissing me) could suddenly say, "I've secretly married somebody else"? I think she was a bit this way, and a bit that way, but I've never forgotten her. I thought she was fantastic.

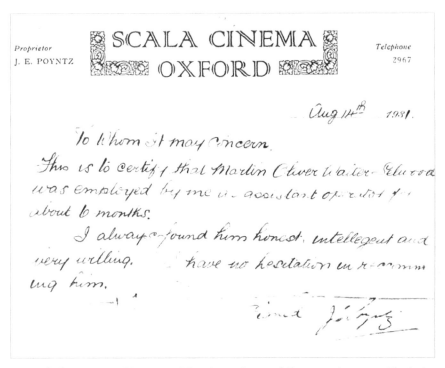

Letter of reference received by Martin Selwood upon leaving full-time employment at The Scala. Courtesy of Martin Selwood.

Maisie's new husband was Eric Bowtell (1908-1999), of whom we'll hear more, as the couple took over the running of The Scala in later years. Happily, Martin Selwood met Eva, with whom he went on to enjoy a long marriage and family.

I never saw or spoke to Maisie again. I know that eventually, when her parents died, they lived up Boars Hill. Whether it was connected with the money they got from their parents when they died I don't know. But, of course, I lost interest then because we had our sons, and a wonderful life. Done a lot of things.

The adoption of art-house programming

Through the course of the 1930s, The Scala continued to develop its reputation for showing foreign-language films, although, since the majority of titles listed in newspaper advertisements were of British or American origin, it seems likely that many of the continental films screened at this time were private performances put on expressly for university students. Nevertheless, the original emphasis on helping students to learn European languages was soon supplemented by an increased focus on the artistry and politics of world cinema.

This was the decade in which the cine-club movement, which had made its first appearance in Britain in the 1920s, burgeoned in popularity. By 1939, there were an estimated forty societies in operation, which had grown to around two hundred by the late 1940s.[6] Oxford proved one of the leaders of the pack; in 1933, a new film society was formed, which screened films at The Scala on Sunday evenings—a day of the week when cinemas used to be closed to the general public. An early membership advertisement card advised film lovers: "If you wish to see films that are different—join the Oxford City Film Society."[7] Later known simply as the Oxford Film Society, this club provided a valuable forum for like-minded art cinema enthusiasts for many years to come. Like The Scala's main public programme, the Film Society programme was structured and advertised according to university term dates, making its target membership quite clear.

An undated 1930s copy of the society's 'Rules and Regulations' states the following objectives:

1. *The purpose of the Society shall be (a) to show films of an educational, cultural and artistic value which would not ordinarily be exhibited, and those which, for one reason or another, have too specialised an interest to appeal to large audiences; (b) to revive films of outstanding merit, which, although they may have been publicly exhibited, have since gone out of circulation, and could not otherwise be seen again.*

Into class (a) will fall foreign (other than American) productions, and shorts, which are largely neglected by the commercial cinema. Class (b) will include mainly British and American feature films.

2. *The season shall consist of ten performances, during the period October-March, five before and five after Christmas (four meetings in each half season will be held in the Michaelmas and Hilary terms respectively). Performances will be given at The Scala Cinema, Walton Street, on alternate Sunday evenings during that time.*

Admission was by subscription, which in 1934 cost fifteen shillings for ten films, payable in advance. Later, the society would offer reduced rates for additional family members. Membership was open to all (except under-16s), but no guests were allowed to attend. The society was a not-for-profit organisation, which pledged to devote all income to the pursuit of its objectives.

An advertisement for the society's second season, beginning 28 October 1934, illustrates the typical range of its programme, including silent classics alongside recent releases. The features listed are *Hunted People* (Nunzio Malasomma, Germany, 1926), *La Maternelle* (Jean Benoît-Lévy and Marie Epstein, France, 1932), *Storm over Asia* (Vsevolod Pudovkin, USSR, 1928), *Poil de Carotte* (Julien Duvivier, France, 1932) and *Morgenrot* (Gustav Ucicky and Vernon Sewell, Germany, 1933).

Society members were encouraged to help select the films. An undated 1930s voting card solicits their opinions on the following options for silent revivals: *Ben Hur* (Fred Niblo, US, 1925); *The Four Horsemen of the Apocalypse* (Rex Ingram, US, 1921); *Greed* (Erich von Stroheim, US, 1924); *Intolerance* (D. W. Griffith, US, 1916); *The Last Laugh* (F. W. Murnau, Germany, 1924); *Metropolis* (Fritz Lang, Germany, 1926); *Mother* (Vsevolod Pudovkin, USSR, 1926); *La Passion de Jeanne d'Arc* (Carl Theodor Dreyer, France, 1928); and *Warning Shadows* (Arthur Robison, Germany, 1923).

It soon became the norm to accompany each main feature with one or two short films, which often included a Disney cartoon and a production from Britain's GPO Film Unit. Many of the films shown by the society in the 1930s are regarded as classics to this day. Examples from the Michaelmas 1936 season include *Battleship Potemkin* (Sergei Eisenstein, USSR,

1925), *Blackmail* (Alfred Hitchcock, UK, 1929), and the short films, *The Song of Ceylon* (Basil Wright, UK, 1934) and *Night Mail* (Basil Wright and Harry Watt, UK, 1936).

By 1937, the selection of films showed an increased emphasis on politics and current affairs. In the Hilary term that year, a selection of German dramas, including *Dr. Mabuse* (Fritz Lang, 1922), *Musik in Blut* (Erich Waschneck, 1934), *Savoy Hotel 217* (Gustav Ucicky, 1936), and Georg Wilhelm Pabst's socialist, antiwar allegory, *Kameradschaft* (1931), sat alongside the documentary, *The Expansion of Germany 1870-1914* (Andrew Miller Jones, UK, 1936).[8]

By 1937 (if not earlier), Eric Bowtell, son-in-law of owner John Poyntz, had assumed the position of Secretary to the Oxford Film Society. This no doubt helped to ease the relationship between the film society and public programming. For instance, a card advertising the 1939-40 season explains that the society had come to an arrangement with The Scala whereby *Das Testament von Dr. Mabuse* (Fritz Lang, Germany, 1933) would be shown for a three-day public run. It was noted that many members had requested this title, but it was considered that too many had seen it already to make it an appropriate selection for a film society slot.

The popularity of *Das Testament von Dr. Mabuse* among Scala customers (a film banned in Nazi Germany, where it was deemed politically subversive) appears to partake of a wider appetite for politically topical themes as the outbreak of World War Two approached. In February 1938, *Der Ammenkönig* (Hans Steinhoff, Germany, 1935) screened as part of the main public programme, "by kind permission of the City Magistrates" (as it had not received a certificate from the British Board of Film Censors).[9] Steinhoff had become associated with Nazi propaganda filmmaking, although this particular film was a relatively innocuous period-set comedy.[10]

Politics were firmly on the programme in December 1939, when the cinema hosted a screening of *A Homeland in the Making* (Georg Engel, UK/Palestine, 1939), which was arranged by the Federation of Women Zionists in conjunction with the newly formed Oxford Zionist Society.[11] In January 1942, the Scala proprietors were presented with a Jewish National Fund certificate as a gesture of thanks for making the auditorium available for another topical film screening by the Oxford Women's Zionist Society.[12]

As Britain entered the war, the Oxford Film Society proclaimed its commitment to business as usual:

Although most other Film Societies have closed down for the duration of the war, the Oxford Film Society has decided to carry on with its meetings, believing that an opportunity of continuing with the type of entertainment which it provides will be welcomed. It is thought that, with a high proportion of the University returning into residence this term, with an influx of a number of students from London University and its hospitals, and with the general increase in Oxford's population since the outbreak of war, sufficient support should be forthcoming to make possible the holding of five meetings before Christmas; and it is hoped that a further five may be held in the New Year. No difficulty over the supply of films is anticipated. [. . .] Any member called away on National Service will be entitled to repayment of the unexpired portion of his or her subscription. Membership is open to all, and those who have been moved to Oxford for the war will be welcomed.

By this stage, Eric Bowtell occupied a dual role as Secretary to both the Oxford Film Society and The Scala Cinema.[13] Although we have not been able to ascertain the date from which he took on responsibility for programming the venue, it seems likely that he began to do so as far back as the 1930s. Certainly, he would come to be recognised as the man responsible for the film choices in later years and, thus, the driving force behind The Scala's emergence as a leading light in the British arthouse scene.

Timothy Gee has shared the following memories of his encounters with Mr. Bowtell in the late 1950s:

I was first secretary, and then president, of the 'Oxford University Film Society.' As such, I probably enjoyed a closer relationship with Eric Bowtell than many of his other customers and indeed, once my association with the OUFS began, he always insisted that I should be admitted without paying, a generous gesture but one I greatly appreciated as I went on a weekly basis. This extended also to his special Sunday evening 'Oxford Film Society' showings, when he screened his own favourites. I remember him showing Henry V *[Laurence Olivier, UK, 1944], and I remember particularly seeing* Trouble in Paradise *[Ernst Lubitsch, US, 1932] there, which I only knew as a title before that.*

Eric was a remarkable man. His day job was as bursar of Summerfields School and his primary interests were playing cricket and bridge. But, despite these varied interests, he was clearly also a film enthusiast, as well as being a keen businessman. In order to get early showing of the Ingmar Bergman films, which were just starting to gain distribution in the UK in 1957, and other major continental releases, which included [René] Clair's Les Grandes Manoeuvres *[France, 1955] and several [Luis] Buñuel films, he had to agree to take the lightly pornographic films on the distributor's catalogue. These he programmed during the vacations and no doubt played to empty houses so that he could show the films the undergraduates wanted to see in term time.*

He also had a favourite double bill, which he showed every August Bank Holiday, which consisted of Monsieur Hulot's Holiday *[Jacques Tati, France, 1953] and, I forget what he partnered it with, but he always booked in the ten-minute short* The Fall of the House of Usher *[James Sibley Watson and Melville Webber, US, 1928], which carried an X certificate and thereby enabled him to exclude children from the cinema when the programme was being screened. He told me more than once that it was a specific policy of his. I think he felt that children wanted ice creams, and so forth, and distracted people from the enjoyment of the film.*[14]

Reconstruction of the building

In 1939, John Poyntz embarked on an extensive programme of alterations to The Scala, introducing many new features that remain in place today. Although the actual work was executed with remarkable speed, the project followed a long period of gestation.

Back in January 1933, E. A. Roberts (the previous proprietor, who remained the leaseholder) contacted St John's College to ask whether it would consider either signing over the freehold or extending his lease to ninety-nine years.[15] Dismissing the freehold enquiry out of hand, the estates bursar, Ronald Hart-Synnot, advised that "the College would consider granting a lease for a long period only in the event of appreciable improvement of the premises."[16] Mr. Roberts (who was resident in Brighton by this time) pursued the matter a little further, but dropped it when advised that, even if he made improvements, it was highly unlikely his lease would be extended beyond its existing 1962 expiry date.[17]

Whether Mr. Roberts' enquiries were made entirely on his own be-half or at the request of his tenant, John Poyntz, is unclear. What is certain is that by the following year, Mr. Poyntz's own ambitious ideas for redeveloping the cinema were starting to take shape.

In October 1934, John Poyntz met with the bursar and announced his plans to build two new cinemas in Oxford; one was to be on the site of the existing Scala; the proposed location of the other is not recorded. The bursar noted:

> *For this purpose he would require to purchase the leases of the houses North of the cinema in Walton and Cranham Streets so as to have a square site. I advised Mr. Poyntz to obtain an option on the leases for a short period during which he could negotiate with the College for the surrender of all the leases and the issue of a new lease for a long period which will permit of the building of a satisfactory cinema. Mr. Poyntz mentioned £50,000 as the kind of figure contemplated.*[18]

Following the bursar's advice appears to have been a protracted process, as almost five more years passed before Mr. Poyntz was ready to embark on building works. By this stage, he had abandoned the idea of a costly new rebuild and had settled on a more economical plan to adapt the existing building. He had, by now, obtained the leases to neighbouring properties (including the house around which the cinema had originally been constructed). This permitted enlargement of the foyer and auditorium, and a widening of the cinema façade to its current dimensions.

The firm selected to design the reconstruction was the London-based Frank Matcham & Co., which specialised in theatre architecture. The late Matcham's own most celebrated achievements had included the London Coliseum, and the Tower Ballroom and Circus in Blackpool.[19] Frederick G. M. Chancellor, who oversaw the design and costings for the revamped Scala, was also an experienced theatre and cinema architect. Locally, he had designed the Oxford Playhouse theatre, which had opened the previous year, and which also stood on land belonging to the St John's College estate.[20] Under his management, the firm had also been responsible for the architecture of the Super Cinema (now Odeon) in Magdalen Street, which became a Grade II listed building in 1994.

Mr. Chancellor advised that the plans would cost at least £3,250 to execute (with an additional £150 for a new canopy); this excluded the cost of any upgrades to the heating and ventilation systems, furnishings, and cinema apparatus.[21] Based on John Poyntz's commitment to spend at least £3,500 on improving the cinema, and an "undertaking to maintain as hitherto a high standard of films produced," the college agreed to extend the lease until 1999.[22] The city authorities also ratified the new plans, on the proviso that the cinema forecourt was "to be surrendered to the City, and become part of the public highway."[23] Mr. Poyntz's idea of creating a car park behind the cinema was rejected by the college, however, with the bursar suggesting the land might better be used for a "suitable war purpose."[24]

Reconstruction began in July 1939, with the building work conducted by a local firm: Messrs Hinkins & Frewin of Cranham Street.[25] These contractors had worked with Frank Matcham & Co. at least once before, when erecting the Super Cinema in the early 1920s.[26]

The timing of the refurbishment meant the screen of The Scala was already dark when war was declared on 3 September 1939, and a leaflet entitled 'War Emergency' was hastily distributed to households across the UK. It advised that, "All cinemas, theatres, dance halls and places of public entertainment will be closed until further notice [...]. They are being closed because, if they were hit by a bomb, large numbers would be killed or injured."[27] This measure was short lived and, with the government recognising their potential for raising public morale, most entertainment venues had reopened within a fortnight, leaving the imminent re-launch of The Scala unaffected.

On 16 October, after a closure period of just three months, John Poyntz was able to welcome the public to The Scala's new 575-seat auditorium. The main attraction, playing for a six-day run, was the frothy comedy-drama, *The Divorce of Lady X* (Tim Whelan, UK, 1938), which featured a top-notch cast led by Merle Oberon, Laurence Olivier, and Ralph Richardson. This was supported by the less memorable British comedy *Yellow Sands* (Herbert Brenon, UK, 1938) and a selection of Walt Disney cartoons. The following Sunday, the Oxford Film Society launched its new season with Marcel Carné's enduring classic *Le Quai des Brumes* (France, 1938).[28]

Memories of The Scala

Among the varied reminiscences of visiting The Scala in this period, two common points of experience recur: the atmosphere of watching films in a specific communal environment, and an awakening to, and appreciation of, the pleasures of different kinds of film.

Given how much time has passed, it's unsurprising that first-hand recollections of the 1930s and 1940s are dominated by childhood memories.

Bernie Burgess: *My father worked at The Scala Cinema in the 1930s. We were living at 100 Cardigan Street at the time. I can remember my sister taking me to the Scala children's matinee on Saturdays, but she was always disappointed because I would want to come out of the cinema if my favourite cowboy was losing in a fight.*

Winifred Jones (née Goodwin): *I was one of many children who were brought up in the children's home The Poplars. Due to the war, we had to be disbanded to different locations in Oxford. Many of us were fostered out, to people who had to take you in, if they had the room, regardless if they did not want you. (Horror!) My second placing was with a couple who lived two doors from the cinema. I had never seen a film, or been inside a cinema before. However, the lady of the house loved to go, so when it was a film suitable for a child to see, she took me along. What magic! I was in another world completely (heaven!) although I used to cry a lot at sad films. To me it was real, not make believe. The year spent with Mr. and Mrs. Morgan was the happiest of my entire childhood, for many reasons—one being my visits to the pictures. These thoughts have stayed with me all my life, being a comfort, you might say. Memories of seventy years ago take me back into a happy period, which is why I am so interested in your forthcoming centenary, and everything planned. If only I lived in Oxford I would have loved to have been a part of things. Simply because of that wonderful period of my childhood, I could capture, perhaps, some of that magic for a few minutes. I'm delighted the Picturehouse is still going strong; long may it continue to do so. Please feel free to include my memories, should you wish to. One little girl's moment of happiness, remembered always.*

Elaine Blerkom (née Tomkins): *I have fond memories of living in Jericho. The Scala was our local cinema. My brothers and I were regulars in the 30s and*

40s. I believe The Scala was run by twin sisters; I can't remember their names. If the cinema was running an 'A' film, or later an 'H,' we had to ask the grown-ups if they would take us in. Some people were kind enough. Sometimes it took a while to get in, but we finally did.

Ann Cole: *My sister took me at four years old to see* Frankenstein *[James Whale, US, 1931] in 1934. I sat with my head in her lap. When I was about twelve or thirteen, in the war, I used to make myself look older so I could get in. I put a bit of lipstick on, and I used to put a turban on—I must have looked hideous! You'd get a child come up to you, and they'd ask if they could take me in. I'd say, "yes, ok," and was taking these children in! It was no problem; they never questioned you.*

We never called it 'The Scar-la.' In my day it was always 'The Scay-ler.' It was quite some time before we called it 'The Scar-la.' For ages and ages we called it that.

The first colour film I saw there was The Garden of Allah *[Richard Bole-slawski, US, 1936], with Marlene Dietrich and Charles Boyer. They fell in love, and he was a priest. I can see her now, and it was very exotic. I wasn't very old, and I thought, "gosh, this is a racy film!" And, of course, the colour was beautiful. It was a very interesting and exciting time for me. It made me have a love of cinema all my life. It also helped to educate me, with all the historical films we saw.*[29]

Very little had changed by the time Jim Wright started visiting The Scala as a young boy in the early 1950s:

I was born in Jericho, and I went there from the age of about nine. I can remember that they didn't sell sweets or chocolate or ice creams, or drinks for that matter. You could bring your own in, but they didn't sell them, so you had to go across to a little shop across the road, called The Chocolate Box, to get all your bits. Mr. Poyntz thought a cinema was for watching films, so there was no advertising, like Pearl and Dean, and things like that at the time. They never opened on a Sunday, and they ran their films for two days at a time, or three days and two days, or three and three. They changed the programme; instead of having two screens [like today] they were doing it by having two-day shows and then three-day shows.

The programme was always two o'clock, and always finished smack on ten o'clock. There were always two films to a show, and most of the shows ran three to three-and-a-half hours. They used to pick up the Walt Disney cartoons—the ten minute ones. The sort of thing I used to watch was things like Burt Lancaster in The Crimson Pirate *[Robert Siodmak, US, 1952]* (lovely film—all colour, beautiful!), and other Bob Hope and Bing Crosby films, and Dorothy Lamour, like Road to Bali *[Hal Walker, US, 1952]* and those sort of things. Adventure films, being a boy.

If you had a favourite film, you might watch it twice through. Pocket money was hard to come by, so you made the most of it. There was an usherette called Elsie, who worked there for many years, and she used to turf us out. The parents used to moan, but we did get the better of her, and we used to hide under the seats until she'd been down, looked with her torch, and then disappeared again.

When I used to go to the cinema, it was ninepence, and you had to sit four rows from the front. You couldn't sit any further back. If we tried to move back a couple of seats, Elsie used to come down and move us back, even if there was nobody in the cinema. You could see the holes in the screen. I used to put my feet up on the seat in front. I used to get told off by the usherette.

We used to stand outside for an 'A' (because you had 'U's and 'A's and 'X's), and for an 'A' we would stand outside and then get an unsuspecting student to take us in. You wouldn't do that today, would you! Very often they'd pay for you as well. It always was quite a surprise if the students used to just pay for you. You'd have your money in your hand but they'd pay for you.

The projectionist that I remember was Peter Del Nevo. I knew him well, because his parents owned the fish and chip shop across the road. He worked there for twenty-seven-odd years, I think it was. He went there as a boy, I think (he told me he was fifteen, sixteen, or something like that), and he was a jolly easy person to get along with. But it was my uncle that used to work there part-time who took me to the projection box and put a wooden box there for me to put the reels on. I was eleven, so I used to get up there and lace the film up, and then you had to change over every eighteen-twenty minutes, with the shutter blade, so you had to be quite quick. And one of the things you watched for was a little dot on the right-hand side in the corner. You saw the first dot—you started the machine up; you saw the second dot—bang, over it went. If you missed, you got all the numbers on the screen.

The films used to break at regular intervals years ago, because the copies used to do the rounds quite a lot, and so they'd run them until they were falling to pieces, really. The joints as they went through—crxch! And you'd get a white screen ("Boo!!!") or a burn hole. There were always loads of joins, and they used *to chuck loads of it in the bin out the back. When we were kids we used to go and round them up and make stink bombs of them—set fire to them!*[30]

Jim Tallett: *I think that going to The Scala was like going to somebody's house, because we all rode up on bikes, would stick them against the wall at the side, and then go in. But there was not a huge great kind of foyer; you just went in and you were in the cinema—no formality at all, apart from the doorman. I seem to remember someone being turfed out for being on roller skates! I suppose he went in with his skates on (clomp, clomp, clomp) and then whizzed down, because it sloped.*[31]

Many of the current Phoenix customers began their visits to The Scala as undergraduates in the 1950s and 1960s, and still remember the profound impressions made on them by the varied foreign-language films on offer. These were invariably shown in their original language, with English subtitles. Indeed, dubbing was regarded as an abomination by the Scala management and regulars, as this February 1963 newspaper article makes clear:

UNDUBBED BEN TO THE RESCUE

CRISIS at the Scala, Oxford last night: while Les Enfants du Paradis unwound the last hour of its pythonic length, the last hour of its pythonic length, the projectionists were engaged in the routine task of checking the brand-new copy of Ingmar Bergman's Through A Glass Darkly for showing today.

They were puzzled not to find any sub-titles. As the last of the audience filed out, the beginning of the film was projected to check. Dubbed English voices rang out.

The Scala and its audiences regard the dubbing of foreign-language films with something like horror, and the contract was for a sub-titled version.

At midnight, the managing director, Mr. Eric Bowtell, sent a telegram to the distributors, following it with a telephone call this morning.

They were equally contrite, and could only suppose that a

dubbed copy, which they had passed on, had been sent by mistake from abroad.

However, they agreed to send instead Volpone, Maurice Tourneur's famous version of Ben Jonson's comedy, which has not been seen in this country for some years and is about to be revived. The revival has not yet been shown to the public or even the trade.

The Bergman film will be shown next term.

LET'S EAT AT
THE ROEBUCK

Courtesy of Oxford Mail / The Oxford Times (Newsquest Oxfordshire).

Patricia Marshall: *I came up to Oxford as an undergraduate in 1951. I can't tell you what your cinema has done for me. As an undergraduate you showed me what European cinema was, as in most of the country it was impossible to see anything but English and American films, and there were no recordings to be had. We used to go once or twice every week, sometimes more when there*

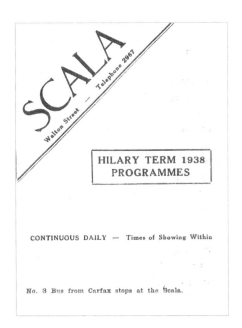

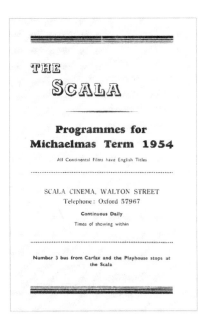

A selection of Scala programmes. 1938, 1949 and 1954 courtesy of Ian Meyrick; 1968 from Syd Taylor's collection.

was a special week of films changing every day. I saw films like Les Enfants du
Paradis *[Marcel Carné, France, 1945], which I have always loved since and
now have my own copy. Then there were so many new films, especially Ingmar
Bergman's and [Akira] Kurosawa's.*

Richard Asser has another reason to remember a busy show of Les
Enfants du Paradis in 1952: *My companion, an undergraduate at St Hilda's,
and I were shown to one of the twin seats that were a feature of the establishment.
At a moment of high drama on the screen, the cast-iron side of our seat fell off,
depositing us both in the aisle. We were just good friends, but the outraged looks
of nearby patrons assumed otherwise.* [32]

Patricia White first attended in 1950: *As undergraduates, we used to frequent The Scala, particularly in the afternoons. It was that period when French
films began to come back to us after the war. We became familiar with the great
stars of the day—Jean-Louis Barrault, Michel Simon, Edwige Feuillère, Jean-
Pierre Aumont, Jean Cocteau's early movies like* Orphée *[Jean Cocteau, 1950]
and* Drôle de Drame *[Marcel Carné, 1937]. (Drôle de Drame was set in
London, with Aumont playing a milkman, muscles rippling, and singing out "le
lait" as he ogled the maidservants; Barrault playing William Kramps the butcher
killer, riding a bicycle and dressed like a Breton onion seller; and Louis Jouvet,
the great classical actor, playing a lecherous Anglican bishop, with a cohort of
children.) My schoolgirl French was enhanced by these movies. I did not go to
France until 1957; I fell in love with France immediately. I have never stopped
following the French cinema.*

Anne Brau: *I was a student at Dorset House in the years 1950-54. The
Scala, as it was called then, was the cinema where many films from around the
world were shown. I particularly remember* The Wages of Fear *[Henri-Georges
Clouzot, France, 1953] with Yves Montand, and* Orphée. *I remember seeing
many French and Italian films there. It was The Scala that sent me on a lifetime
love of films which are not shown in the big commercial cinemas.*

Timothy Gee was a weekly attendee from 1957-60: *I was reading history, but it was always my intention to make my career in film so I regarded the visits
to The Scala as part of my education. Having grown up in Leicester, where there
wasn't a specialist cinema, I managed to see a number of standard classics, but that*

was just a beginning, so Oxford broadened my education. One regarded French, Italian, and (particularly at that time, of course) Swedish and Japanese cinema as a part of the canvas of films, of cinema history, and I wanted to know more.

You probably realise the impact of The Seventh Seal *[Ingmar Bergman, Sweden, 1957]. I think it had just opened in London when I got up to Oxford, so I was impatient to see that; it was the annual Bergman new film.* The Seventh Seal *was followed by* Wild Strawberries *[Bergman, Sweden, 1957]. Plus they were, of course, going through the back catalogue, so* Summer with Monika *[Bergman, Sweden, 1953] I think was certainly one that I saw at The Scala. Bergman struck with an enormous force; it was the Promised Land. But, particularly, I remember seeing both* Les Grandes Manoeuvres *[France, 1955] and* Porte des Lilas *[France, 1957]: two wonderful René Clair films.*

I also remember seeing Throne of Blood *[Akira Kurosawa, Japan, 1957] there. I think that was probably a film society one-off on a Sunday evening. I seem to remember that the final climactic scene of* Throne of Blood *actually provoked laughter in the audience. He's stumbling around being pierced by arrows, and one realised that an arrow probably didn't kill you outright as it always did in a Robin Hood film, and that it was only when you actually did get stuck with several arrows that you bled to death or whatever. Kurosawa was probably right in what he did, so it may have been the emotional realisation people were going through, but I do remember people laughing.*

Eric Bowtell obviously had very good projectionists, because I never remember there ever being any technical problems. Just before I came up to Oxford I had reason to stay overnight in Preston, and I found that Sawdust and Tinsel *[Ingmar Bergman, Sweden, 1953] was playing in a back-street cinema and, as I remember, the projection broke down twice or three times in the course of the screening. But that never, in my experience, ever happened at The Scala.*

They were a bit inclined to play repeatedly Vivaldi's 'The Four Seasons' as the pre-screening and interval music. I don't know whether this was the only record in the box or just a particular favourite of Eric's. It was quite radical for the period, though I grew somewhat over-familiar with it over three years. [33]

Mr. Gee realised his dream of a career in the film industry, and later edited many well-known pictures, including *The Stepford Wives* (Bryan Forbes, US, 1975), *International Velvet* (Bryan Forbes, US/UK, 1978), *Clash of the Titans* (Desmond Davis, US/UK, 1981), and *Salome's Last Dance* (Ken Russell, UK, 1988).

Jan Rae first attended The Scala in 1955: *I remember the '3 shows in 1' evenings—a 'B' feature (usually an Edgar Lustgarten crime story), the main feature, and the Pathé news. We enjoyed at that time all the great French and Italian cinema—The Scala (and The Phoenix) has always shown great continental films. No snacks or hot drinks then (just cigarettes, chain-smoked) but, whether in a double seat or a single seat, you usually ended up reclining more during the course of the programme as the thick pall of smoke from Gitanes and Gauloises threatened to obscure the top half of the screen. Witty catcalling was 'de rigueur' if the 'B' feature was laughable (it usually was!) Happy days...*

Susanna Pressel and James Fry: *Like many people, I'm sure we have very happy memories of sitting in that double seat in the back row of the cinema in the 1960s. It was when we were students, and soon after we had first started 'going out' together. We've been together ever since—partly thanks to those wonderful evenings at the pictures, watching all kinds of films. We've been coming back regularly ever since.*

Patrick Moles: *My first visit to The Scala was in 1965 with a group from my class at Cheney School, led by our form and Liberal Studies teacher Robert Catterall, whom we nicknamed 'Bobcat.' We saw Jean-Luc Godard's* Bande à Part *[France, 1964]. I had not been to any cinema much, and certainly not to an 'art house' to see a subtitled film. Although I didn't thoroughly understand it, I was intrigued by the black and white 'anarchic' film and subsequently made many further visits to see other films, mostly on my own. I well remember the barrel-like ceiling of the cinema, and the clock with an octagonal face, and the fact that the lighting was always subdued. I, like many other young men and women, exchanged some kisses with a member of the opposite sex while watching in the double seats at the back, before they were removed in 1970 when The Scala was refurbished and turned into a multi-screen cinema.*

I cannot remember all the films that I watched, but Viridiana *[Luis Buñuel, Mexico/Spain, 1961],* Kanal *[Andrezj Wajda, Poland, 1956], and* Closely Observed Trains *[Jiří Menzel, Czechoslovakia, 1966] stick in my memory, as well as French old favourites like* Jules et Jim *[François Truffaut, 1963],* Les Vacances de M. Hulot *[Jacques Tati, 1953] and* Mon Oncle *[Tati, 1958]. I well remember the efforts of the main character in* L'Homme qui Aimait les Femmes *[Truffaut, 1983] to chat up and find out who the woman telephonist with the sexy voice was who gave him his morning alarm call. What a man!*

June Parker: *Arletty was in one called,* Huis Clos *[Jacqueline Audry, France, 1954], which is about somebody who dies, and heaven or hell (whichever it is that they go to) is like a very grand hotel, and everyone has their own room. It made a tremendous impression on me, and I still every now and again think, "I wonder if heaven or hell is like that," you know. Is it going to be like that?* [34]

Jan: *As a student I saw* Z *[Costa-Gavras, France / Algeria, 1969], an amazing film. I'd seen nothing like it and it had a huge impact on my thinking about the world—a political awakening you might say. I followed it by seeing* L'Aveu *(The Confession) [Costa-Gavras, France / Italy, 1970] shortly after.*

The quality of the films shown in the 1950s and 1960s (at least during term time) encouraged regular visits and a generally forgiving attitude towards certain shortcomings of the viewing environment.

Peter T. started watching films at The Scala in 1951: *It has come through various stages of 'personality.' When I was a student it was known as 'the fleapit,' and frequented by 'strange' people to see questionable films.*

Elisabeth Salisbury: *As a student here I came frequently from 1956-59. It was pretty much a fleapit but showed fantastic films. I particularly remember* The Seventh Seal, Miss Julie *[Alf Sjöberg, Sweden, 1951],* The Wages of Fear, *and, of course, the Marx Bros.*

Elisabeth remembers the auditorium did not always smell good, and particularly recalls an occasion on which a rat ran over her friend's foot. After reporting this interloper to the manager, she enjoyed free tickets for a good two or three years.

During a conversation with Jim Tallett and Ann Cole, Jim Wright recalls, "they used to call it 'the bug house' because you came out with an itch."

Jim Tallett adds: *I didn't ever find that, I must say. It was disinfected. I do remember that the screen was often more or less obscured by a huge pall of smoke, because everyone was smoking in there, and then you could see the [projector] rays. It was gradually rising, so by the end of the evening I should think you'd be choking pretty well!*

Ann Cole: *They used to come round with the 'flick gun'. Either it was for fleas, or just to freshen the atmosphere. I never found out why they did it.*[35]

Sue Bateman first attended in 1966: *When I first came it was The Scala—a real fleapit (you literally got bitten) but renowned for showing avant-garde films. I saw* Ivan the Terrible *[Sergei Eisenstein, USSR, 1944] and* The Seventh Seal: *good old classics. It was very popular with students, and* <u>red</u>.

Timothy Gee offers a more sympathetic account of the state of the auditorium at that time. *Certainly I never would have used the word 'fleapit'. I mean, it was not a picture palace, in the sense I think probably not a great deal of money was spent on redecorating and so forth. But technically it was always in good shape. We're talking about 1957-60, and probably a lot of cinemas were not spruced up, because carpeting and that sort of thing was in short supply, if it wasn't actually on coupons. So it was clean, and the rubbish was always cleared away. I don't think he sold ice creams or anything of that sort, so there wasn't that sort of litter. Certainly not popcorn, but popcorn wasn't 'in' in cinemas in those days anyway.*[36]

James Leheny certainly had no complaints. *It was the academic year 1965-66 and I was living in digs in Wellington Square. I'd never spent a winter in Britain before, so the small gas fire in my bed sitter, which required shilling coins (which were hard to come by, since nearly all the shilling coins in the realm were in gas meters), was barely sufficient to warm the room, with its high ceiling and drafty windows.*

So, on cold winter nights, I had only a few alternatives: I could return to the Bodleian Library's Upper Reading Room, where I'd spent most of the day, or I could huddle by my fire, drinking tea and listening to the BBC Third Programme, or I could climb into bed, under a duvet that kept me warm, and read books—which is what I'd been doing most of the day.

OR, I could go to The Scala Cinema on Walton Street, buy an inexpensive stalls ticket, remain warm, and be entertained with some quite wonderful films—and all for less than the gas meter would have consumed in a comparable period of time!

I'd always loved films, even mediocre Hollywood fare, and The Scala enabled me to stay warm, and to become engaged and entertained, both mentally and visually.

These days, I think of the old Scala cinema whenever I walk down Walton Street on my visits to Oxford, or when I join friends there to see a film at The Phoenix. It's a great institution. I shall always harbour very fond memories of my winter nights there in the 1960s. Long may it thrive!

The final years

On 11 December 1962, John Poyntz died aged seventy-five, followed, almost exactly two years later, by his wife May.[37] Chairmanship of The Scala Cinema (Oxford) Limited passed to their daughter Daphne, who continued to run it in partnership with Eric Bowtell.

Public perception was that business at the cinema continued as usual but, behind the scenes, great changes were afoot. On 4 January 1966, an Extraordinary General Meeting was held, and a special resolution passed: "That the company be wound up voluntarily, and that Sydney Ernest Clark, of Boswell House, 1-5 Broad Street, Oxford, be and is hereby appointed Liquidator for the purposes of such winding up."[38] Three years later, Mr. Clark invited members of the company to a further meeting "on Friday the 28th day of March 1969, at 11.30 o'clock in the forenoon precisely, for the purpose of having an account laid before them, and to receive the Liquidator's report, showing how the winding-up of the Company has been conducted and the property of the Company disposed of."[39]

By this time, Jim Wright was working as a part-time projectionist at The Scala. Business seemed steady to him.

Like today, it was always quiet in the afternoons, but in the evenings you'd get quite a few people in, especially if they were running new continental films, and things like that. They used to do very well with the students. There were always queues.

Nevertheless, he had begun to suspect that Mr. Bowtell's involvement might be drawing to a close.

I asked him. I said, "Are you thinking of packing it in, by any chance?" because he was getting on a bit. He told me that he'd just had enough, real-

ly—that he'd "done his share," as he put it to me. I don't think any of the other staff knew because, apparently (as [projectionist] Peter Del Nevo told me), they came in to go to work one day and the place was all locked up. Just like that! Usherettes turned up; the projectionist turned up; everybody. Even the films were left outside.[40]

"It was very sudden," says cinema historian and ex-Scala projectionist Ian Meyrick.

This was the way Star [the buyers] operated. One of the conditions that Mr. Bowtell was given was that they didn't tell the staff or anything; the whole thing was completely secret, and The Scala changed over without warning. In fact Peter Del Nevo told me that he read about it in Kine Weekly. *Almost every week (I can remember in those days) in the* Kine Weekly *there would be an announcement that Star had taken over circuits and individuals. They were on a massive acquisition drive at that time.*[41]

On 24 June 1970, a short article in the *Oxford Mail* announced the news to local cinemagoers:

As The Scala changes hands in Walton Street, Oxford, cinema economics seem to be getting trickier and trickier. The Regal in Cowley Road now has to run bingo half the week, and only strong local action prevented The Regal at Abingdon from tearing out the projection equipment and providing bingo every day.
But the policy of The Scala—which shows good, if not generally spanking new, films—has been proved a success. The last private owner says it still makes a profit. Today it belongs to the same firm that runs the Regals in Bicester and Abingdon. Although the new owners have not yet declared their plans, it is to be hoped they do not include more bingo. They should Carry On Projecting.[42]

After retiring from the cinema, Mr. Bowtell was able to give more time to other activities, including the Oxford Bridge Club, among whose members he remains respected and fondly remembered.

Michael Robinson: *I knew him through Bridge, which I started playing when I was at school in the sixties. I suppose he was involved with the cinema at that time but, although I was movie-crazed in my teenage years, I wasn't aware at that time that Eric was involved with the cinema. He would, I guess, keep the things in separate compartments a bit.*

He was a very charming, very gentlemanly person. When we started up he

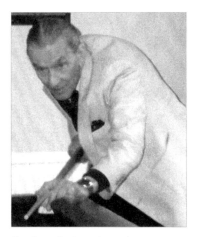

was very, very kind to us; he would drive us to away matches when we started playing for the county, and that sort of thing. It was very sad he never had any children.[43]

After the death of his wife Maisie, Mr. Bowtell became reacquainted with his childhood sweetheart, Mary Forrester, whom he married at the age of ninety.

Judy Brown: *The next part of the story is so romantic. She and Eric had known each other in their late teens, but then I think they sort of went their separate ways.*

Eric Bowtell relaxes during his retirement. Courtesy of Michael Robinson.

The Scala in 1970. Photograph by Ian Meyrick.

She played Bridge and came upon a problem, so she wrote to Eric and I think he rang her up. They met and got on extremely well. Eric was, by this time, pretty frail. He ended up in hospital, and she took him home with her because he needed somebody to look after him. They had a terribly happy few years together.[44]

Eric Bowtell's retirement marked the end of The Scala's forty years under a single family's ownership—years in which its enduring reputation as one of the UK's leading art-house cinemas were firmly established. So ended an era.

Chapter Three
Studio 1 & 2: 1970-1977

The Scala's new owner was Star Associated Holdings Limited. For the first time in its history, Oxford's Walton Street cinema was brought under the umbrella of a large national chain.

From a customer perspective, few changes were instantly obvious. Aside from the first day glitch reported by Peter Del Nevo, there was no period of closure, says Ian Meyrick.

> *Star just took over, and then they ran it as The Scala for a while. They ran through the summer in the same kind of way, showing—well, certainly one of the films was* Camelot *[Joshua Logan, US, 1967], and things like that. Nothing really changed in the programme because The Scala used to show normal revivals. The only thing that I remember they did was to take out the little slide projector they had, which was quite a historic little thing, but they had some kind of thing against slide projectors apparently.*[1]

Bigger changes were on the horizon, nonetheless. Star's business plan and company ideology could hardly be more different from that of their predecessors, and the change of ownership would have tremendous consequences for The Scala and its customers.

Star Cinemas

The Star group of cinemas started life in 1931 when Walter Eckart (1899-1964), an Essex-born toy importer, purchased The Majestic Cinema (formerly The Star Picture Palace) in Castleford, Yorkshire. The New Star, as he renamed it, subsequently doubled as head office for his other rapidly growing cinema acquisitions. Twenty years later, his cinema empire had swelled to fifty venues, which spread across central and northern England. As the business grew, Walter inducted his sons, Derek and Rodney, into the firm. An apprenticeship period working front of house helped to teach them the trade from the bottom up, before they rose through the ranks to become joint Managing Directors, based in Star's expanded headquarters in Leeds.[2]

By July 1958, the number of cinemas controlled by Star had reportedly exploded to 118. Despite this rapid expansion, and the announcement of "a £300,000 deal which shows [Walter Eckart's] faith in the future of the movies," by 1958, the British cinema business was facing some very real problems.[3] Between 1950 and 1960, the amount spent on cinemagoing by the British people fell a massive 64%.[4] Star responded to this threat by taking advantage of a change in legislation, in order to diversify their business operations and property portfolio.

On 1 May 1961, the Betting and Gaming Act of 1960 came into effect, legalising gambling for small cash prizes. Britain's entertainment landscape changed radically, as casinos, betting shops, and bingo halls sprung up in communities of all sizes. In December of that year, a government report estimated a turnover of £762 million for all forms of gambling in 1961, of which at least £25 million was reckoned to have been taken in the newly-opened commercial bingo clubs.[5]

Star was one of the first cinema operators to adopt bingo on a large scale. Although bingo was not the only form of non-cinematic entertainment it supplied (around the same time, Star also experimented with ice-skating rinks and discotheques), it would have the greatest impact on the future of its cinema business. Some cinemas were converted entirely to bingo, while others became mixed-purpose.[6] A classified advertisement placed in the *Daily Express* in December 1964 is a good indicator of the range of Star's business interests at that time. "Top salaries and excellent career prospects await men with personality and a flair for showmanship. Activities within this rapidly expanding company include:- cinemas; bingo and social clubs; entertainment centres; night clubs; catering."[7]

By the time Star purchased The Scala in Oxford, bingo had become the largest part of its business. The lease of twenty-five new bingo clubs in May 1969 brought its total to 144, while the number of cinemas it ran had dropped to sixty-eight by this point.[8] Luckily for film fans, The Scala escaped the craze for converting cinemas to bingo clubs. Nevertheless, the ways in which Star sought to modernise the building and the nature of its business gave rise to dramatic changes.

From one screen to two

Between 1950 and 1969, annual UK cinema admissions fell from just below 1,400 million to 215 million, within which period around two-thirds of cinemas closed down. As many owners of those that survived found their large, traditional auditoriums an ever-greater struggle to fill, a new fashion emerged among those opting to retain movies as the main part of their business. In 1965, Rank, one of the major circuits, opened a two-screen cinema in Nottingham, and subsequently embarked on a programme of converting their other cinemas to twin and triple screen venues. The largely empty and hard-to-heat screens of earlier years were replaced by smaller, more intimate spaces designed for ease of staffing and maintenance, while these multi-screen venues offered customers a wider choice of films.[9]

By 1969, the fashion for splitting traditional cinema screens into two or more smaller spaces was becoming the new norm, and Star set about their own conversions with gusto. Cinema historian Brian Hornsey reports that by November 1971 they had sixteen twin cinemas, one triple, and two four-screens. Around the same time, they also created a five-screen cinema in Manchester, which they claimed to be the first five-screener in Europe.[10] In many cases, Star renamed their newly subdivided cinemas 'studios.'

Ian Meyrick: *For the twinning, if I remember rightly, they closed on 24 October. By the next Monday everything had gone. Helen (who is now my wife) and I went to a film, which was* Spartacus *[Stanley Kubrick, US, 1960]. We*

went up [to the projection box] at half time, because it was a film with an in-
terval; I started the last half off, and we went back downstairs. Helen managed
to lose a glove (we were in on Saturday night), so I went in on Monday to try to
find it, and the whole place had just been torn apart. You wouldn't have believed
anyone could have got going so fast! All the equipment, the projection, had been
pulled to one side. The actual auditorium had been completely stripped.[11]

Star's favoured technique for subdividing cinemas allowed them to
complete conversions very quickly and at low cost. The redevelopment
of The Scala, achieved during a closure of just two months, followed
their normal practice. A press release announcing its redevelopment (reproduced opposite) explains the process, which is illustrated by a graphic
that appeared in *The Oxford Times* on the week of reopening.

Courtesy of Oxford Mail / The Oxford Times (Newsquest Oxfordshire).

Splitting the auditorium in two was not the only modification made
by Star, who also added a new canopy and signage to the building façade,
and refurbished the interior according to the fashions of the time. An
advertising feature in *The Oxford Times* described the ways in which they
sought to enhance the cinemagoing experience.

Studio 1 has a 25 foot "floating" screen backed by gold-coloured curtains
draped from floor to ceiling and lit by concealed lighting above and below. Be-
tween performances there is no curtain in front of the screen. Instead the screen
is decorated with psychedelic lighting.

The Star Group of Companies

Incorporating Star Associated Holdings Ltd and Associated Companies

Britains Leading Entertainment Organisation

CINEMAS ★ BINGO & SOCIAL CLUBS ★ CATERING ★ PENNY FARTHING CLUBS

<u>NEW TWIN CINEMA DEVELOPMENT FOR OXFORD</u>

Opening during the holiday period in Oxford is a new luxurious dual cinema unit incorporating a 240 seat cinema and a 140 seat cinema. These new cinemas — Studio 1 and Studio 2 — have been built from the shell of the old Scala Cinema, in Walton Street, Oxford. They will open to the public on Monday, December 28th.

Behind the project is the Star Group of Companies, the Leeds based national entertainment organisation which operates over 250 branches of various facets of entertainment throughout the country.

The final transformation from the former Scala to the new luxurious twins has taken only eight weeks. A tremendous combined building operation which brings Oxford two intimate and luxurious cinemas, comparable with cinema operations anywhere in the country. This supreme achievement has only been made possible by the use of revolutionary new system of projection which has been pioneered and developed by the Star Group.

Both cinemas are at ground level in 'tandem' formation — with Studio 1 in the front half of the building and Studio 2 to the rear. A single projection suite serves both auditoria — an operation which could only be achieved by deflecting the projected image from its normal direct route. To do this the 'periscope' idea of angled mirrors has been incorporated into the projection system. This enables the projected image for Studio 2 to be beamed into and out of a false ceiling and subsequently onto the screen. Studio 1 is reached by direct projection, via the whole of the false ceiling above Studio 2 and through a glazed aperture into the auditorium and onto the screen.

Thickly carpeted and luxuriously upholstered throughout, both auditoria are designed to ensure the maximum comfort for the cinema going public. Studio 1 has the very latest 'floating' screen with illuminated curtains draped behind. Studio 2, with a curved, slightly angled screen, is smaller but just as luxurious.

The opening choice of films will be of great interest to the general public. Studio 1 offers advance booking facilities and an extended run for the critically acclaimed 'Anne of the Thousand Days' starring Richard Burton as Henry V111 and Genevieve Bujold as Anne Boleyn. Studio 2 will open with the new anti-western 'There was a Crooked Man' presenting a contrasting selection of entertainment to cinema-goers.

Star Cinemas press release. Courtesy of Oxford Mail / The Oxford Times (Newsquest Oxfordshire).

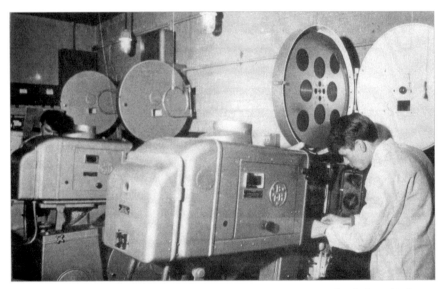

Chief projectionist Roy Cox in the revamped projection booth. Courtesy of Oxford Mail/The Oxford Times (Newsquest Oxfordshire).

The Scala reopens as Studio 1 & 2. Courtesy of Oxford Mail/The Oxford Times (Newsquest Oxfordshire).

In Studio 2, the screen is surrounded by illuminated translucent panels in brilliant orange. Comfortably upholstered seats in a velvet material have been installed in both cinemas.

The most striking thing about the cinema—apart from the new, imposing frontage—is the intimate atmosphere inside, particularly in Studio 2, which is more like a cosy club than a public cinema. This effect is heightened by thick wall-to-wall carpets in both cinemas, the linking corridor, and in the foyer.[12]

The two screens allowed Star to cater simultaneously to The Scala's established audience for serious, upmarket cinema and those seeking lighter entertainment. It reopened on 28 December 1970. In Studio 1, the acclaimed British historical drama *Anne of the Thousand Days* (Charles Jarrott, 1969) brought together a heavyweight cast including Richard Burton, Geneviève Bujold, Anthony Quayle, Michael Hordern, and Irene Papas. In Studio 2, Kirk Douglas starred alongside Henry Fonda, Hume Cronyn, Warren Oates, and Burgess Meredith in director Joseph L. Mankiewicz's enjoyable Western romp, *There Was a Crooked Man...* (US, 1970). It was a good start, but there were further changes in store, and not all would be widely welcomed by long-standing Scala regulars.

Courtesy of Oxford Mail / The Oxford Times (Newsquest Oxfordshire).

A new kind of programming

From 1930 to 1970, The Scala had been a family concern whose business model centred on the provision of art-house and foreign-language films to a predominantly student audience, and which had built and maintained customer loyalty by providing a type of programme unique within the local area. For much of that time, Eric Bowtell's own cinephilia had contributed to the film choices, with commercial considerations sitting alongside a highly visible programming integrity. Things were different under the ownership of Star.

As one might surmise from the wide-ranging fields of entertainment in which Star engaged by the time it purchased The Scala, celebration of the art of film lagged some way behind the driving commercial interests. With the company firmly ensconced in the world of show business, a pamphlet

Left to right: Rodney Eckart, Bernard Rains, and Derek Eckart at the 1968 Star Parade Awards. Courtesy of Pat Church.

celebrating the 1968 'Star Parade Awards' features the joint Managing Directors, Derek and Rodney Eckart, and Director Bernard Rains, pictured alongside the swimsuit and sash-clad glamour girls, 'Miss Star Cinemas' and 'Miss Star Bingo.'

The sparseness of customer reminiscences of the Star years suggests that some of The Scala's world cinema fans drifted away during this period (although many would return to The Phoenix in the late 1970s and beyond, when new operators reinstated a programming policy featuring an extensive array of art-house titles). The most extensive accounts of the cinema's incarnation as Studio 1 & 2, therefore, come from staff members—whether based at the cinema itself or at the company's booking office in London. Although it's hard to think of these years as the cinema's glory days, their recollections paint a vivid portrait of the hard slog of trying (successfully, to the benefit of all of us) to keep the venue afloat, as

British film exhibition headed into its darkest period. Several still work in the cinema industry today and, whatever one's personal opinion of Star's style of operation, their film knowledge and committed professionalism played an important role in keeping things running through tough times.

Three former film bookers for Star (Ron Nicholson, Alan North, and the company's first Oxford booker, Mike Vickers—all of whom worked at its Soho office in the 1970s) have shared their recollections and insights into the company's approach to cinema programming. Former chief projectionist Bob Ord offers another perspective: an informative and often humorous account of life on the front line.

Ron was the first booker to share his memories, providing an overview of the operation and climate of Star's booking office:

When I replaced Mike Vickers in 1973, the London office was based in Gala House, Old Compton Street, and came complete with resident ghost. It's now Soho House [a private members' club for film and media professionals], but I'm not sure if the spook is still in residence!

The team consisted of myself, Alan North, and a secretary, Sheila Campbell, who, incidentally, I later married. Ken Newton was the booking manager. He was based in the Leeds office but came to London for a couple of days most weeks to meet distributors and keep an eye on us. [Director Bernard] Rains was a hard-bitten Yorkshireman, who had a dim view of Londoners and only accepted the London office as a necessity because the distributors were based here. He was also deeply suspicious of Ken Newton and, when Ken became ill, took the opportunity to replace him with John Gregory. John was a lovely guy in his late thirties, with one of the sharpest movie minds I've ever encountered. He was always looking for an angle on any deal, and knew everybody in the industry. He brought Jacky Simons with him as his PA, and it transformed the way the office worked. He was the one who negotiated Emmanuelle *[Just Jaeckin, France, 1974], which was enormously successful. The office relocated to the Studio Cinema in Oxford Street around 1977 and, finally, to Wardour Street. By then, I was the only one of the original team left.*

The company ethos was basically to make as much money as possible with limited resources. Certainly there was no national programming policy; it was up to the bookers to get the best possible movies available. In those sites that were barred by the large chains we had to be very inventive with programming. Double bills were very popular—anything with Bruce Lee or Clint Eastwood usually hit the spot. We also played a lot of sex movies that the mainstream exhibitors wouldn't touch.[13]

At this time, two circuits (ABC and Rank, the latter operating both Odeon and Gaumont halls) dominated British cinema exhibition. Making the most of their substantial market shares, these companies used their strong negotiating position with film distributors to gain exclusive screening rights to the strongest titles, thereby exercising a stranglehold that denied other operators the cream of the first-run movies. For smaller companies, such as Star, a great deal of ingenuity was required in order to populate their schedules with box office hits, which is why securing the rights to show *Emmanuelle*, and other successful adult titles that ABC and Rank eschewed, became so crucial to the company's operation.

Alan North: *I recall that the Oxford site had a strong student audience and was programmed accordingly—relying on a mix of reissues, double bills and repertory titles. Once the city's two first run ABC cinemas had played the film, for what was then normally just a two- or three-week booking, we would capitalise on any remaining box office.*

I recall two examples in particular: 1) a double bill of the very popular David Essex musical dramas Stardust *[Michael Apted, UK, 1974] and* That'll Be The Day *[Claude Whatham, UK, 1973], and 2) an extended engagement on* Cabaret *[Bob Fosse, US, 1972], after it had picked up its Oscar nominations and subsequent wins. Ron is quite correct about long engagements on what were at the time quite controversial titles. As well as the aforementioned* Emmanuelle*, I also recall* Last Tango in Paris *[Bernardo Bertolucci, France/ Italy, 1972] and* The Night Porter *[Liliana Cavani, Italy, 1974] being two of them. Ron is also correct in his praise of John Gregory, who really did know everyone in the industry. I recall one very notable day when his good friend, the 'Carry On' actor Charles Hawtrey, turned up unannounced at the office with a box of champagne... but that really is another story!!!*[14]

Mike Vickers, who booked the films for Oxford's Studio 1 & 2 for several years, recalls that subtitled films were pretty much dropped from the programming agenda, but that contemporary student tastes remained an important determinant of the kinds of films that were shown. Double bills featuring quality studio productions such as *Cabaret* were a popular draw. In continuing to cater to a strong student audience, the programming responded to wider changes in the cultural and cinematic landscape. American independent films such as *The Graduate* (Mike Nichols, 1967) and *Midnight Cowboy* (John Schlesinger, 1969) proved perennial favourites and were brought back time after time, and The Scala's routine of closing at 10.30 p.m. gave way to regular late shows.[15]

As Ron and Alan's recollections make clear, the main job of Star's film bookers was to find avenues of programming mainstream titles that catered to the demands of the local population while working within the restrictions of being barred from top product by larger cinema chains. Mike offers a fuller account of the challenges he faced in trying to strike a balance between the expectations of his bosses, the restrictions posed by the operators of the local ABC, and his personal sense of what was right for the cinema.

I remember I was booking 141 screens, and I calculated I had eight minutes per week to spend on each screen, so there wasn't much chance to customise the programme. The only time we ever played any major releases was when there was a falling out between Paramount and Warner Bros. and ABC. We got There Was a Crooked Man... *because ABC had had a falling out with Warners. We got that in all the competitive slots around the country.*

Studio 1 & 2's booking of *Anne of the Thousand Days* was the product of another disagreement about rental terms between ABC and the film's distributor, Mike explains. In those days, when the biggest cinema chains had the upper hand over film distributors, smaller chains, such as Star, would sometimes benefit from these conflicts, but such incidents certainly couldn't be relied on as the mainstay of programme product. Unable, and to a degree unwilling, to compete on an equal level with the major cinema chains, The Scala had prioritised foreign-language titles. Star, as noted above, took a different approach.

Mike: *Star had a policy of showing sex films. They made a lot of money showing the softcore, light stuff, and they wanted to play them in Oxford. I'd have fights to try not to do that, and to show more upmarket films instead. You see, the audience there was mostly students in those days. In your heart of hearts, you'd know that sex films weren't right for that venue, and they didn't do par-*

ticularly well there, but there were certain films I had to play. Certain films had to play in a certain number of screens. I can remember on the odd occasion trying not to play some of the films in Oxford, but if I had to I would put them in for the shortest possible time. Where I had the opportunity I'd play them somewhere other than Oxford.

There was, he says, no discussion with cinema managers about the selection of films that would be shown; each week's programme would be presented to them as a done deal.

Bob Ord, who transferred to Oxford from Star's Colchester venue, recalls:

When I started at the cinema in 1974, I only expected to be there about three months, as they were having staffing troubles in the projection room, and a Star Group area manager asked me to go and sort out the problems. I liked it so much I stayed there thirteen years! The cinema was called Studio 1 & 2 when I joined, soon to become Studio 1 & X. Remember this was about the time of another decline of cinema after colour TV had got more popular, so the Star Group resorted to that old thing called Sex. In a photo I took the first week I was there, one of the films was called Can You Keep it Up for a Week? *[Jim Atkinson, UK, 1974] (with* Blazing Saddles *[Mel Brooks, US, 1975] in the other cinema).*[16]

Studio 1 & 2 in 1974. Photograph by Bob Ord.

Few customers have shared their memories of visiting the cinema at this time. "No one wanted to admit even thinking of going to those sorts of films!" he observes. One of the few kind souls to do so was Alison Gomm:

I have been a loyal customer of The Phoenix since I first came to Oxford as an undergraduate in 1974. In those days it was Studio 1 & 2, one of which became, late on a Friday night if I remember correctly, Studio X, and showed horror and what I think would be classified as soft porn. I was rather a naïve eighteen-year-old who had led quite a sheltered life. Late one Friday night, after a party, I was walking past Studio X with some friends who suggested that it would be amusing to go in and see the film that was then showing. I don't remember the title, and I've not been able to trace it by googling, but I remember that the plot concerned a female vampire and a blond male hero who was only able to overcome her by impaling her with his enormous silver penis. The film was sparsely attended (bunches of giggling students and a few solitary men, as I remember) and I believe that I was the only person in the cinema who noticed that the projectionist put the reels on in the wrong order—because I was following the plot!

Alison's recollection paints a vivid picture of the mid-70s milieu (although, as is often the case, mythology has muddied historical detail, and it seems probable that the late show she attended was a 'regular' public performance, rather than one belonging to members-only club Studio X). Yet the slide into sleaze would indeed come to define the cinema's image in the mid-1970s, reaching its apotheosis with the launch of Studio X in 1976. In the interim, Alison certainly wasn't the only customer to be somewhat perplexed by the movie on offer, as an amusing story in the *Oxford Mail* described:

After watching the erotic goings-on in Emmanuelle *in Studio 2 with increasing embarrassment, one of the two old ladies in front of a colleague finally turned round and asked him: "Excuse me, is this a love story?" Eventually the penny dropped that what they thought they were seeing was* Love Story *[Arthur Hiller, US, 1970] in Studio 1. But for the moment all he could stammer out was: "Well, there is a bit of love in it."*[17]

A 'conveyor belt of sex films'

Sex films, Mike Vickers explains, had two big advantages. One was that the major chains boycotted them, so those cinemas showing them would often have exclusivity in the local area. The other was that the cinemas only paid 25% of the box-office takings to the distributors, which allowed cinemas a much higher profit margin than did many of the more mainstream titles. In the 1970s, numerous companies specialised in distributing this kind of product to independent cinemas, taking advantage of the burgeoning number of private cinema clubs where uncensored titles could legally be shown, and catering to a popular demand in the pre-home video days.

By the mid-1970s, Mike had moved on from Star and, under his successors, the programming emphasis edged towards increasingly salacious material.

Bob Ord: *Star did have cinemas showing first runs over the country, but in Oxford I think they found it hard running with the big boys like ABC, who had the monopoly. Star probably thought—sex always sells, even in the Roman days! When I joined Studio 1 & 2 we did not have sex films all the time, then all of a sudden we had the conveyor belt of sex films. Week after week, they all seemed to merge into one, but I do remember that the main films were from USA, Germany, and the Swedish type! After people got fed up with them, Star Group thought they would set up the Studio X club cinema to tantalise the public to think they were getting something a bit stronger.*

Studio X was a club type cinema showing very soft porn compared with today (2012). To become a member, the person had to wait twenty-four hours. A lot of people tried to persuade us to let them into Studio X before they were a member, but they never got in as they could have been the Mystery Shopper from the authorities! We had to have a person on the door to the cinema all the time. The outside exit door had a switch on it, so when opened a light would come on to warn us to check the door and that no one was being sneaked in!

Films in the mid-1970s were more like the 'What the Butler Saw' in the 1920s in comparison with today's standards of porn that everyone, even school teenagers, can view online. A film just popped into my head: Chesty Morgan— the woman with the seventy-three-inch bust. I believe she suffocated her victims with her boobs [in Deadly Weapons *(Doris Wishman, US, 1974)]. The thing is, some of the films were so tame that sometimes we had films arrive that had been passed by the BBFC and had an 'X' certificate, so that was spliced out and not shown!*

Studio X launched on 11 July 1976. Writing for *The Oxford Times*, Peter Bradley managed to contain his enthusiasm:

> *Studio 2 becomes Studio X this weekend, and celebrates its new status with a couple of productions which the BBFC have never even seen, still less certified. I can find no information about* Animal Love, *although I am assured that it is not an RSPCA documentary, and* The Ramrodder *is even more inscrutable: its connection with the art of musketry seems to be tenuous in the extreme.*[18]

Whereas *Animal Love* (Kenny, US, 1969) remains relatively obscure, *The Ramrodder* (Van Guylder, US, 1969) would acquire minor notoriety for having been shot at the Spahn Movie Ranch during Charles Manson's occupation; two 'family' members, Bobby Beausoleil and Catherine Share, appear in supporting roles.

A cinema in crisis

In July 1975, Star's joint Managing Directors, Derek and Rodney Eckart, pleaded guilty at Leeds Crown Court to a £47,000 tax fraud. According to a contemporary newspaper report, "Mr. Derek Clarkson, for the prosecution, said the brothers had houses and cars on an expensive scale, owned boats, bought thousands of pounds worth of paintings and jewellery and one had a villa in Spain. But they were motivated by greed and used many methods to cheat the Inland Revenue." Clarkson went on to explain that "both brothers had work done on their homes, but [...] bills for the work and for household heating were put through the company accounts to avoid paying tax." The brothers' convictions for conspiracy and six offences of making false statements resulted in each receiving a two-year jail sentence, a £14,000 fine, and liability for prosecution costs of up to £2,000.[19]

Bingo still represented the major part of Star's business at this time, and government regulation of gambling operators was strict. Although this wasn't the first time Star had fallen foul of the law (in 1961, The Coliseum Cinema in Whitby had been fined for allowing a girl under eighteen to play bingo), the implications of the tax fraud convictions were on another scale entirely.[20] Derek and Rodney Eckart were smart businessmen, recalls Mike Vickers, but this episode resulted in the loss of their bingo license. With bingo halls generating the largest part of the company's revenue, its future outlook was bleak.

Even before the trial took place, it seems the company realised that the fallout from the charges would be grave. Earlier that year, it sold its 158 bingo halls to EMI, which already held a 50% stake in fifty-four of the sites.[21] On 27 February 1975, an Extraordinary General Meeting was convened and a resolution passed that Star Associated Holdings be wound up.[22] This voluntary liquidation was part of a reorganisation under which business was transferred to the newly formed Star Group of Companies Limited.[23] Star continued, but as a shadow of its former self.

Bob Ord recalls the climate at Studio 1 & X in Oxford:

I don't think things were going well for Star after their tax problem. If I remember rightly, as for attendances, the cinema just ticked over, and by the time Mr. and Mrs. Cooper [the next operators] had taken over, the manager even had to use a payphone fitted in the office to make their calls. (Do you remember... put the 10p in after hearing the pips?) What image did that give?

After just seven years, the time had come for another change of ownership, and the cinema was sublet to Charles and Kitty Cooper. In the eyes of many customers, this was a felicitous new beginning, as The Phoenix rose from the ashes of the struggling Studios.

The Studio 1 & 2 projection booth, circa 1977. Photograph by Bob Ord.

Chapter Four
The Phoenix Cinema: 1977-1989

The cinema's new operator was Contemporary Films, which had started out, and was still very active, as a London-based film distribution company. It was founded by Charles Cooper (1910-2001) in 1951, and, in 1964, his wife Kitty also joined the firm, with which she remained until her retirement in 2008. Still operating today, it now claims the position of the UK's oldest extant film distributor.[1]

Contemporary Films specialised in art-house and foreign-language cinema, and was responsible for bringing many of the most important works of new and classic world cinema to the UK. By the 1980s, Charles Cooper was able to boast, "Of the fifty to sixty film-producing countries in the world we distribute films from more than thirty countries."[2] Acquisitions included films by Ingmar Bergman, Luis Buñuel, Sergei Eisenstein, Miloš Forman, Werner Herzog, Yasujiro Ozu, Satyajit Ray, Andrei Tarkovsky, and Andrzej Wajda, to name but a few. In the 1950s and 1960s, their films had made regular appearances on the screen of the Oxford Scala, before being edged out by the more mainstream policy of Star Cinemas in the Studio 1 & 2 days.

In the late 1960s and 1970s, Contemporary Films diversified into exhibition, and took over the operation of three cinemas, beginning with the Paris Pullman in South Kensington, which it ran from 1967 until its closure in 1983. Its second venue was The Phoenix in East Finchley, and Oxford would be its third and final site.

As a cinema operator, Contemporary's programming was not limited to the films it distributed, but its catalogue titles would become staples of the schedules once again. Kitty Cooper estimates that these films represented around 30-40% of the films screened at The Phoenix in Oxford. Given the importance of Contemporary's role in promoting world film culture locally and across the UK, we were delighted when Kitty agreed to contribute to the Phoenix centenary programme by curating a retrospective of key films from the their catalogue, which screened across the course of 2013.

Charles and Kitty Cooper outside The Rex (soon to be The Phoenix) in East Finchley, shortly after they acquired it. Courtesy of Kitty Cooper.

The Phoenix rises

Kitty describes Contemporary's move into cinema operation, and the decision to take on Oxford's Walton Street venue:

It was always an ambition to own cinemas, because the problem with being a distribution company is that you buy the films, and then who's going to show them? For many years, we had a very close association with *The Academy in Ox-ford Street [London]*. At that time, there were quite a few art-house cinemas, and *The Academy* was probably one of the finest. There was *The Cameo in Regent Street*, there was *The Continental*, and another cinema at the bottom of Totten-ham Court Road. There was *The Curzon [Mayfair]*, of course... So there were far more foreign-language films being shown in those days (the fifties, the sixties) than now. And so we always had the ambition, as you can't rely just on one cinema to show your films. Often we bought films they weren't keen on showing.

The first cinema we bought was the *Paris Pullman in South Kensington*, and we ran that as an art house. After the *Paris Pullman*, we were looking for other cinemas to buy. We had associations with Oxford because a very close friend of mine lived in Oxford, so we were often visiting. Having a twin cinema was a great advantage to having single cinemas, because single cinemas are not very financially viable; you've got all the overheads but only one cinema carrying it.

So we went, and at that time the cinema was owned by the Star Company. Robert Ord was the projectionist. The funny thing was that the first time my husband Charles and I went down there to visit (the Star people had just no idea about foreign-language films, or art films or anything) when we wanted to have a look at the screen in Number Two, I'll always remember this was early in the morning, and the only film that Bob had to show us was a porn film! I'll always remember that because I thought that was very funny!

So then we acquired the cinemas from Star but, of course, they weren't selling them. It was only on a lease, so we had to pay them rental. With the other two cinemas (*The Phoenix in East Finchley* and *The Paris Pullman*) we owned the properties outright, but the Oxford one was only on a lease arrangement, I think for twenty-one years.

It wasn't making any money. [Star] had no idea about what sort of films to show to bring in the students. It was just making a loss. They were glad to get rid of it. Jericho was pretty grotty in those days—it wasn't like it is now, and it just wasn't a very desirable area, you know. There were the major cinemas as well, weren't there, in town? There were quite a lot of cinemas, and they would get first pick, so unless you were going to show a completely different type of programming there was no point in having a cinema.[3]

Contemporary Films entered into discussions with Star in 1976, and commissioned an insurance valuation, which was delivered that Octo-ber. Ivor F. Martin of the London-based estate agency Harvey & Wheeler reported: "General condition is good and provides very acceptable facilities [...] We were very impressed by the standard of finish and decoration in both Cinemas which are in the style of the smaller luxury West End Cinemas. This was one of the most attractive Cinema complexes we have seen for some while."[4]

A deal was struck and the cinema reopened with a new name on Sunday 17 July 1977. The name and logo were (and still are) shared with Contemporary's East Finchley venue, which the Coopers had renamed from 'The Rex' for reasons Kitty explains:

I was thinking of the advertising and lineage. We had the Paris Pullman, and I wanted to have a name which would be close to Paris Pullman, so in the 'what's on and where to go' the two cinemas would be close together. And that was The Phoenix. It was very simple reasons! People always ask, and they think there was some great reason behind it all, but there actually wasn't!

Reshaping the cinema's identity

The films selected for the cinema's first week as 'The Phoenix' sent a clear message to Oxford's filmgoers that the name was not the only thing to have changed. Gone were the kinds of films shown earlier that month, such as *Lisa's Folly* (John Alderman, US, 1970)—a sexploitation thriller whose tagline ran, "She lived for love and loot... taking both in fiery, lusty abandon." Any patrons expecting similarly salacious pleasures from *The Lost Honour of Katharina Blum* (Volker Schlöndorff, West Germany, 1975) in Phoenix 1 may have been sorely disappointed to find themselves watching a thoughtful and award-winning political thriller. Meanwhile, the selection of the sharp socio-political satire, *Xala* (Ousmane Sembène, Sengal, 1975) for Phoenix 2 fortified the message that a new era of intelligent and cultural film provision had begun.

The array of drinks and snacks on offer was also modified with a new clientele in mind. Bob Ord (who had stayed on as chief projectionist, before becoming manager circa 1979) remembers: "As well as the usual popcorn, sweets, and ice cream sold at the cinema, we introduced 'whole food' cakes and savoury snacks. Our bestsellers were the chocolate fudge cake and rum truffles."

SUNDAY, 17th JULY for 7 days
STRAIGHT FROM ITS SUCCESSFUL LONDON RUN!
VOLKERS SCHLONDORFF'S

THE LOST HONOUR OF
KATHARINA BLUM (AA)

". . . an innocent at large in a hostile and hypocritical society! . . Guardian

Programmes: 4.0, 6.15, 8.30

The rise and fall of a black middle-class businessman in a newly independent African state

XALA THE CURSE (AA)

A funny savage social satire by Africa's best known director Sembene Ousmane

Programmes 3.45, 6.15, 8.30. Contemporary Films Releases

Courtesy of Oxford Mail / The Oxford Times (Newsquest Oxfordshire).

The Coopers set out to regain the student audience that had proved so important to the business operation during the Scala years. Although they were quick to abandon the sex films associated with the more recent Star period, they kept up the regular late-night shows Star had introduced. Times had changed; student tastes and cinemagoing habits were not the same as they had been in the 1960s. The Coopers' response was to launch a new and distinctive type of programming that combined foreign-language cinema with the best new British and American independent titles, retrospectives of classics from around the world, and regular themed seasons.

With the Coopers, Bob says, there came "strange student type films like *Pink Flamingos* [John Waters, US, 1972]."

Polyester [John Waters, US, 1981] was an X-rated film and came with a scratch 'n' sniff card with about ten smells on it. When you got to a certain place in the story, a number would flash on the screen and you would scratch and sniff that odour. I sent the film info out to all the local media, including a card each. Two days later, I was at home in the shower when I had a phone call from Jeff Mead, who was then the local news reporter on ITV, who wanted to do an interview with me for the six o'clock news. We did the interview, and Jeff even stopped people in the street to ask if they knew what the smells were!

Bob Ord at The Phoenix. Courtesy of Bob Ord.

Ian Hunter's account of attending The Phoenix (and the rival Penultimate Picture Palace across town) illustrates the importance of this kind of programming to students at that time:

I was at Oxford from 1982-85 and then as a post-grad 1986-91 and spent rather too much of my time at The Phoenix and The Penultimate Picture Palace. What immediately comes to mind is how different it was in the 1980s from now for a budding cinephile, and how important rep cinemas were. Like most students, I didn't have a TV and video, and so the only way to learn about films was actually to see them in cinemas, at a time when European art-house films and the New Hollywood made up the canon.

I certainly remember watching a triple bill of (I think) [Pier Paolo] Pasolini all day at the PPP and then literally running down Cowley Road and across town to see Eraserhead *[David Lynch, US, 1977] on a late-night double bill at The Phoenix. This was the end of the 'midnight movie' years when cult films were still to be seen at exciting one-off screenings in cinemas, and The Phoenix certainly introduced me to lots of those.*

*I also remember buying a load of posters and stills from The Phoenix—*Pretty Baby *[Louis Malle, US, 1978],* Manhattan *[Woody Allen, US, 1979],* Tess *[Roman Polanski, France/UK, 1979],* After Hours *[Martin Scorsese, US, 1985],* Scarface *[Brian De Palma, US, 1983],* Blow Out *[De Palma, US, 1981]—which decorated my digs off the Cowley Road, and most of which, to my eternal chagrin, I managed to lose. But two stills, of* Scarface *and* Tess, *are now framed behind me as I write in my living room—a little link to The Phoenix.*

Did I mention the screenings of the Talking Heads film Stop Making Sense *[Jonathan Demme, US, 1984] in the eighties with people dancing in the aisles, including one very out of place hippy? Went back two nights in a row to enjoy that spectacle.*

Anthony 'Grim' Hall recalls his first visit to The Phoenix, where he was struck equally by the programme and the general ambience:

I dated a Poly student I'd met in the college canteen (used to sneak in for cheap food) and I first went with her and her college friends. I think it was my first 'art house'/independent cinema, so it made quite an impression. I had only known the usual local cinemas until then, so it was quite something to see cool movies in cool surroundings. I remember it as a little shabby, but cool in a stu-

dent bohemian way. Back in the late '70s/early '80s, the cinemas tended to be quite run down and not exactly nice places to go to watch a movie. Now it's the same but in the completely opposite way—the flash and shiny multiplexes but with no personality. The Phoenix, I remember, had personality.

Meanwhile, the Penultimate Picture Palace proprietor kept a close eye on The Phoenix, recalls projectionist David Powell. "Bill Heine used to come in quite a lot, just to see what was going on. He used to pop in and say, 'Hi! How're you doing? Just having a look round…'"[5] "He was always phoning me every week to see how films were doing," adds Bob, "and he did come to see the odd films at The Phoenix and to spy on us!"

Until the mid-1980s, Kitty was the programmer for The Phoenix in Oxford (as well as for Contemporary's London venues).

Fundraising for Muscular Dystrophy. Projectionist Stephen Pill and Manager Sandra Welch as Yogi and Boo-Boo, with Bob Ord (right). Courtesy of Oxford Mail/The Oxford Times (Newsquest Oxfordshire).

We built up The Phoenix and The Phoenix became an important feature in Oxford. I think it still is. We changed the whole character of The Phoenix, the films they were showing. We were able to show films that would never have been seen in Oxford otherwise. It was very satisfying. We could have lesbian and gay seasons. We did all the sort of work that the BFI does. It's like another BFI cinema in many ways, with seasons and everything.

Bob recalls a well-received Buster Keaton retrospective in the early 1980s: *For the press show, we got the piano from the Prince of Wales pub up the road. There we were pushing the piano up the street to The Phoenix! We must have looked like something out of Laurel and Hardy. Luckily there were no steps to go up and no bowler hats!*

Building this new audience didn't happen overnight, he says: *Even years after Mr. and Mrs. Cooper took over, the ordinary person on the street that didn't go to the cinema much thought The Phoenix was still the old Studio cinema. At any opportunity, I would try to do some sort of competition in the local free paper to promote the films and cinema.*

In the late 1980s, the days of Studio 1 & 2 would be recreated for the filming of the second episode of the *Inspector Morse* television series, *The Silent World of Nicholas Quinn* (1987), where attending a film in Studio 2 provides a murder alibi. The front of the cinema was decked out with posters for risqué movies once again, and Kitty recalls Bob's amusement at this, after all their efforts to shed the cinema's old image. Ironically enough, the film that provides the alibi is Bernardo Bertolucci's erotic 'art-house' classic, *Last Tango in Paris*. Although it enjoyed two runs during the Studio 1 & 2 days, it made far more regular appearances on

Filming Inspector Morse, as viewed from the projection room exit. Photograph by Bob Ord.

the Phoenix screens, when it was revived almost twenty times between 1978 and 1988 (and subsequently went on to play several times more in the Picturehouse era).[6]

David Powell recalls the early days of The Phoenix, as its new programme structure began to take shape.

I was working for Contemporary Films in the film library, and I was the preview projectionist there, so they actually asked me to work in their cinemas. I used to go down and do relief projection at all three. I started in Oxford seven or eight months after they took it over. It was quite slow to begin with, if I remember rightly. I can remember matinees were reasonably quiet. Thinking back, it used to be a fairly elderly audience in the afternoons, and I remember they always asked us to play the films low— "Can you turn the sound down just a little bit?"

In the daytimes, before the cinema opened to the general public, colleges would regularly hire The Phoenix for education screenings.

David: *I used to ride down on my motorbike from London, and on a Friday it would be something like nine o'clock in the morning doing Shakespeare films for the colleges (doing two of them up to lunchtime). We used to go through 'til about one o'clock, have a break for an hour (hour and a half sometimes), and then on with the afternoon matinees—up to half past ten, quarter to eleven. Then we used to start the late shows! Fridays and Saturdays it used to be a double bill, so you didn't used to get out until three o'clock in the morning.*

The battle over late-night performances

Late shows were very much the fashion of the day. Their regular presence in the Phoenix programme would become a central feature of its operation in the late 1970s and 1980s.

David: *From what I can remember, the late-nights were quite popular. They used to do films at the time like* Sitting Ducks *[Henry Jaglom, US, 1980],* Barbarella *[Roger Vadim, France/Italy, 1968], and things like that, which was quite normal for the late-night circuit round about that time. We used to do* Pat Garrett and Billy the Kid *[Sam Peckinpah, US, 1973] and I think it was* Midnight Cowboy *and things like that which were doing the rounds. We used to do the late show in both screens, not just one. They were supposed to start at eleven o'clock, but one of them always started at about five past, almost ten past, simply because we had to make sure they were finishing apart.*

I'll allow you one of my faux pas. I made up a film. It was done quite quickly, but I put my hand up to it. It was Barbarella, *and I put one of the reels in upside down. I was watching the other film, and it took ten minutes before people realised it shouldn't be like that. Someone came and told me, and I had to stop the film, rewind it, put the reel round the right way, and start again. I think that's the fastest I've ever broken down a film and made it up again. It took me about fifteen minutes to get it back on screen. I felt so embarrassed by that! Because it was a science-fiction film out of that era they thought it was how it was supposed to be!*

David Powell wishes a happy birthday to manager Sandra Welch. Photograph by Bob Ord.

An application to run late shows on a daily basis proved controversial. Although they were popular with students, some of the local residents were less enthusiastic. Kitty explains the case from the Contemporary Films perspective:

With students there was a ripe audience for late-night shows. The council didn't want to give us permission because of the people living nearby, and that was a big struggle. I suppose people did object, but there weren't that many people living round the cinema at the time, because there was the pub next door, then shops opposite, obviously. We had a very good solicitor, Jack Gaster, who came down to Oxford to represent us at the council. I think first we got permission for two nights, and then three. He finally managed to get us seven nights a week, which was good. It was terribly important for us to get the license. It was such a good source of income for the cinema, which, at the time, was an important factor. You needed every source of income you possibly could find.

Phoenix 1 & 2. Photograph by Bob Ord.

The local campaign against daily late shows centred on allegations of noisy and otherwise antisocial behaviour on the part of student patrons. A forty-strong residents' petition against the proposals read: "As local ratepayers we do not feel we should be expected to pay towards the grants of students and then put up with their late-night revels—they would be better to get to bed earlier and therefore be brighter and more able to study."[7]

Dave Richardson of the *Oxford Star* summarised the specific charges levied: "Students were accused of kinds of atrocities ranging from shouting, urinating and slamming car doors, to consuming Chinese take-away meals while sitting on walls and discussing films in an obscene manner."[8] "I'm sure all of that took place!" Kitty concedes. While assiduously disputing the magnitude of alleged disruptions, Contemporary also took steps to minimise the disturbance caused by late leavers, remembers David Powell. "They used to have someone out in the front just asking people to leave quietly if they thought they were getting a bit loud."

As anyone staffing or attending late shows will know, they do indeed have a tendency to generate weird and wonderful moments. David recalls one night that was a little out of the ordinary:

We were all ready to go home after a late show and the manageress did a search of the ladies and Bob [Ord] did a search of the gents, and he found someone in there—an old tramp, and he wouldn't come out! He said, "I'm staying in here." Bob said, "You can't stay in here; we're closing up." But he said, "I'm going to sleep in here. This is where I'm sleeping tonight." This went on for about fifteen minutes, and in the end they had no choice but to call the police to get him out. The police came along; they knocked on the door. He came out very quietly and walked away. It's silly the way you have to call the police when you're going to go anyway. No one saw him come in, because there are people coming and going all the time. It's just one of those silly things that happen from time to time.

Bob: *Most cinemas had the cat, to keep the mice away, but at The Phoenix Oxford we liked to be a bit different, so we had a dog from a puppy and we named him Kaspar, after* The Enigma of Kaspar Hauser *[Werner Herzog, West Germany, 1974]. He was good company for the staff, especially on those long double-bill late shows. Walton Street can be a very eerie place at 2.00 a.m. (well, it was in the late seventies and eighties; in the early days Jericho was a bit of a red-light area). Kaspar would help lock up each cinema, checking in between the rows of seats and picking up the dropped popcorn!*

One late show, we were quite busy and these two lads turned up with a big pizza. We said, "Sorry, you cannot take that inside as it will smell out the cinema." The lads were perfectly okay with that and we said they can collect it on the way out! We put the pizza in the stock room and closed the door. Everyone went in and the films started. Later we started to pack up, the stock room door was opened, and... yes, Kaspar slipped in and pounced on the pizza before we could do anything! At the end of the show, the lads came out to collect the pizza. We explained what happened, and said that old cliché, "Your dinner's in the dog!" The lads laughed about it. We gave them comp tickets and they were happy to see another film.

Kaspar. Photograph by David Powell.

While the roundabout of license applications and local objections dragged on, The Phoenix continued to make use of a legal loophole.

Bob: *The cinema resorted to a club system (not to be confused with the Studio X club). This was just to get around the law to show seven-day late-night shows, so that meant we were able to show a lot of John Waters films like* Pink Flamingos *and* Female Trouble *[US, 1974], which were popular with the students. When we were busy I was forever making peace with the local neighbours because of the bikes parked outside their houses.*

Public late shows were programmed on three nights each week, with members-only late shows running on the other four. The reason they were so important to The Phoenix was that the student audience was crucial to the cinema's success, and strong term-time business was needed in order to offset the lower trade during vacation times.

Kitty: *The big problem I found with Oxford, thinking about it, was that we depended on the students. I mean that was our core audience, and, of course, the students are only there for six months of the year. Oh dear! And what do you do over Christmas? And what can you do over the summer?*

I think I did repeats. Sometimes I brought in new films, but you didn't want to use the best films in the summer. You wanted to wait until the autumn when they all came back again. So it was tough, I think, especially in Oxford, where there's only six months that they're there, and it takes a few weeks before they find The Phoenix, as well. So you've got six months to make enough money to carry you for the rest of the year.

If you couldn't get the students you tried to get other audiences, such as chil-

dren's shows. *Of course, we had a big catalogue of films, and I was able always to fall back on our catalogue, and we were continuing to buy new films. But it was still hard—you had two cinemas and fifty-two weeks of the year.*

Dark days for the cinema business

The years in which Contemporary Films operated The Phoenix were the toughest ever experienced by British cinema operators. When Star had bought the venue in 1970, annual admissions for the UK stood at 193 million; by the time Contemporary acquired it in 1977, this figure had dropped to just 103 million. After rallying briefly at the end of the decade, attendance went into free fall during the early eighties, reaching its nadir in 1984, when just 54 million admissions were registered.[9]

The responses to a survey conducted that year showed that, for a medley of social and economic reasons, less than a third of the population considered a cinema the best place to watch a film. Most people preferred to see films at home, either on television (42%) or on the newly popular home video recorders (22%)—a device installed in the homes of 33% of British adults by 1984 (up from less than 1% just three years earlier).[10] Although aficionados of foreign-language and other 'specialised' films were nearly three times as likely as the general population to describe the cinema as their preferred viewing environment (91%), the attendance drain took its toll on art houses as well as mainstream cinemas.[11]

Kitty: *At the beginning, the cinema did do very well. We had the very good years, I mean the cinema made a profit. We had some good years with all the cinemas, and then we got into that terrible patch in the eighties when nobody was going to the cinemas any more, and we just couldn't afford to keep them. It hit all our cinemas and that's why we sold them.*

In 1984, Contemporary was approached by the Cannon Classic cinema chain. A letter to the Coopers advised, "I have pleasure in informing you that my company is prepared to offer £45,000 for your leasehold interest." Cannon Classic was, at this time, negotiating to purchase the Star chain of cinemas—a transaction concluded the following year, when they paid £4.4 million for thirty-seven other Star venues and, in doing so, became the second largest cinema circuit in the UK.[12] As Contemporary was still subleasing The Phoenix from Star, it seems likely that Cannon's offer was connected to this larger acquisition.

Although Cannon Classic was a large, predominantly mainstream chain, the manner of its approach to The Phoenix suggests some sensitivity to its value as an art house. Programmer Tony Jones recalls:

Kitty Cooper was approached by Ken Rive on behalf of Cannon. He was one of their programme consultants. He used to run cinemas of his own under the banner of Gala Films—there was The Gala in Edgware Road, The Barclay, and another one on Tottenham Court Road. Cannon took him on as (a) an art-house distributor (they had some good films, Gala), and (b) as a sort of programmer, basically, when they were thinking of taking over The Phoenix.[13]

Whatever the reasons behind Cannon's offer, their money was certainly tempting to the Coopers, but when news of a potential sale leaked out to the press, uproar swiftly ensued. "As soon as you want to sell a cinema, everybody is up in arms. You know, they don't come to the cinema when it's running. That's all you expect from people, is to attend the cinema. But God forbid you decide then to sell it," laments Kitty.

In October 1984, an *Oxford Star* 'exclusive,' entitled "Cinema to be sold," opened with the rabble-rousing announcement that "Oxford's major arts cinema may be sold to a big American chain." In the face of this threat, it reported, "businessmen from Oxford and other parts of the country are trying to arrange an alternative sale so that The Phoenix can go on showing the rare artistic films which have made it successful."[14]

While negotiations to do just this unfolded behind the scenes, a public campaign was launched by three local cinemagoers, with backing from the *Oxford Star*. In early December, John McGrath reported:

A busker who sings at The Phoenix Cinema in Oxford has raised £45,000 to buy it. Part-time teacher Alison Bentley was upset when she heard the arts cinema on Walton Street was likely to be sold to a commercial chain. She told the Star: "I wanted somewhere to carry on busking—and I thought buying the cinema was the easiest way!"

Alison went in with two partners, Jonathan Flint, a medical researcher, and

Bill Raeper, a teacher. Between them they raised the asking price of the lease through promises of loans from friends and from a bank.

However, their startling plan has come temporarily unstuck. Alison said Mr. Charles Cooper [...] had raised the asking price to £70,000. Now Alison, Jonathan and Bill are looking for film fans to back them to raise the extra £25,000. The three friends only have about a week more to raise the money. Then it looks likely Mr. Cooper will go ahead and sell to the Cannon Classics Chain.[15]

Jonathan Flint recalls the strength of feeling behind this campaign, but downplays the idea that they came as close to buying the lease as the news article suggests.

When I was a student at Oxford, I lived in the North Oxford area. The programme of the cinema was always interesting (you got to see films from around the world) and we wanted the cinema to remain independent. We certainly did not try to buy the cinema, but we wanted to do something—something that could raise the social attention towards this campaign. We just didn't want the cinema to be sold, that's all, so we tried to at least do what we could. We didn't know the story would go in the newspaper. [To raise funds] Alison played some music in front of the screen before the films started, and Bill and I would go around to collect money. (Unfortunately, he died in a plane crash a few years ago.) People were very supportive, and kindly donated money when they found out what we were doing, but we could never raise that amount of money.[16]

'Cinema must not die in Britain'

In December 1984, Contemporary announced that it would not be selling the lease to Cannon Classic, but, still struggling with declining audience numbers, instigated a series of changes in the hope of turning the cinema's fortunes around. One was the appointment of a new film programmer as Kitty was, by now, finding this duty increasingly arduous.

I used to do the programming, and the majors were so difficult. When it went well, and when we had people who came down to Oxford to appear with a film, and there was a good audience it was really exciting, exhilarating. But I found a lot of the time was pretty much a slog.

Talking from my own experience, I find there's the enthusiasm and the ideas, but as the years go by it becomes more difficult. I mean, I was programming all three cinemas, and the late-night shows. I would come home and I'd start doing all the lates—because there were seven nights late-night shows, and the daytime shows, and I would say I got stale. You get stale after a time.

The new programmer was Tony Jones, with whom the Coopers already had a business relationship; Contemporary's films often screened at the Cambridge Arts Cinema, which Tony booked and managed.

Tony: *I started off programming the East Finchley Phoenix, and then Kitty Cooper asked me to take over looking after The Phoenix Oxford for them, so I did that alongside Cambridge. Cambridge was outperforming Phoenix Oxford, and it still does on the right sort of films. The programming was done a lot better by me in Cambridge and Oxford than it would ever have been just with Ken Rive showing Cannon's selection of art-house titles, and then whatever else fitted in.*

Although Cambridge Arts was run quite independently from The Phoenix, there were definite advantages to booking them together. As Tony explained to the local press, "With the Oxford and Cambridge cinemas working in tandem we have effectively double purchasing power so we can set up a mini-circuit and get films out of the distributors quickly."[17]

Several employees have described what would become a long-standing ritual: meeting in motorway service stations to trade film prints between the two venues. "Do you remember that scene in *Cinema Paradiso* [Giuseppe Tornatore, Italy, 1988] where they're showing a film, and a cinema over the hill or whatever's also got the film going on, and they're swapping reels of the print?" asks former Picturehouse manager John Hughes. It felt a bit like that, he says![18]

Tony: *Rather than rely on an unreliable film transport service to do a Thursday night crossover for a Friday screening, it was a lot easier to go over first thing in the morning and meet someone near Milton Keynes—particularly if there were only one or two prints. Then you could be sure that they would actually get there. So it was a very reliable system. And, of course, it's about 120 miles over the motorway to Oxford; it's a bit of a trek, so meeting somebody half way is not too bad. Bob Ord would sometimes come over in his Rover; I think 37 or 67 ORD was his registration number.*

Another new initiative launched at this time was the 'Friends of The Phoenix Association.' The main purpose, Kitty says, "was to try and get people to come to the cinema, because audiences were falling off. The eighties were a terrible time. It was a fight to keep cinemas open, so we tried all ways and means."

When announcing to the press that the cinema would not be sold to Cannon Classic, Charles Cooper took pains to emphasise that for the venue to remain viable it required the continued support of all the Oxford cinemagoers who had campaigned so passionately against the sale. He told the *Oxford Star*, "The last thing we wanted to do was dispose of The Phoenix, but it is a question of getting a larger audience."[19]

The proposed 'Friends' scheme was designed to raise funds through paid subscriptions. These fees were to be put towards building improvements, while Friends would benefit from discounted ticket prices and invitations to exclusive free events. Contemporary hoped to accrue, in this way, at least £10,000 to help secure the cinema's future.[20]

Further details of the scheme were provided on the application form:

A number of improvements are planned for the cinema and we hope that with your continued support The Phoenix will maintain its position as a major regional showcase for European and independent cinema, satisfying both the cultural and entertainment needs of the community.

Recently there has been a considerable degree of interest in the future of The Phoenix and we wish the cinema to play a larger role in the life of the community. With this in mind we have decided to introduce the FRIENDS OF THE PHOENIX ASSOCIATION. There will be an annual subscription of £10. Part of this income will be devoted to improving the facilities provided at The Phoenix. A small bar/restaurant will be created off the foyer, Dolby sound installed, also new seats, carpets and other decoration.[21]

The association launched on 28 April 1985, when Charles Cooper made an impassioned speech about the crisis afflicting The Phoenix and other British cinemas. Pleading for the co-operation of film lovers to

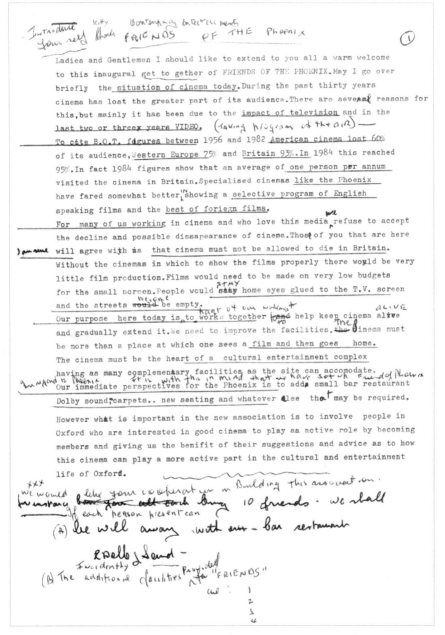

Introduce yourself Kitty Phone *Contemporary entertainments* **FRIENDS** *of* **THE** Phoenix ①

Ladies and Gentlemen I should like to extend to you all a warm welcome
to this inaugural get to gether of FRIENDS OF THE PHOENIX.May I go over
briefly the situation of cinema today.During the past thirty years
cinema has lost the greater part of its audience.There are several reasons for
this,but mainly it has been due to the impact of television and in the
last two or threex years VIDEO. (taking programs off the air) —
To cite B.O.T. figures between 1956 and 1982 American cinema lost 60%
of its audience,Western Europe 75% and Britain 93%.In 1984 this reached
95%.In fact 1984 figures show that an average of one person per annum
visited the cinema in Britain.Specialised cinemas like the Phoenix
have fared somewhat better, *in* showing a selective program of English
speaking films and the best of foriegn films.
For many of us working in cinema and who love this media *are* refuse to accept
the decline and possible dissapearance of cinema.Those of you that are here
I am sure will agree with us that cinema must not be allowed to die in Britain.
Without the cinemas in which to show the films properly there would be very
little film production.Films would need to be made on very low budgets
for the small screen.People would *stay* stay home eyes glued to the T.V. screen
and the streets would *become* be empty.
Our purpose here today is to work *that of our workout* together *and* *to* help keep cinema *the* *ALIVE* alive
and gradually extend it.We need to improve the facilities.the Cinema must
be more than a place at which one sees a film and then goes home.
The cinema must be the heart of a cultural entertainment complex
having as many complementary facilities as the site can accomodate. *set up Friend of Phoenix*
In respond to Phoenix Our immediate perspectives for the Phoenix is to *it is with this in mind that we have* add small bar restaurant
Dolby sound,carpets.. new seating and whatever else that may be required.

However what is important in the new association is to involve people in
Oxford who are interested in good cinema to play aa active role by becoming
members and giving us the benifit of their suggestions and advice as to how
this cinema can play a more active part in the cultural and entertainment
life of Oxford.

xxx *We would* like *your cooperation in Building this association.*
For instance *If each person present can* buy 10 friends . We shall

(A) *be well away with our - bar restaurant*

& Dolby Sound -

(B) The additional facilities *provided* *for* "FRIENDS"
are : 1
2
3
4

*Extract from Charles Cooper's draft of his speech for the inaugural 'Friends of the Phoenix'
meeting. Courtesy of Kitty Cooper.*

give the venue a new lease of life, he urged them to "support and assist us in becoming 'Friends' and bringing in more friends." Before welcoming director Alan Bridges to introduce a screening of his latest film, *The Shooting Party* (UK, 1985), he announced the slogan of the new association: "Cinema must not die in Britain."[22]

The last stand

Despite the revenue brought in by the 'Friends of The Phoenix' scheme, the pressures of the business continued to take their toll, and the struggle to raise the standard of the building proved an ongoing source of strain.

Kitty: *It was always a difficulty not having enough money, not being able to bring the place up to the sort of standard one would have liked. I think we solved the problem of the sound travelling from Number Two into Number One. When we bought the cinema, you got two films for the price of one! There were a few times, of course, we replaced the seats. I still have plans of what we wanted to do with the cinema, but the problem was that the money was never there.*

In the late 1980s, a range of architectural plans and sketches were drawn up by the Oxford-based architect Reg James to show different options for the proposed bar and restaurant, as well as for a new front entrance and canopy, but none would be realised. One of the things that discouraged the Coopers from investing heavily in the building was the contract under which they were subleasing from Star. "Of course, we couldn't do anything to the building without their permission," Kitty says, although she doesn't recall them being particularly difficult to deal with. The more significant issue was that the lease arrangement offered no long-term security and made them vulnerable to escalating rental costs.

Kitty: *We used to pay our rent in to Star, and whenever we wanted to renew the rental period, we had to go back to Star. I think our lease ran for twenty-one years, but there were breaks in it. I think every seven years my husband had to renegotiate the rents with them, and those went up every time. It became more and more onerous on us, you know. In time, we got fed up with it all.*

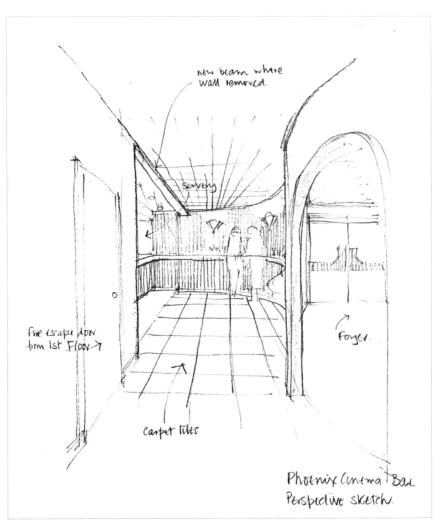

new beam where
wall removed.

screens

Fire escape door
from 1st Floor →

Foyer.

carpet tiles

Phoenix Cinema Bar
Perspective sketch.

Sketch for a downstairs bar, by Reg James. Courtesy of Reg James and Kitty Cooper.

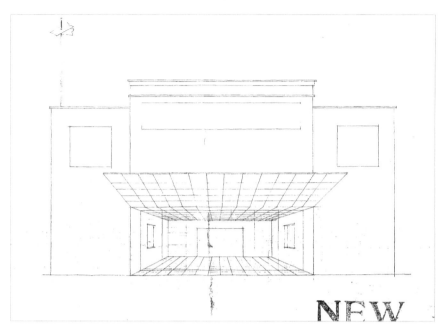

Unrealised plans for a new entrance, by Reg James. Courtesy of Reg James and Kitty Cooper.

We tried to buy the cinema. We put our solicitor on to it but weren't terribly successful. The Star people just didn't want to know. They didn't want to sell it, or there was a problem with St John's College. We were sorry that St John's College were not interested in selling the freehold of The Phoenix Cinema. We thought: it seems a long time to wait until 1999 [when Star's lease expired]; perhaps they'll come up with something sooner.

Increasingly wearied, Charles and Kitty looked seriously once again at giving up the cinema, and entered into discussions with their programmer, Tony Jones.

We knew that he was looking for cinemas. I think it was probably right at the beginning of City Screen, wasn't it? I think it was probably their first cinema. So we knew he was interested. And, you know, the cinemas, they're a big responsibility, aren't they? And especially, of course, they weren't in London—so we went to Oxford; every week we went down to Oxford. We did have somebody from our office who took care of the cinema, but it was still hard work. And then we met Lyn [Goleby] through him, and it just went along. And they were very keen, of course, to start their own sort of group of cinemas, their own chain, which they finally seem to have achieved.

Contemporary's ownership of The Phoenix came to a close in 1989. Despite the tribulations of steering it through the eighties doldrums, Kitty retains many fond memories of her time there, as well as an unabated passion for films and for cinemagoing culture.

It was fun. It was also fun times. I think the highlights were when I saw the queues round the block. And we did. It was very successful to begin with. It was just the satisfaction of booking a film; showing a film where you get an audience; the audience responds to the film. This is why I always campaign for cinemas, and for seeing films in cinemas rather than at home on DVD. It's not the same experience. It's a great experience, you know, when you think of lots of other people, and they're all responding to the film.

As distributors, we brought films into the cinemas, and we showed them. We resurrected two cinemas, come to think of it (The Phoenix in Oxford, and The Phoenix in East Finchley), both of which were showing mediocre films. And it was much appreciated. It was just that decade in the eighties that really killed us, I'm afraid. And it killed other cinemas, you know, and distributors, as well. Even today, when you think of it, how many foreign-language films are actually released in this country now? Very few. Whereas, with Contemporary Films, we alone used to acquire at least twelve new films a year. And then Artificial Eye came much later, and they did as well, and other people. So it was a real blossoming: a real blossoming of art cinema. And now we've become so insular we don't show films from the rest of the world. It's mainly American films, some of which are very good, but there's a whole world out there, and we don't even see their films, and we don't know their culture.

And it's just sad, but I think for young people now it's all different with them with their interests with films. There's not the same concern with the films per se as there used to be—for the art of cinema. I mean, the fifties, sixties, and seventies were really the heyday of cinemagoing. We really had that, which was wonderful. It was a great time for going to see foreign-language films, which was our main interest, Contemporary's main interest.

It could be very stressful. There were ups and downs, you know. But on the whole it was a wonderful experience, a great adventure. It was certainly something I never thought I would be doing. But, of course, the greatest pleasure, or what made it so pleasurable, was that I was doing it with my husband. He brought me into the business; I was at Edinburgh doing a diploma in social work before that, but when it looked as though we were going to stay together he suggested I come and work with him. I think at one time, one way or the other, the whole of Contemporary Films was more or less made up of family members.

Our whole life was the cinema, and the distribution, and going to festivals, and at the same time, of course, raising a family, because we had two small children, as well as the older children [from Charles's first marriage]. But it's the fact that we did it together: that was the great part of it, what made it so wonderful. It was a real team—you were a team.

Charles and Kitty Cooper with director Satiajit Ray and his wife Bijoya. "This was taken at a party we gave at our home in his honour, and to which we invited many of his friends who lived in London, including Pamela Cullen, Marie Seton, film critic David Robinson and others." Courtesy of Kitty Cooper.

Chapter Five

The Phoenix Picturehouse: Since 1989

In 1989, Tony Jones and Lyn Goleby purchased The Phoenix from Contemporary Films, under the auspices of their newly formed company, City Screen. It would be the first full-time venue in what was soon to become the Picturehouse group of cinemas. Lyn explains how it all began, and the original idea behind this new venture:

Tony Jones was the programmer for Kitty and Charles [Cooper], and Tony had offered to them that he would buy the cinema. I was working freelance with Working Title at the time, and Tony Jones came through my door saying he needed to raise the money to buy this cinema. I think he may have been introduced to me by Roger Wingate. I was raising money for films at the time, trying to be a film producer and doing all that kind of stuff. So I was raising money, and I was out there. I agreed I would help him. I think we tried to get something like £100,000 together to start the company up. We ended up with three seed investors, and Roger Wingate was one of those who put the first £100,000 into the company.

We also took a loan from the BFI, which it turned out really needed to have been a grant. But a loan it was, and it was repaid. Wilf Stevenson was the boss of the BFI at the time, and he was a big supporter of the ideas behind City Screen, which Tony and I started up in order to buy the cinema.

So we got a small loan from the BFI, seed money from initial investors, and started City Screen. Tony was programming The Arts Cinema in Market Passage, Cambridge, as well as Oxford, and he had the Ely part-time cinema. What we did was we bought his interest in Ely, bought Oxford new (that was the core of the new company), and kept an affiliation with him as programmer of Cambridge. That didn't fully come into City Screen until later on when we took over Cambridge Arts.[1]

Tony Jones: *It was quite a complicated lease deal. Contemporary's interest was bought out and St John's College was closely involved with the changes so they could issue a new lease directly to City Screen.*[2]

Lyn: *At the time, I wanted to produce films, but I was also really interested in the bricks and mortar aspect of cinema. The concept was: I was going to raise this fund; part of the fund would invest in film production, and part would be the absolute, secure, bricks and mortar investment in cinemas. I wrote business plans around that, but that concept never really came off.*

The first day I went to visit the cinema, to see what this money was all going to be spent on, we'd done the deal with Kitty and Charles. I was going to go and say "Hello! We're the new owners." Everybody was in the foyer sitting on the floor, and I remember thinking "Ooh! This is not how it's going to be run in the future!"

The Phoenix lost money for two or three years after we'd first bought it. It was absolutely losing money hand over fist when we bought it, and I remember thinking "What have I done?" because we didn't have a clue what the cinema was worth. I was only just doing it as a fundraiser; I wasn't even working within City Screen. I was just going to be a director of the company, responsible for bringing in the investment, and Tony was going to run the whole company. I thought he was going to know all that, and I was going to do my film production.

Bringing the facilities up to date

With new capital invested in The Phoenix, it finally became possible to make some of the improvements to the building that had proved out of reach for Contemporary Films, although ongoing budget limitations meant that developments were somewhat piecemeal.

Lyn: *St John's wanted [the cinema to be given] a new lease of life and money to be spent on the place, which is what we, with the seed money for City Screen, wanted to be able to do. We were going to transform it.*

We had very grandiose plans, which were drawn up by an architect called Simon Smithson, who is now a very high-up person within the Richard Rogers partnership. We never did those grand plans because they were actually too ambitious and we only had £100,000 in the company, so by the time we'd bought it, and it lost money for a couple of years, there wasn't much money left.

The plans involved new doors, a new awning, and a new bar upstairs—all of which happened, but just on a much less ambitious scale, really, and it happened more gradually. We were never in a position of having hundreds of thousands of pounds to spend on actually doing it, so it was done bit by bit.

Alastair Oatey (now director of operations at Picturehouse Cinemas) began working at The Phoenix shortly before the sale. *I went there as a student, and I was watching lots of films there. One day, the manager (who was Stuart Jarvis) said, "Do you fancy doing some work here?" I said, "Yes, I'll do it if you give me some free tickets." He said, "Yes, and I'll pay you as well!" So that's where it all started.*

I came in one day and they said, "We've got new owners." I do also remember when Lyn and Tony came to visit in their separate ways. The company at that stage was very small. They knew the staff, and they knew the managers, and they were intimately concerned with how the cinema worked, which was nice.

The film programme didn't change dramatically. What we did see was the building being invested in. It was done up. The box office was under the stairs, where the disabled toilet is now, so that moved to the other side of the room with the new kiosk. Then the bar was built upstairs, which wasn't there when City Screen took it over. The box office and kiosk moved places about three times in the years with City Screen, at least.[3]

Lyn: *In two phases of time I spent quite a lot of time up there. Phase one was when we were first tidying it up: really basic stuff. It was very tacky when we bought it, so we re-seated it, and we re-carpeted it, and we did the first manifestation of new toilets. I think we've done the toilets about three times since we've had The Phoenix. We completely re-seated and re-tiered Screen Two, as well. I made the black felt masking, and the curtains that go to the left of the screen in Screen One as well. I put those together on my sewing machine!*

In the second phase, I think I spent a whole summer staying with friends out at Oxford and doing the façade that has the stained glass phoenix on the front, and doing the bar.

John Hughes joined the cinema as an usher and, after his promotion to manger in 1991, became intimately involved in the process of expanding the level of service on offer to Phoenix patrons.

Making the cinema bar was a big idea, really: to try to keep people engaged with the cinema for longer, and not just be a film house. I think around that time we were probably developing Exeter [Picturehouse], as well, or it may have been developed. They'd had quite a big success in building a very popular bar and gallery, although we didn't have the same sort of space or aspect that they had. So we were trying to capture people as they came in, and put them in an environment that they felt safe in as well, and offer them an alternative to the pub culture that was still really strong in Jericho. Our space was going to be intimate, and plans to see the inner workings of the projection booth would make it unique.[4]

Installing a bar had been a long-cherished idea of Contemporary Films, but the money had never been in place to do it. When City Screen eventually created one in 1994, it was based on an entirely new design idea, which transformed a previously unused area of the building.

Lyn: *There was nothing on the roof behind the parapet. There was a void (a sort of a roofscape), and then there was the projection box. I can't remember how you accessed the projection box in those days, but we basically filled in what was a void to make a kind of conservatory, if you like. It was quite radical, I suppose. We created a space where there wasn't one.*

The bar, I remember, was done with jobbing builders, and sort of air rather than money, to be honest. It was all reclaimed church materials from a Suffolk reclamation yard. We used recycled floorboards, which we bought from a merchant. And we used one of Simon [Smithson]'s ideas, which was to create a visibility between the bar and the projection box. That was his original idea (it was going to be grander than that), and that still exists to this day. You were able to see the sort of shadow of the projectionist going through, and the idea was that you'd feel as if you're part of the projection action.

The bar (featuring a now iconic stained glass window designed by Chris Sanders) proved a well-received addition. Many regulars report enjoying the facility even when not attending a film, while its relaxed intimacy has made it popular for private parties and events. "I had my wedding after-reception there," says Alastair Oatey. "Now that's company loyalty! And we got good takings for that day!"

Stormtroopers take over the Phoenix bar during an event run in association with the Make-a-Wish Foundation. Photograph by Matt Taylor.

By the time the bar was installed, changes in the projection booth itself had improved the technical standards of film presentation. Although the periscope system introduced by Star was ingenious in concept, the quality of image it delivered to Screen Two left much to be desired.

Tony: *When we took it on, the equipment was rubbish. We just put a pair of refurbished Westar projectors in there, and they're still there right to this day. The mirror system was so bad it was hanging on chains. It wasn't fixed, really, so any vibrations and the screen would move and the picture would go out of focus; the picture would be like a BananaScope! If you're in an art house, you want to be able to read the subtitles. You could say that The Phoenix was the forerunner of Smile Vision, because you had strange shaped subtitles, but all that was improved with a good engineer: a chap called Billy Bell.*

Billy was, John Hughes recalls, "the most amazing old engineer, who looked like something out of the *Lord of the Rings* trilogy. He used to turn up with this little brown suitcase, a bit like the chancellor's briefcase, and he'd only have a handful of tools in there, but he could fix anything." Tony makes what John describes as "quite a major engineering project" sound remarkably simple:

The Westar projectors there have a pedestal about three feet high, but it's only on legs and a tin skirt. It's got a cast iron top and a cast iron bottom, and steel screw legs. All we had to do, therefore, was just chop those down to about one foot rather than three foot, and then we were able to get the projector beam directly on to the screen, and so the focus was 100% improved. I mean, it's fantastic, and you get more light, as well, as you're not going through a dust-mirror.

John: *The sound improvements, and all those technical things, would have been maybe unseen by lots of people if we were just showing subtitled films or vintage films that were probably not shot with the same kind of technical expertise, but when we had a good film on like* Blade Runner *[Ridley Scott, US, 1982] or some of the [Stanley] Kubrick films that really were quite grand in terms of the CinemaScope sort of landscapes that he shot in, then Phoenix 1 was a great place to see it.*

The last major alteration to the building was the restoration of the cupola in Screen One.

John: *We knew it existed, as there was a way to get above the ceiling, so you could see the reverse. There were these great bulbous things inside the quite cheap ceiling and roof that we had on the cinema, but we didn't know what they were going to look like and how much repair they'd take.*
Peter Johnson, and another guy called Simon who was his plasterer extraordinaire, worked through the night and across one whole Christmas period to restore the ceiling to as it was, rather than these tiles that used to fall down on

people during late shows. We put absolutely tons and tons of sand and cement and plaster on that ceiling, and you just thought, "it's never going to take it," but obviously it did. And the guys just worked so phenomenally hard to get the cinema going.

It was just a really special thing. With every major refurbishment, and the more money that we ploughed into the cinema, I think we gradually started to compete in terms of not just being a fleapit or a has-been. We were making big improvements, which people were starting to get used to when they went to other art-house cinemas—maybe in London, or some of the purpose-built ones, like Cornerhouse Manchester, for instance.

With things like the cupola, they were always trying to restore the cinema and take it back to how it was. I think as Lyn had taken on cinemas like The Duke of York's [in Brighton], we always felt that trying to restore them to their former glory (if they weren't new builds) was probably the way forward. People wanted to see those grand old houses looking the way they were. That was our USP, because we certainly couldn't put stadium seating in, and THX sound, but we could add a touch of boutique cinema nostalgia.

The return of the glory days

The energy invested in refurbishment works in no way diminished the efforts to maintain a vibrant programme of films and events.

Alastair: *The programming was very diverse. There were split screenings all the time. There were lots of late shows. There were morning shows. It was a stuffed full and exciting programme. At the time I was there, Not the Moulin Rouge [in Headington] had closed, but The Penultimate Picture Palace was open and had an equally diverse programme, so there really were two cinemas very active where cinema lovers could go, and where you could see something interesting every night. It was just the sheer breadth of things that you could see there...*

Tony: *The PPP was purely a club, so it would show anything you wanted really, but the business was done down at The Phoenix, so the key art-house releases would have played there. I mean, I'm not the sort of person that would play second fiddle to somebody else, so we had what we wanted—I'm almost certain of that!*

John: *We were one of the main art-house cinemas, I think, in the UK at the time. If there were prints around for the big art-house films, we would be one of the key cities getting them almost day and date with London, which was really important. People saw us as quite a cutting-edge cinema. I suppose we've got Tony Jones to thank for that.*

The first films I think we showed on my first day as a manager in 1991 were Silence of the Lambs *[Jonathan Demme, US, 1991] and* Ai No Corrida *[Nagisa Oshima, Japan/France, 1976], which had been brought back out after some time in hibernation. It played to full houses for weeks and weeks; it felt like the glory days were back to the cinema.*

Lyn: *I'd say the programming became more energetic once Tony had an ownership interest in it. He programmed it incredibly aggressively. Aggressive is the wrong word, but with enormous energy and passion. I mean, he was going to make the Oxford cinema the equivalent of a Regional Film Theatre [one of a network of art cinemas established by the British Film Institute during the 1960s and 1970s]. It was going to have a reputation alongside Cambridge, and it was going to be better than every RFT that was out there. So he pushed an enormous number of films through it, and as many visits by filmmakers as he could get through, as well. He was always pulling people like Michael Palin into it, because of their links to Oxford.*

John remembers it being a vibrant era for special events with visiting filmmakers: *I sort of knew what I'd like from the cinema moving forward, which was probably a lot more interaction with the filmmakers. That was a big thing. I was quite keen to deal with PR companies—you know, Rogers and Cowan, McDonald and Rutter, Corbett and Keene, and people like that from way back, who had access to talent as they were coming over on their road shows. I was quite keen to integrate that and build our membership as well, which I thought was key to the success of the cinema at the time.*

We did an awful lot of screenings where we got people in who were either on a junket, touring around the UK, or they were just in town for a short time and we managed to get them up. Those sort of links extended to famous people who may well have also gone to the Oxford Union for the infamous Union Talks, so we interacted with them quite a lot, as well. If they had people in town who had a film connection, we'd talk, and we'd try to do the talk at the Oxford Union and put a film on at the cinema as well.

Sir Ian McKellen at The Phoenix for a screening of Gods and Monsters (Bill Condon, UK, 1998).

All photographs of Q&A guests courtesy of Martin Jennings-Wright.

Director Mike Newell in the Phoenix bar
after a Q&A screening of Donnie Brasco
(US, 1997).

Phoenix manager Martin Jennings-Wright talks to
producer Ismail Merchant about Le Divorce (James
Ivory, US, 2003).

Director Robert Altman brings Gosford Park
to The Phoenix.

Director Stephen Daldry (pictured with
manager Martin Jennings-Wright) at a Q&A
screening of The Hours (US/UK, 2002).

*Pete Postlethwaite at The Phoenix for a Q&A screening of The Usual Suspects
(Bryan Singer, US, 1995).*

I think, going back, some of my favourite times really were getting the people along, like Peter Greenaway, William Friedkin, and hosting the premiere of Wilde *[Brian Gilbert, UK, 1997]. We had Stephen Fry there, and some of the cast, and put on a great screening. Dickie Attenborough came for a re-release of* Brighton Rock *[John Boulting, UK, 1947]. He turned up in his Rolls Royce, but he was a really nice guy. They're the sorts of things that I remember really fondly—having such talent arriving, and being at the cinema. I know the members just absolutely loved that, and the fact they were there in Oxford (seventy-odd miles from London), but they were brought these amazing people, and we managed to put that on for them.*

Whit Stillman was really, really good fun. He's obviously made quite a few big films like Metropolitan *[US, 1990] and* Barcelona *[US, 1994], and we had him on a circuit. I think he did Brighton, Cambridge, and Oxford, and I was his designated driver for the trio of shows. He was one of the greatest guests I've ever had because, I spent so much time with him in the car, I got to know him outside of film—you know, what he was like as a person.*

I think one of the most nervous trios of characters we had on the stage were three guys called Hodge, Boyle, and Macdonald, who were the writer, director, and producer of Trainspotting *[Danny Boyle, UK, 1996]. I think we were doing their second public showing where they were actually physically there, and they were really nervous. We went for a meal at a place round the corner from the cinema, and they were just so nervous. They were: "What are they going to ask? What if they don't like it?" Obviously Danny Boyle is phenomenally famous now, and John Hodge, who was the writer of it, went on to great things as well. So they're a phenomenally successful trio really. It just felt like they were sort of growing up, and we had them at the cinema. Not many people would have been able to meet the filmmakers, especially from a great film like* Trainspotting*, and what it did for cinema at the time. So it was good to be part of it, and putting The Phoenix on the map.*

I think filmmakers did like to get closer to the audiences. If you get an intelligent audience asking cerebral questions it can really work well, although there were lots of other directors and producers who were very much self-centred, and focused on themselves, and it was absolutely so much hard work just trying to get anything out of them. One of the producers we had did nothing but talk about himself the whole time, and didn't really want to engage with the audience, which was almost the total opposite of Peter Greenaway, who stood up and didn't want to be 'Q&A'd. He didn't want someone on stage with him, and just sort of dismissed me with abandon, saying, "I don't need you now." And he sort of took them apart like part Hannibal Lecter, or a well-oiled comedian! He was absolutely phenomenal—a very articulate, intelligent auteur. And obviously they loved that interaction with such a famous filmmaker at the time.

Encounters with filmmakers (whether famous or lesser known) certainly feature among the favourite memories shared by customers and staff alike. For Christopher Gowers, "one highlight was sitting behind the director of the film we were watching! (*A Room with a View*—James Ivory [UK, 1985].)" George recalls the occasions on which "Robert Altman and Pete Postlethwaite came to *Gosford Park* [Altman, UK, 2001] and *The Usual Suspects* [Bryan Singer, US, 1995] respectively and were both delightful! I'll never forget these events." Scott Ellis singles out "meeting special FX master Ray Harryhausen."

In January 1992, one guest film producer was Lyn Goleby herself, who visited with actor David O'Hara for a screening of *The Bridge* (Sydney Macartney, UK, 1992), a Suffolk-set period drama that also featured Saskia Reeves and Joss Ackland. Alas, the next film she had hoped to bring to The Phoenix, *Tiger Rag*, would never come to fruition.

It never got made! I've still got the script. Michael Thomas, the guy who wrote Scandal *[Michael Caton-Jones, UK, 1989] wrote it. It's a great script. It was going to be shot around Cochin in South India. I got loads of money from Columbia for development of the screenplay, plus a couple of great trips to Los Angeles, and that's about it. But then David Puttnam was no more at Columbia, and* Tiger Rag *was no more.*

The plan to use City Screen as a source of finance for film production fell by the wayside, and the company's future efforts were planted firmly in the development of its cinema business.

A cinema for the whole community

Although students remained a significant part of the Phoenix audience in the 1990s, as they had been in the Contemporary period, as the tone of the area started to change, the cinema catered to an increasingly mixed crowd.

John: *The cinema was very much seen as part of the makeup and the canvas of the bohemian part of Jericho that was trying to re-establish itself, I suppose. It was quite a student area when I was there, and the sort of chichi restaurants like Raymond Blanc's Petit Blanc had just moved in not so long before, so the whole area was really changing dramatically. I'm sure neither you nor I could afford a house there any more! It's very expensive.*

It was quite interesting when people who starred in the films were actually just there as customers. Jodhi May was one, and Jeremy Irons came in with his family quite a bit; he used to live nearby. So there was Sinead Cusack—I think that's who he was married to, wasn't it? Anyway, they both turned up at the same time. They came to watch a matinee—we may have had Die Hard *[John McTiernan, US, 1988] on, or something which he was in as a villain. It was quite an interesting cinema. Ian McEwan was there quite a bit. We had him for* The Cement Garden *[Andrew Birkin, UK, 1993] and another film I can't remember. But anyway, he was still a regular at the cinema. He lived up the road, and I used to still see him at preview screenings and chat to him. He obviously remembers the cinema quite fondly, I'm sure.*

Elizabeth Jennings, the poet, was our sort of resident bag lady, who used to come in the afternoon looking rather dishevelled, with just hundreds of plastic carrier bags. I think she had dementia towards the end of her days, but she was an amazing customer of ours who absolutely loved coming into the cinema. We had a lot of eccentrics that used to come in, that I suppose made it interesting, mixed with the students and the old-fashioned North Oxford middle classes. They were definitely fun days. You never knew what was going to happen really.

The mixed audience didn't always combine happily with the range of films on offer.

John: *We were attacked a few times. With* Ai No Corrida, *the front of the cinema was daubed in paint and posters stolen. They didn't like that. They particularly didn't like the Russ Meyer season because, of course, we had a phenomenal archive of posters and, at the time (before the foyer was done up, anyway), it would literally be full of posters. It was probably quite a sight—a film fanatic's dream! For the Russ Meyer season, the top tier of that foyer drew a few gasps, and not many people liked those. We didn't want to upset certain crowds of people, but we were showing a season of films, and obviously we weren't trying to be biased. It was about trying to show a freedom of speech, I suppose.*

Occasional mishaps in the projection booth also led to a few raised eyebrows. Fortunately, such incidents seem to be remembered with a spirit of forgiving and amusement.

Sharon Woodward: *The memory that sticks in my mind the most is when I worked at The Phoenix. Must have been around 1992/93. I was running the Kids' Club and we were short-staffed. A number of parents were in the cinema so I was filling up on the kiosk.* The Singing Ringing Tree *[Francesco Ste-fani, East Germany, 1957] and Jackie Collins'* The Bitch *[Gerry O'Hara, UK, 1979] were mixed up and put in the wrong tins. I'll always remember the embarrassed father pushing a Yorkie into his son's hand in an attempt to distract him as the young boy asked, "Daddy, why was that lady taking all her clothes off?" Lots of red faces that day!*[5]

Alison Gomm: *I turned up on a Sunday lunchtime to see a French film I had been looking forward to. The lights went down, the film started, but it was not the one we were expecting. I thought it might be an extra short. Then everything stopped and the manger came to the front and announced that the distributor had sent the wrong film and, since* The Human Centipede *[Tom Six, Netherlands, 2009] was not a film she was prepared to show to an audience who had not knowingly chosen to see it, she was going to refund our money. I'd never heard of* The Human Centipede *but, of course, went straight home to google it!*

Suzy Sheriff: *Yes, I was on duty. Thank God it was a fairly quiet Silver Screen and our stalwart customers showed a great sense of humour over the whole thing. The only real red face in the cinema was mine—and the projectionist's when I'd finished with him.*[6]

Through the course of the 1990s, the Phoenix management launched a series of initiatives designed to cater to different sectors of the Jeri-cho community—some of which would be rolled out to other venues in the growing Picturehouse group. This period saw the start of the Silver Screen shows for senior citizens, 'Big Scream' shows for parents and babies, and Saturday Kids' Club performances.

Particular effort was invested in enhancing the Junior Friends' (later Kids') Club, for reasons described in a 1997 funding application.

Cinema presents a wondrous and uniquely creative experience to a child—the viewing of projected sound and images in the space of a dark auditorium is in itself a fascinating, cultural and educational experience. Therefore, we decided to promote the club through various ancillary events to not only increase the attendance level of the Saturday screenings but also to encourage children to become directly involved with the Cinema and to view it as a social and accessible activity within the community—an impression which they could project through to future generations.[7]

John: *I think we may have started the Kids' Club revolution. I think there may have been a Kids' Club at the High Wycombe Six, but it didn't have the same sort of interactivity, or the games and things like that beforehand. We had June Brown [who played Dot Cotton in EastEnders] open our one for us, because she used to be in the Navy Wrens in the war, and she was a projectionist, so she was keen. We got her down and did a photo call with the local press. Everyone does Kids' Club now, and all the Picturehouses have it, don't they?*

We had a girl called Sharon Woodward who used to run the Kids' Club, and do the games and stuff. To be honest, after starting it I didn't want any more involvement with the kids! Lots of the parents would just duck next door to the Jericho Tavern and get lashed for about two and a half hours before the kids would come out screaming!

In 1995, after the appointment of Ian Christie as visiting lecturer in film at the University of Oxford, film education courses became a popular addition to the Phoenix programme, with modules including 'European Cinema' and 'Language, Film and the Media.'[8]

John: *We struck up a partnership with Tony Smith, who was the ex-head of the BFI, who went on to be President at Magdalen College, so he still had very strong film ties. We struck up a relationship with him and a curator called Ian Christie, from the BFI, along with Stanford University. We did a number of these courses with students who were coming over to study, and we got to show the most amazing films that were out of the archives from the BFI—films that probably haven't been shown since, but Ian was desperate to get them there. I remember our two projectionists doing an awful lot of work to try to make sure they'd go through the machines. They were maybe at weird shutter speeds, and we brought in these special motors to be able to play all sorts of different lengths, including*

CITY CINEMA KIDS SAVE A LIFE

Hedgehog adopted

A HEDGEHOG'S prickly problem was solved when young cinema fans came to the rescue.

The mild winter has stopped hedgehogs from hibernating properly and they are being taken to St. Tiggywinkles wildlife hospital in Haddenham for care.

Children at the Phoenix Cinema's Saturday Kids' Club, based in Oxford, have adopted a hedgehog which was in danger of starving to death after emerging from hibernation too early.

By REBECCA SMITH

Linda Hunter of the cinema said: "Every three months we can raise money to adopt an animal. It costs about £20 to adopt a hedgehog for three months. St Tiggywinkles then tell us how the animal is doing.

"It's a worthwhile and educational project for the Phoenix to be involved with."

Every three months the 130 members of the kids' club can adopt anything from deer to badgers and will visit the hospital twice a year.

When the animals are well enough, they are returned to the wild.

Wildlife link . . . Phoenix cinema manager Martin Jennings

A cute story from the Oxford Star in March 1999. Courtesy of Oxford Mail/The Oxford Times (Newsquest Oxfordshire).

a resounding silent picture of Napoleon *[Abel Gance, France, 1927].*

We had a pianist, Andrew Youdell, who was at the BFI as well, and we got him down to do piano accompaniment. It was things like that that were just magical. They were films that would have come out when the cinema first started, and we managed to show them almost a hundred years later. It was quite amazing. Some of the films we've shown were phenomenal.

Peter Schofield recalls an amusing incident: *When I retired to Oxford in 1994, one of the pleasures of retirement was the possibility to go to the cinema in the afternoon, just like when I was an undergraduate. At the time, The Scala was showing, on Wednesday afternoons, vintage movies as part of a film studies course offered by the university. Introduced by a short lecture, these showings were very popular, not only with students.*

On one occasion, standing behind me in the queue was an undergraduate who was explaining to his female companion: "Film Studies is a genuine subject on a par with Language Studies, History Studies, Music Studies, and so forth. It is very theoretical." After a pause, he added, "Of course, I am not doing the theory—it is too difficult."

Other local partnerships developed in this period included the newly opened Petit Blanc. "We did a sort of dinner-film thing," says John. "We used the cinema for the film and then diners went up pre and post. It was their sort of warm up event at Petit Blanc before it officially opened." Regular fundraising activities took place for local and national groups, and a wide variety of screenings were scheduled as part of local and touring festivals.

In 2007, The Phoenix became host to two new festivals in partnership with the *Oxford Mail*. The six-day Oxford Mail Film Festival now runs annually in late spring, and features themed retrospectives curated by its features editor, Jeremy Smith. Each December, the festive season kicks off with the Senior Citizens' Film Festival, 'Merry Christmas Matinees,' when the paper's older readers can enjoy free drinks and mince pies alongside a selection of the year's most popular films. More recently, 2011 saw the launch of 'Parky's Pics': a new programming strand curated by Oxford-based film critic and historian David Parkinson, which features an eclectic range of classic titles and 'under the radar' art-house treats from around the world.

The Phoenix grows up

As the twenty-first century dawned, further changes were afoot, both locally and nationally. Audience demographics began to shift as Jericho's gentrification proceeded, and nationwide viewing habits adjusted to the growing provision of new forms of home entertainment. It was time for The Phoenix to readjust, as it had done so many times before. Alastair Oatey describes his perception of a significant change that has taken place since he first joined The Phoenix in the late 1980s.

Phoenix manager Suzy Sheriff and Oxford Mail features editor Jeremy Smith launch the 2012 Oxford Mail Film Festival. Courtesy of Oxford Mail / The Oxford Times (Newsquest Oxfordshire).

It was very studenty, and you could see the difference between term time and the university holidays incredibly differently. There were always the university students, plus university 'people' (the academics, and their families, and that), so it wasn't just a student place, but it was much more noticeable than it is now that the figures were in line with term time. It's broadened its appeal since then, and I guess it's growing up with the market.

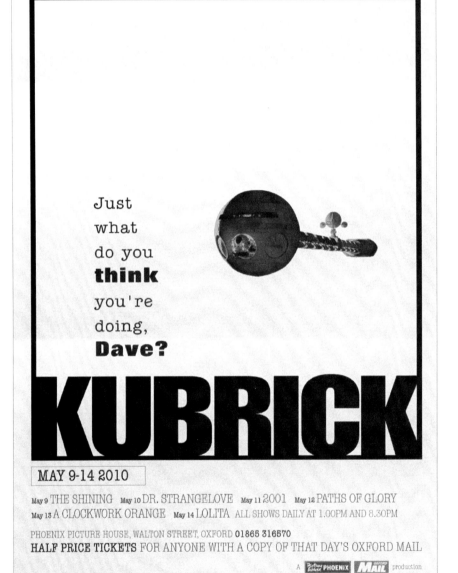

Poster for 2010 Oxford Mail Film Festival. Courtesy of Oxford Mail / The Oxford Times (Newsquest Oxfordshire).

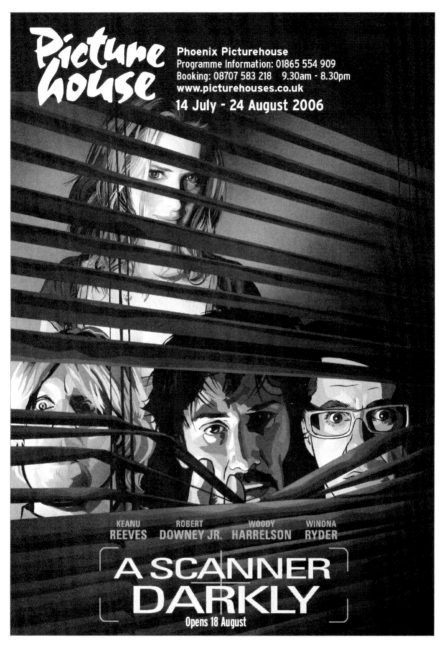

Phoenix brochure cover, 2006. Courtesy of Picturehouse Cinemas.

I think the other thing is, in our days at university [late 1980s/early 1990s], there weren't DVDs, there wasn't TV on demand, and Sky, and going to the cinema to watch your Sunday matinee (your Bill Douglas Trilogy *[My Childhood, UK, 1972;* My Ain Folk, *UK, 1973;* My Way Home; *UK, 1978], your* Unbearable Lightness of Being *[Philip Kaufmann, US, 1988])—that was the way you learned film. The way you learned film was by watching it at eleven o'clock at night until bloody o'clock in the morning!*

Learning film history and seeing that breadth of films in there, and seeing it on the big screen, with people, as well—that attracted the student audience for Sunday matinees. The Bill Douglas Trilogy *I first saw in the wrong order (I think it was one, three, and two), but no one minded. By the end, we'd all worked it out. So Sunday matinee stuff was there regularly, and the late-night shows, and that kept a real student core to the audience. Of course, as student habits have changed universally (people not going out to see those types of films any more) that bit of it's changed. I guess that's had an impact on the rest of the audience.*

The Phoenix team in February 2000. Back (from left)): James; James; Mike; Michael; Dylan; Steven; front (from left): Katrina; Gloria; Jackie; James; Soizik; Julian; Helen; Sarah; Andrew; Martin (with Bodie); Bente; Kathleen; Sam; Jennifer; Pip; David; Neil. Photograph by David Fisher Photography.

Clare Binns, Picturehouse's director of programming and acquisitions, elaborates: *I think audiences now are much more driven by marketing, and marketing has become much more sophisticated in the way that it sells films. Also, with the choices that people have (whether it be with cinema, theatre, online—very different activities they can choose to spend their money on), I think they're far more picky. In days gone by, people would be much more driven by taking a chance on something, and now I think they want to leave the venue feeling a particular way, so that they're less prepared to take a risk.*[9]

As well as shifts in the relative popularity of different kinds of films and events (at The Phoenix and elsewhere), expectations of the viewing environment have changed dramatically in recent years.

Clare: *Very definitely the audience has changed in what they expect from the comfort when they go and see a film. I think that was driven by the multiplex (the multiplex opened a site in 1985 at Milton Keynes), whereas our audiences were pretty much prepared to put up with anything. They would be in uncomfortable seats; perhaps the sound quality was not as good as they certainly would expect now, and they could pretty much get a cup of instant coffee (that would be fantastic if they could do that!) and maybe a bag of sweets if they were lucky.*
It was the independents who first started offering perhaps a cake and different things to eat. But really, in terms of comfort, it was multiplexes coming from the US with their comfortable seating and great sound, and physical facilities that cinemas in the UK had never had, that meant everybody had to up their game. Suddenly, audiences had expectations of sound quality, seating quality, and the environment they went to see the film in.
I think we at Picturehouse have taken that, but given our absolute own skew on what that is, which is all the comfort, all the technical expertise that we put into providing a good show (for sound and vision), and good food and drink, and the ability to take wine into the auditorium. It's really a night out, offering something they're never going to get on the home entertainment system, quite frankly.

Alastair: *In the old days, under the Theatres Act, theatres were automatically covered; people could take their drinks into theatres with them. The kind of audience we have is a theatre-kind of audience, who appreciates that kind of culture. So, when the Licensing Act (2003) came out, it gave us the chance to*

The Phoenix Screen 1 and foyer in 2012. Both photographs courtesy of Picturehouse Cinemas.

The Phoenix bar in 2012. Both photographs courtesy of Picturehouse Cinemas.

submit a new application for the licensed area, which we just did throughout the whole building, enabling customers to take drinks from the bar into the auditoria. It just adds to the experience of the cinema, and marks it out even more from the multiplex cinemas. It treats people as adults, which you don't get elsewhere. People appreciate it and, anecdotally (at The Phoenix and elsewhere), it's one of the reasons why people come to watch films in our cinemas. That's the experience that they want. And, of course, now having the latest in luxury seats just backs up that experience.

Fortunately for fans of The Phoenix, recent changes have all been designed to enhance the cinema's ambience and the overall experience offered. Things could have been very different, jokes Lyn Goleby. "Around 1999 or 2000, I did have an offer once from Tesco. I just tucked it away in a drawer and didn't tell anybody. It could have been a Tesco Metro!"

The dawn of the digital age

In 2001, Britain's first high-definition digital cinema projector was installed in London's Odeon Leicester Square. The following year, the UK Film Council secured a £17 million government grant designed to enhance the provision and attendance of 'specialised' films in UK cinemas. The backbone of this ambitious initiative was the launch of the 'Digital Screen Network.'

Digital cinema was looked on as a way of reducing distribution costs for film companies, because striking 'prints' in digital format costs less than duplicating them on 35mm (the industry standard up to that point). It was hoped this would benefit small, cash-poor art-house distributors, and allow their films to be shown in a larger number of cinemas within a shorter space of time. Thanks to the DSN, the UK would become the European leader in rolling out this new technology across the nation.

Under this scheme, cinemas competed with one another for recognition as the worthiest recipients of Film Council-funded digital projectors. In May 2005, the first 209 successful applicants were announced, of which The Phoenix Picturehouse was one. Indeed, The Phoenix was among less than a sixth of successful applicants to receive more than one projector—an achievement that still yields benefits today. Alastair

Oatey summarises the reasons why City Screen felt it was so important to go down this route.

We wanted digital. We could see that the future for the industry was digital projection, and it was the way that we could afford to digitise. I can't remember what the costs were in those days. Now they're £50,000 apiece; I think they were probably more than that then—hugely expensive. So when the Film Council came out with a scheme to do it, it was the obvious (and, frankly, only) way that we could afford to do it.

Obviously, we were looking across the whole group, but in Oxford it had a strong art-house/independent programming content, which it's always had. It was part of the Europa network of cinemas (so it had a pedigree already), and so it was fairly easy to know that it would become part of the scheme. The difficult thing was that the scheme was built for the multiplex cinemas to show that they were increasing the amount of independent films they were showing, and so you had, therefore, to commit to increasing the number of shows you were doing of that kind of content. This was pretty much impossible at Oxford, because we were doing 100% of that, but we put in an application, and we were successful, and the kit's still there.

From our point of view, it was a really successful scheme. It kick-started the transition from celluloid to digital, which wouldn't happen at the pace it happened if it wasn't for that Film Council intervention. So it was a good thing for small cinemas, it was a good thing for big cinemas, and it was good for the industry. It was a useful intervention.

The Phoenix's long-standing chief projectionist, Mike Warner, describes what the change has meant in terms of the technical presentation of films, and explains how the system works.

When I first started in 1987, it was a period when 16mm began to die out. The majority of films then was on 35mm, and occasionally on 16mm. Around about 1989, when the current company took over the business, the film format was completely dominated by 35mm. Around about 2005, digital projection technology came in and, gradually, it has become the main film format instead of 35mm.

A digital projector has two main parts. The first one is a computer server, where we store all the films, advertisements, and trailers. It's basically like a

Chief Projectionist Mike Warner in 2012. Photograph by Hiu M. Chan.

computer, but it has a huge memory. For example, we now have about forty-three films stored on the server, excluding the trailers. There is some software on the computer, which allows me to create a playlist—to put the films into a screening schedule. The server is then connected to a projector head, where all the light is coming out. The projector head receives signals from the computer server, and projects whatever the server sends out.

Digital has much better quality. It's always in focus; for 16mm and 35mm projectors you have to focus the lens manually. Because a digital projector does not contain a physical film reel, it doesn't shake when it's projecting; it's very stable and quiet—although if something goes wrong with a digital projector there is nothing you can do. As it's a computer, you have to wait for some profes-sional people to come in. As for 16mm and 35mm, at least you can cut the films or put them back together again.[10]

Initially, The Phoenix's new digital projectors were used solely for screening films in what would have been (from a customer perspective) a very traditional way. That would change in 2006, when an early ex-periment with a live satellite link paved the way for regular broadcasts of what has come to be known as 'alternative content.' It was a development made possible by a combination of technological advances and the financial economies and negotiating capability of City Screen's burgeoning number of cinema venues. Marc Allenby, Picturehouse's head of commercial development, describes how this new phenomenon came about:

> *As we went digital across the estate (as in one screen in every cinema was digital), Lyn really saw the opportunity that non-film content would start to have more of a presence on the cinema screen.*
>
> *Through an existing relationship, we started talking to Amnesty International about their* Secret Policeman's Ball, *which they were re-launching for the first time in fifteen years. I guess they were aware also of this possibility, but didn't know what was happening because it wasn't happening in the UK. We built up the idea of broadcasting the* Ball *into cinemas, and installed the kit to enable us to do it, and that was the first live satellite event we actually ran with.*
>
> *That was in October 2006 and, after that, because we had the infrastructure, we approached the New York Met through an intermediary, Marc John, to do* The Magic Flute *on Boxing Day of the same year. We dipped our toe in (I think with six or seven sites), not sure what would happen. It sold out, or was 80-90% occupancy. We then took the rest of the season through 2007, and the rest is history.*
>
> *[Installing the equipment] wasn't hugely challenging, but it needed a lot of technical management because everybody was new to it, so understanding how we tune it, how we use it, how you test—that kind of thing. So we just threw people's time at it, rather than a massive technical breakthrough. All the technology, all the components existed already. It was just a matter of applying them to cinemas, rather than inventing a particular format.*[11]

> Mike: *It works basically like the digital television we have at home nowadays. We have a satellite digital box, which allows us to pick up signals sent out by satellite. It's able to pick up all the free digital channels as well. But when we show a specific live performance, for example the Met Opera, we will receive a special sequence number from the broadcaster so that we can tune into this particular channel. The satellite server is connected to our digital projector head, which projects the received signals on to the big screens. However, to screen the live performance successfully, I also have to make sure the framing adjustment looks accurate on the big screen after we receive the signals; I will have to adjust the pictures with the right ratio, and also make sure the sound level is accurate.*

The introduction of 'alternative content,' and the opportunity to experience some of the most acclaimed opera, ballet, theatre, and concert productions from around the world quickly gained popularity with the arts-savvy audience that had come to define The Phoenix in the twenty-first century.

After attending the second Met Opera broadcast, *Eugene Onegin*, at The Phoenix Picturehouse on 24 February 2007, Oxford-based opera reviewer Peter Schofield described his initial impressions:

> *I was totally bowled over. This is a completely new way to experience opera. It is neither just a film show with a superior music score nor a music drama accompanied by visual imagery but a true synthesis of both elements. On the other hand, it is not cinema: the words are sung, the action confined to a stage set; it is not opera: the images are two-dimensional, the sound reproduced. But whatever the analysis, one was totally engrossed, with the ability to view the singers in close up and to read the text without having to raise one's eyes while hearing the glorious music. The peripherals added to the enjoyment: the camera roving round the auditorium and orchestra before the start, the ability to study the conductor during the overture, the backstage tour, interviews and rehearsal scenes during the intermission (but no Met Opera Quiz).* [12]

A selection of Mr. Schofield's reviews, many of which first appeared in *Oxford Magazine*, are now available online, and describe the various ways in which "over the seasons the presentation for the audience has developed and matured in professionalism." [13]

The perennially popular broadcasts from the New York Met now sit alongside productions from the National Theatre, the Bolshoi, and other cultural organisations to enrich a programme that continues to offer a wide range of films, but which is increasingly diverse in form and origin.

> Marc: *What I think's interesting is our success, and by 'our' I mean independent cinemas across the board. It's not just the content which is coming through, but it's also independent cinemas' knowledge of their customers and their ability to talk to them directly. All the work we've done pre-alternative content in audience development and diversity of content means alternative content just works very naturally within our programme, whereas I think that the multiplex cinemas is quite a contrast. It's very different, and they don't have*

the same relationship with their customers; their customers don't have the same expectations. So, I think the success is celebrated more because of those reasons, which is an important thing, and it's great for Picturehouses and great for independents in general.

Sold, but not sold out

On 6 December 2012, Picturehouse Cinemas launched its twenty-first venue: The Duke's at Komedia in Brighton. That day would also bring another big announcement:

Cineworld Group plc ("Cineworld" or the "Group") today announces that it has acquired City Screen Group, which trades as Picturehouse ("Picturehouse"), for £47.3 million in cash. [...] This acquisition will enable Picturehouse to unlock more than 10 new locations already in the pipeline. Picturehouse will operate as a separate business entity within the Cineworld Group and will continue to be run by the existing Picturehouse management team. [...] Lyn Goleby will continue in her role as Managing Director of Picturehouse.

Lyn Goleby said: "The opportunity to be part of a public company is great news for Picturehouse and our customers. We are known for our high quality city centre cinemas and our distinctive, wide-ranging programming. The unique character of Picturehouse cinemas will remain and our team will continue to bring the widest range of film to customers. This acquisition by Cineworld will accelerate the development of further Picturehouse cinemas around the country."[14]

Steve Wiener, Cineworld's founder and CEO, describes the development and shape of Picturehouse's new parent company. After beginning his cinema career as a part-time usher in Miami, Florida, Steve progressed to running (what was then) RKO Theatres in New York City. His next job, as managing director of Warner Bros.' European cinema operations, brought him to London.

I moved here in 1991. It went reasonably well. I was with Warner Bros. for three years. When they decided to change their strategy about expansion, which would have meant that if I stayed with them I would basically be living out of a suitcase almost full-time, I decided to leave. So I had to figure out what I was

going to do next. I came up with this crazy idea that everyone was building cin-
emas in the UK in the 'catchment area'; the catchment area is a twenty-minute
drive time. They were all building them in all the major cities only.

There also was a book that came out at the time, which, when I was at Warn-
er Bros., I contributed to. The book was the Monopolies and Mergers Commission
investigation into the movie industry. I read the book (looking to see what titbits
I had given them ended up in print, and there weren't very many!) but one thing
that came across early in the book was that the average person in the UK would
not drive more than twenty minutes for their entertainment. Later in the book,
another piece was that 60% of all people in the UK lived more than twenty
minutes from a modern multiplex, and it started me thinking.

I knew I couldn't compete with established cinema chains, so what I did was
go into markets with less than 250,000 people, because there was no one doing
it. I guess you could say the rest is history. Today we have eighty multiplexes
here in the UK, and we're on a programme of building another twenty-five.[15]

Although Cineworld (or Cine-UK, as it was called at first) was born
from the same kind of lateral thinking and entrepreneurial spirit that has
shaped the development of the Picturehouse group, the kind of cinema experience it offers could hardly be more different. Despite official
reassurances that it would be "business as usual," initial reactions from
Phoenix customers were dominated by feelings of apprehension.[16] A series of anxious posts on the cinema's Twitter page that day conveyed a
widespread worry that its unique and cherished identity would be lost:
"A little concerned by Cineworld's purchase of Picturehouse cinemas.
Oxford's wonderful @PhoenixPH is a cinematic haven"; "I was dev-
astated to hear the news earlier. I don't believe them when they say it
won't change"; "Don't let them touch the bar!"[17]

"We have no intention of screwing things up," Steve Wiener assures.
"We're not the bad guys. As Lyn put it at the Komedia opening night,
'We just get to use all that multiplex money to open new Picturehous-
es,' and that's exactly what she's doing."

Eight months after the sale (at time of writing) the ownership change
has made no discernible difference at The Phoenix (although the cinema has recently benefited from the execution of existing plans for a
much-welcomed spending spree on new doors and a new roof).

Clare Binns: *The only change you will see is that Picturehouse is now a very robustly financed company, which just allows us to do more of what we're good at. Cineworld has no influence on the programming; it has no influence on the kind of cinema we are and how we go forward. It just means we can probably do what we do better because we've got very strong supporters in Cineworld.*

Throughout its existence, The Phoenix Picturehouse's greatest assets have been its customers and staff, who, together, have shaped its unique identity as what many have come to regard as a kind of home from home. Their passion for the place, and a real sense of community spirit, has created some extraordinary moments. One such occasion came at the Christmas Eve screening of *It's a Wonderful Life* (Frank Capra, US, 1946) in 2011, when, with a bit of help from the cinema management, the screening of a 'fake trailer' helped Richard Smith propose to Holly Lawton Smith.[18] "The cheering when she said yes was fantastic," an anonymous audience member reported.

The ardent interest shown by Phoenix customers in contributing to its ongoing development has played an enormous role in making the cin-

Christ Church alumnus Richard Curtis at an August 2013 preview screening of About Time in aid of Maggie's Oxford. Photography by Ric Mellis.

ema what it has been, what it is, and what it will become. Clare Binns describes her vision for the future:

Just listening to what our audiences want, and trying to deliver that. Picture-house is always at the forefront of technical innovations and programming inno-vations. I think we're leading the field. We're always prepared to take chances, and we're always prepared to look at all the exciting things out there, so I don't think we will stop still.

Part Two

Appreciation

Among the themes that emerged as we researched the cinema's history were the passions inspired by films seen there, whether recently or many years ago, and a sense of affinity with the venue itself. The essays collected here expand on these topics, providing further accounts of the reasons underlying The Phoenix's long-standing and continued popularity.

In 'The Phoenix History of World Cinema,' David Parkinson looks back at some of the 21,000 films that have flickered across the Walton Street screens during the past 100 years. His lively jaunt down memory lane takes in many much-loved favourites from around the globe, while also offering a fascinating insight into the broader artistic, political, and economic environments that helped to shape the range of films on offer to cinemagoers.

In 'A Place Like Home,' Dr. Daniela Treveri Gennari takes a closer look at the ways customers feel about The Phoenix. Drawing on the theories, approaches, and findings of other contemporary scholars working in the field of audience studies, she seeks to give context to the various audience reminiscences and observations collected here.

We end our book with a further selection from the wonderful array of memories contributed in response to our public appeal by those who have joined us in 'Celebrating The Phoenix.'

The Phoenix History
of World Cinema

by David Parkinson

Since it opened its doors on 15 March 1913, the little cinema at 57 Walton Street has provided Oxford with a window on the world. Thousands of films have screened there over the last century and, not only have they allowed audiences to see places they could once never have hoped to visit, but they have also introduced them to great works of literature and informed them about historical and contemporary events. They have also fired their imaginations, touched their hearts and provided them with an escape from the daily grind. As one- and two-reel shorts gave way to features, patrons also built up relationships with the stars and directors who made them laugh, cry, thrill and think. The various incarnations of what is now The Phoenix Picturehouse enabled locals and scholars alike to witness the evolution of the motion picture, and the lists contained in Hiu M. Chan's monumental *100 Years at The Phoenix: Archive of an Oxford Cinema 1913-2013* provide a compelling alternative history of the 20th century's most potent form of art and entertainment.

It's safe to say, however, that there were no enduring classics in the inaugural programme. The three main attractions were Ralph Ince's Vitagraph drama, *The Wood Violet* (1912), which starred Anita Stewart and Edward Klink Lincoln; Gilbert P. Hamilton's *The Trail of Cards* (1913), in which Lillian Christy played the abducted daughter of a ranch-owner, who is rescued by cowboy hero Edward Coxen; and Joseph Levering's *The Red Cross Nurse* (1913), which featured Marian Swayne attempting to thwart the robbery of a courier.

The supporting programme contained a couple of scenics or travelogues (depicting a Scandinavian city and the Scottish Highlands) and three comic cuts. Ernesto Vaser and Marcel Perez took the title roles in the Italian knockabout *Friscot* and *Tweedledum Fight a Duel*, while the tangled affairs of Mexican landowner Russell Bassett's daughter Betty Keller and her beaux Lee Moran and George Field were chronicled in Al Christie's romp *When Hearts Are Trumps*. Finally, the larger than life comedian John Bunny took centre stage in George D. Baker's *The Lovesick Maidens of Cuddleton*, which included future silent siren Norma Talmadge among the lovesick lasses.

Moving images had been flickering on screens across Oxford for 17 years when The North Oxford Kinema opened for business. It had plenty of competition in The Palace Picture House on Cowley Road, The Electric Palace on Castle Street, The Picture Palace on Jeune Street, The Electra Palace on Queen Street and The Cinematograph on George Street. As a consequence, it didn't always have access to the latest 'flickers'. Yet, in its first year, the Kinema presented several films by the most innovative American filmmaker of his day, D. W. Griffith. It also screened numerous Westerns starring G. M. 'Bronco Billy' Anderson, and Mack Sennett's earliest Keystone slapsticks. But, in these pre-star system days, the actors on the screen would have been largely unfamiliar to most moviegoers, let alone such prolific pioneers as Thomas Ince (who devised the 'film factory' method of production) and J. Searle Dawley (whose literary adaptations were designed to entice a 'better class' of audience), émigrés like Scot Colin Campbell and Irishman Herbert Brenon, and such neophytes as Allan Dwan, who would remain active until 1961, and America's first notable woman director, Lois Weber.

The reliance on American imports is readily evident, although British talents like Cecil Hepworth and Lewin Fitzhamon (who had teamed on the landmark chase film, *Rescued by Rover*, 1905), and A. E. Coleby (who made over 240 films in his 22-year career) proved perennially popular, as did Fred Evans in the knockabout comic role of Pimple. But, despite occasional Italian superspectacles like Giovanni Pastrone and Luigi Romano Borgnetto's *The Fall of Troy* and Mario Caserini's *Napoleon* (both 1911), European pictures appear to have been few and far between before the outbreak of the Great War in August 1914. During the war years, new comic icons like Charlie Chaplin, Mabel Normand, and Roscoe 'Fatty' Arbuckle became the big draws, alongside such emerging British directors as George Pearson (an early advocate of moving camera shots) and Bert Haldane, whose crime films, social dramas and literary adaptations were noted for their realism.

The cinematic landscape had changed dramatically by the time The Scala was launched on 19 April 1920, with Anita Stewart once again topping the bill, this time in George Loane Tucker's *Virtuous Wives* (1918). The wartime collapse of so many nascent continental film industries had allowed Hollywood to seize control of the world market, and it is no surprise to see the programme being packed with American titles. The emphasis was on crowd-pleasing mainstream fare and slapstick starring such new clowns as Buster Keaton, Larry Semon, and Harold Lloyd. The venue occasionally hosted marquee names like 'America's Sweetheart' Mary Pickford in Paul Powell's *Polly-*

Douglas Fairbanks. All card illustrations courtesy of David Parkinson.

anna, her swashbuckling spouse Douglas Fairbanks in Fred Niblo's *The Mark of Zorro*, and stage legend John Barrymore in John S. Robertson's *Dr. Jekyll and Mr. Hyde* (all 1920). But such prestige features were comparatively rare.

As a result, the first D. W. Griffith feature to screen there was *Way Down East* (1920) in March 1924. But there is no sign of such other Hollywood titans as Cecil B. De Mille or Erich von Stroheim until much later in the decade. Swedish maestro Victor Sjöström's sombre melodrama, *The Secret of the Monastery* (1920), screened in December 1921. But, with the exception of the March 1923 screening of Fritz Lang's *Dr. Ma-*

buse, The Gambler (1922), German Expressionism bypassed The Scala, as did French Impressionism, apart from the December 1923 presentation of Jean Epstein's *The Faithful Heart*. Unsurprisingly, given the establishment fear of Bolshevism, nothing from the Soviet montage experiment reached Walton Street, either. British cinema also took a back seat, in spite of the emergence of the technically astute and dramatically audacious Graham Cutts, the polished populist Herbert Wilcox, and Alfred Hitchcock, whose only potential contribution in this period is an unconfirmed showing of his 1927 boxing saga *The Ring* in March 1929.

Thus, for much of the 1920s, Scala regulars had to make do with the odd vehicle starring dashing heartthrob Rudolph Valentino, 'Man of a Thousand Faces' Lon Chaney, glamorous siren Gloria Swanson, or 'It Girl' Clara Bow. Yet, they were also treated to the early directorial efforts of such studio era dependables as Raoul Walsh, Howard Hawks, Michael Curtiz, Frank Capra, and William A. Wellman. Nevertheless, it was only after sound became the norm in Hollywood that the cinema began, with any consistency, to show films that have stood the test of time. In 1929, for example, the crop included Danish director Carl Theodor Dreyer's first feature, *The President* (1919); Cecil B. De Mille's typically lavish and sin-filled *The Ten Commandments* (1923); Paul Leni's Expressionist

"BABES IN TOYLAND"

Babes in Toyland brought laughter to The Scala in 1935. Laurel and Hardy would later appear in A Chump at Oxford.

chiller, *Waxworks* (1924); Josef von Sternberg's stark gangland duo *The Dragnet* and *The Docks of New York*; and F. W. Murnau's now lost drama, *4 Devils* (all 1928).

Talkies came to The Scala on 6 October 1930, with Fred C. New-

meyer's short Helen Twelvetrees showcase, *The Grand Parade*, supporting Benjamin Stoloff's musical comedy, *Happy Days* (1929). As British
studios were still converting to the new recording processes, Hollywood
provided the majority of the newly wired cinema's first sound features.
Audiences quickly became acquainted with such fresh faces as The Marx
Brothers, Laurel and Hardy, James Cagney, Edward G. Robinson, Jean
Harlow, Barbara Stanwyck, Marlene Dietrich and John Wayne. However, they had to wait until December 1931 to see their first winner of the
Academy Award for Best Picture, Wesley Ruggles's *Cimarron* (1931),
and until May and December 1933 before Universal horror arrived in the
form of James Whale's *Frankenstein* and Tod Browning's *Dracula* (both
1931). Alongside entries in such new genres as the musical and the gangster film, occasional silents still cropped up, including African-American
pioneer Oscar Micheaux's *Body and Soul* (1925) and Alfred Hitchcock's
The Lodger (1926), which finally reached The Scala in May 1932.

By this time, continental pictures had also started to appear more
frequently. Dr. Arnold Fanck and G. W. Pabst's mountain epic, *The*

Leni Riefenstahl

White Hell of Pitz Palu (1929), led
the way in April 1931. But it wasn't
until November 1932 that Pabst's
pacifist classic *Kameradschaft* (1931)
and Erik Charell's elegant oper-
etta *Congress Dances* (1932) were
shown, to be followed in the first
months of 1933 by Fritz Lang's
brooding underworld drama *M* and
Leontine Sagan's contentious lesbian saga, *Mädchen in Uniform* (both
1931). Even after Adolf Hitler
came to power in January 1933,
more German films played at The
Scala than those from any other Eu-
ropean nation. The standout screening came in 1934, when actress Leni
Riefenstahl introduced her directorial bow, *The Blue Light* (1932), and
addressed the Oxford University German Club on 'the spirit of the New
Germany' that would inform her controversial masterpieces, *Triumph of
the Will* (1935) and *Olympia* (1938).

The winter of 1933-34 brought a trio of inventive sound gems by the versatile René Clair—*Sois les Toits de Paris* (1930), *Le Million*, and *A Nous la Liberté* (both 1931)—while Sergei Eisenstein's documentary *Thunder Over Mexico* (1933) debuted in May 1934. But the emphasis remained on populist Hollywood movies, although there was often a lengthy delay between the original US release and the time that prestige pictures and programmers alike reached Oxford. The bulk of the titles were serviceable time-passers, but the mid-1930s also afforded audiences the opportunity to catch up with such acclaimed pictures as Merian C. Cooper and George B. Schoedsack's stop-motion creature feature *King Kong* (1933); Robert Flaherty's controversially stylised documentary, *Man of Aran*; Frank Capra's multi-Oscar-winning road movie, *It Happened One Night* (both 1934); John Ford's powerful IRA drama, *The Informer* (1935); and *Becky Sharp* (1935): Rouben Mamoulian's Technicolor take on Thackeray's *Vanity Fair*.

Dance duo Fred Astaire and Ginger Rogers, and teenage soprano Deanna Durbin (whose musicals respectively saved RKO and Universal during the Depression) were also Scala regulars, while Charlie Chaplin made an overdue return with *Modern Times* (1936) in November 1938. Disney cartoons began enlivening many a programme, along with comic shorts and March of Time newsreels. But the highpoints came in the springs of 1937 and 1939. Screwball comedy was at the heart of each selection, with Ernst Lubitsch's *Design for Living* (1933), Frank Capra's *Mr. Deeds Goes to Town*, and Gregory La Cava's *My Man Godfrey* (both 1936) showing alongside Archie Mayo's gangster drama *The Petrified Forest*

OGDEN'S CIGARETTES

"TOP HAT" (RADIO)

(which made a star of Humphrey Bogart) and William Dieterle's Os-
car-winning biopic *The Story of Louis Pasteur* (both 1936). In the same
period, Mitchell Leisen's *Easy Living*, Leo McCarey's *The Awful Truth*
(both 1937), and Howard Hawks's *Bringing Up Baby* (1938) coincided
with Fritz Lang's trenchant fugitive lovers drama, *You Only Live Once*
(1937), and William Wyler's simmering period piece, *Jezebel* (1938),
which earned an Oscar for its star, Bette Davis.

Carol Reed.

Hedy Lamarr.

By the late 1930s, British directors like
Michael Powell, Anthony Asquith, and
Carol Reed were becoming as familiar to
Scala patrons as Hitchcock. At the same
time, the programme always contained
generous helpings of comedy, featuring
such household names as singers Gracie
Fields and Jessie Matthews, stage farceur
Tom Walls, the husband-and-wife team
of Cicely Courtneidge and Jack Hulbert,
and the peerless Will Hay, whose bungling
know-alls invariably managed to get the
better of authority figures and even ruth-
less Nazis.

A growing number of actualities also
found screen space, including Basil Wright
and Harry Watt's *Night Mail* (1936), with
its famous score by Benjamin Britten and
verses by W. H. Auden. Produced by the
documentary movement launched by John
Grierson, these shorts often accompanied
the features selected by the Oxford Film
Society, whose termly choices introduced
an art-house feel to the Scala programme
in the latter half of the 1930s. Eleven years
after it had premiered in the Soviet Union,
Sergei Eisenstein's revolutionary masterpiece *Battleship Potemkin* was presented by
OFS in October 1936. Georgi and Sergei
Vasiliev provided more Soviet mytholo-

gising in the Red Army biopic *Chapayev* (1934), while other selections included Carl Theodor Dreyer's stylistically austere and emotionally harrowing courtroom recreation, *The Passion of Joan of Arc* (1927), and Czech Gustav Machatý's adultery drama, *Ecstasy*, (1933), whose nude scenes earned it a certain notoriety and led to Hedy Kiesler being reinvented in Hollywood as Hedy Lamarr. A strong bias towards German films like Fritz Lang's *The Testament of Dr. Mabuse* (1933) remained until the 1938 Munich Crisis, when they were replaced by lauded French pictures by Julien Duvivier, Jacques Feyder, and Sacha Guitry, and such masterworks of pessimistic poetic realism as Jean Renoir's *La Grande Illusion* (1937), Jean Grémillon's *The Strange Monsieur Victor*, and Marcel Carné's *Le Quai des Brumes* (both 1938).

The Scala closed for renovation in July 1939 and, by the time it reopened in October, Britain was at war with Germany. It now had stiff competition from the Headington Cinema (opened 1923), The Super Cinema on Magdalen Street (1924), The Ritz on George Street (1936), and The Regal on Cowley Road (1937). The L-shaped Electra Palace continued to operate in the city centre and, until September 1940, Oxford also boasted the biggest cinema in southern England outside London: the short-lived Majestic on Botley Road (1934). The Majestic was converted into a hostel for workers at the Pressed Steel plant, leaving its surviving rivals to inform and inspire with propaganda shorts produced by the Ministry of Information and to boost morale and provide much-needed escapism with flag-waving dramas, comedies and action adventures extolling the heroism of the armed and auxiliary forces at home and abroad.

Access to new films proved something of a problem, however, and The Scala was heavily reliant on re-runs for the first few years of the war. The bulk came from Hollywood's mini-majors and Poverty Row studios, with B crime franchises featuring Sherlock Holmes, The Saint, The Falcon, The Whistler, The Crime Doctor, Boston Blackie, and Charlie Chan rapidly becoming staples. Low-budget Westerns and broad comedies were also in plentiful supply, with Stan Laurel and Oliver Hardy delighting local audience in Alfred J. Goulding's *A Chump at Oxford* (1940). Yet, there was still room for occasional quality dramas like William Wyler's *Wuthering Heights* (1939), John Ford's *The Grapes of Wrath* (1940), and Orson Welles's *Citizen Kane* (1941). These tended to arrive

upwards of two years after their initial release, although the window narrowed after America entered the war in December 1941 and US military personnel began arriving at British bases.

Inevitably, home-made features were more readily available, with comedies starring George Formby, and Arthur Lucan as Old Mother Riley, showing alongside such compelling docu-realistic accounts of the war as Pen Tennyson's *Convoy* (1940), Pat Jackson's *Western Approaches* (1944), and Humphrey Jennings's *The Silent Village* (1943), which paid moving tribute to the decimated Czech mining community of Lidice. As much of the continent was under Nazi occupation, only a handful of foreign films reached the Scala screen, with the most unusual being Egyptian Ahmed Galal's *Dangerous Woman* (1941), and the most surprising being Géza von Bolváry's *Premiere* (1937), which was made in Germany and starred Hitler's favourite actress, Zarah Leander.

Indeed, the occasional German film cropped up in the post-war period, including Gustav Ucicky and Emil Jannings's adaptation of Heinrich von Kleist's blank verse play, *Der Zerbrochene Krug* (1937). Among the other continental offerings were Sergei Eisenstein's period epic *Alexander Nevsky* (1938), Carl Theodor Dreyer's morality tale *Day of Wrath* (1943) and Alf Sjöberg's provocative Ingmar Bergman-scripted ménage, *Frenzy* (1944). The majority of subtitled films came from France, with Marcel Pagnol's charming rustic comedy *The Baker's Wife* (1938) contrasting starkly with Jean Renoir's brooding take on Maxim Gorky's study of slum life, *Les Bas-fonds* (1936), and his seething reworking of Émile Zola's tale of treachery and murder, *La Bête Humaine* (1938).

The latter anticipated the new vogue in Hollywood for *film noir*, as directors who had witnessed the atrocities of the war attempted to present (as far as the Production Code would let them) a more realistic view of the world and humanity's baser instincts. Before the end of

the decade, Scala audiences had become familiar with hard-boiled private eyes, thanks to Edward Dmytryk's *Farewell, My Lovely* (1944) and
Howard Hawks's *The Big Sleep* (1946), and seductive femmes fatales,
courtesy of Billy Wilder's *Double Indemnity* (1944) and Charles Vidor's
Gilda (1946). They had also seen the less wholesome side of American
society in 'problem pictures' like Wilder's *The Lost Weekend* (1945) and
Elia Kazan's *Boomerang!* (1947), which respectively dealt with alcohol-
ism and prejudice. But the decade ended with a return to back catalogue
titles, as Hollywood responded to a 75% *ad valorem* tax on American
films (the so-called 'Dalton duty') by withholding its latest releases and
offering older, frozen asset pictures instead. The loser in this 'bacon or
Bogart' feud, as Clement Attlee's Labour government sought to restrict
the amount of capital leaving the country, was the British film industry,
which invested heavily in prestige pictures to fill the gap left by US titles,
only to see them swept away on a tide of fresh imports when a truce was
brokered in March 1948.

For the first four decades of its life, the little cinema on Walton Street
had been a neighbourhood venue. Despite the regular influx of students
and OFS members, the patrons were primarily residents of Jericho and
employees of the Eagle Ironworks, Oxford University Press and the various boatyards. Ben Jay had recognised this during the brief New Scala
interlude in the mid-1920s, when he introduced community singing between programmes and offered free tea and biscuits at matinees. But his
Welsh successor, John Edward Poyntz, was determined to make The
Scala the best cinema in Oxford, and his plan finally came to fruition
during the 1950s and 60s, when son-in-law Eric Bowtell was placed in
charge of programming. He gradually moved away from the often cheap
and cheerful commercial British and American fare on which the cinema had subsisted and started introducing more of the art-house pictures
that were increasingly securing UK theatrical releases after their screenings at such festivals as Cannes, Berlin and Venice and their new British
equivalents in Edinburgh and London.

The transformation didn't happen overnight, however, and audiences in the early 1950s would still have been just as familiar with the horse
operas of George Archainbaud, the comic romps of Charles Barton or
the little bit of everything churned out by Lew Landers as they were with
more critically acclaimed A pictures. Similarly, the low-budget thrillers

of John English and music-hall comedies of Marcel Varnel would have entertained regulars as much as works by loftier British directors. Not that The Scala was always one of the first on the list for classics in the making. David Lean's timeless romance *Brief Encounter* (1945) didn't appear until February 1950, while Michael Powell and Emeric Pressburger's celestial fantasy *A Matter of Life and Death* (1946) and Carol Reed's Viennese thriller *The Third Man* (1949) didn't arrive until June and November 1953 respectively. Similarly, although there were plenty of Frank Launder and Sidney Gilliat outings, the Ealing comedies arrived late on the scene, as did the satires of Roy and John Boulting.

Even the tributes to wartime derring-do that so fascinated post-war British audiences, such as Michael Anderson's *The Dam Busters* (1955), turned up several years after their original release. New-fangled American technologies like CinemaScope and 3D, which had been devised to coax the public away from their television sets and back into cinemas, also went elsewhere. Even after the Coronation in June 1953, few Scala regulars would have owned a TV and they seemed content to rely on the cinema for their entertainment. But the calibre of Hollywood pictures

ORSON WELLES

began to improve noticeably from the mid-1950s, as the Bob Hope comedies and B franchises began competing with the latest Fords, Wilders and Hitchcocks. There was also an increase in the number of weighty dramas like George Stevens's *A Place in the Sun*, Elia Kazan's *A Streetcar Named Desire* (both 1951), and Otto Preminger's *The Man With the Golden Arm* (1955), as well as psychological Westerns like Fred Zinnemann's *High Noon* (1952), and such big-screen versions of lauded teleplays as Delbert Mann's *Marty* (1955) and Sidney Lumet's *12 Angry Men* (1957).

Most of these classics were shown long after their release, as The Scala came to operate as much in a repertory as a first-run capacity. But the biggest change in its programming policy involved foreign-language films. Although the cinema had screened European titles outside the Oxford Film Society remit, they had been infrequent and had tended more to the middlebrow than *grande culture*. The OFS often continued to point the way, with a May 1958 screening of *The Seventh Seal* (1957) prompting a flurry of Ingmar Bergman pictures over the next year. By this point, Eric Bowtell had already started devoting entire weeks to admired directors (both American and European), such as John Huston, Frank Capra, Orson Welles, Jean Cocteau and René Clair, and he soon began showing international features as part of the core programme.

The trickle of French films in the early 1950s became a flood as audiences discovered the intimate spectacle of Marcel Carné's celebration of the national spirit, *Les Enfants du Paradis* (1945), the joys of Jacques Tati's meticulously constructed comedies, *Jour de Fête* (1949) and *Monsieur Hulot's Holiday* (1953), the elegantly staged humanism of Max Ophüls's *La Ronde* (1950) and *Madame De...* (1953), and the minimalist realism of Robert Bresson's *A Man Escaped* (1956). Many of the titles on view were being dismissed across the Channel by the acerbic young *Cahiers du Cinéma* critic François Truffaut for forming part of a 'Tradition of Quality' that represented a '*cinéma du papa*' rather than the more personal brand of *auteur* filmmaking that he championed. Nevertheless, Oxford audiences flocked to see René Clément's poignant study of wartime innocence, *Jeux Interdits*, Jacques Becker's slick crime drama *Casque d'Or* (both 1952), and Henri-Georges Clouzot's nerve-shredding duo, *The Wages of Fear* (1953) and *Les Diaboliques* (1955).

Despite showing Wolfgang Staudte's harrowing 'rubble film', *The Murderers are Amongst Us* (1946), in January 1950, neo-realism made little impact on The Scala until several years after it had been proscribed by the Italian government, which disapproved of the negative image of the country portrayed in such films. The first films in Roberto Rossellini's masterly war trilogy, *Rome, Open City*

Actress Magnani was a favourite of Italian neo-realist filmmakers, and star of Rome, Open City.

(1945) and *Paisà* (1946), showed in reverse order a year apart in the early 1950s, but the concluding part, *Germany Year Zero* (1947), has never played at the cinema at all. Indeed, Vittorio De Sica's *Bicycle Thieves* (1948) only just made it before Juan Antonio Bardem's dark social realist saga, *Death of a Cyclist* (1955), brought Spanish cinema to a wider audience, along with Luis García Berlanga's astute satire, *Welcome Mr. Marshall!* (1953), which shared its neo-realist approach.

Spain's foremost director, Luis Buñuel, was in exile in Mexico at this time, but he reintroduced himself to international audiences with *Los Olvidados* (1950) and *The Adventures of Robinson Crusoe* (1954) around the middle of the decade. Akira Kurosawa became the venue's first Japanese director when *Rashomon* (1950) screened in October 1953, but a further decade elapsed before Kenji Mizoguchi and Yasujiro Ozu made their bows. Similarly, Satyajit Ray had to wait until 1963 for his debut, almost a decade after Mehboob Khan had introduced Jericho to Bollywood with *Aan* (1953) in May 1954. Films from Hungary, Poland, Brazil and China had graced the Scala screen by the end of the 1950s, by which time a new generation of filmmakers was starting to make its mark. Among them were Lindsay Anderson and Karel Reisz, two of the founders of the OFS journal *Sequence*, whose documentary, *March to Aldermaston*, screened in May 1959 and formed a link between the Free Cinema movement that had launched at the National Film Theatre in London in February 1956 and the 'kitchen sink' boom that was about to change the landscape of British cinema.

The 1960s was when The Scala became the cinema most Phoenixites would recognise. It was a golden decade, with each month's programme being strewn with future classics by emerging talents who would dominate the art house scene for the next 30 years. There were indeed gaps. Little African cinema was shown, while the Japanese *nuberu bagu*, the Third Cinema of Argentina, Bolivia and Chile, and Brazil's Cinema Novo were largely overlooked. But such was the volume of masterpieces from the various European new waves that even Oxford-educated 'angry young men' like Tony Richardson (*Look Back in Anger*, 1959), Lindsay Anderson (*This Sporting Life*, 1963) and John Schlesinger (*Billy Liar*, 1963) had to doff their caps to the new masters from France, Italy, Poland, and Czechoslovakia.

Claude Chabrol's *Les Cousins* heralded the arrival of the *nouvelle vague* in May 1960, with Alain Resnais's *Hiroshima, Mon Amour* (both 1959) introducing the Left Bank variation in October. But, while the short *Les Mistons* (1957) screened in April 1961, it wasn't until February 1963 that Scala audiences got to see their first François Truffaut feature, *Shoot the Pianist* (1960). They had to wait a further 11 months for Jean-Luc Godard's venue bow, *Le Petit Soldat* (1963), and until February 1965 for his landmark debut, *A Bout de Souffle* (1960). Indeed, a lingering commitment to the old guard and populists like Roger Vadim initially limited the opportunities for audiences to become acquainted with such other *Cahiers* alumni as Jacques Rivette and Eric Rohmer. Free spirits like Louis Malle, Agnès Varda, and Jacques Demy also had to bide their time, as did older non-*vaguers* like Georges Franju, Robert Bresson, and Jean-Pierre Melville, whose stark stylisation eschewed the jump cuts and self-reflexivity of the younger brigade. But, eventually, they all became familiar to the growing cadre of cineastes.

Although it produced its share of incipient iconoclasts like Pier Paolo Pasolini, the Second Italian Film Renaissance was led by more experienced filmmakers whose roots lay in neo-realism. Vittorio De Sica and Luchino Visconti respectively abandoned authentic snapshots of everyday life for such acerbic *commedia all'italiana* satires of sexual manners as *The Gold of Naples* (1954) and lavish costume dramas like *Death in Venice* (1971). Similarly, Federico Fellini switched to surreal swipes at the élite in *La Dolce Vita* (1960) and *8½* (1963), while Michelangelo Antonioni used the landscape to explore urban alienation in such brooding dissertations as *L'Avventura* (1960) and *The Red Desert* (1964). Yet Scala regulars were deprived of sword-and-sandal epics, spaghetti Westerns, Mafia crime dramas and gory *giallo* thrillers. Curiously, even though they saw lots of British genre cinema, they also missed out on the Hammer horrors that had been such an influence on *giallo*. However, they were treated to plenty of Carry Ons, Scotland Yard mysteries, and weightier dissections of a rapidly changing Britain by Basil Dearden, Bryan Forbes, and American *émigré* Joseph Losey, who had been blacklisted during the House UnAmerican Activities Committee investigation into Communism in postwar Hollywood. Pole Roman Polanski also eventually found sanctuary London, where he produced one of the decade's most indelibly disturbing films in *Repulsion* (1964).

Before seeking greater creative freedom abroad, Polanski had made a vital contribution to the Polish new wave with *Knife in the Water* (1962), which drew the country's first Oscar nomination. However, its leading light was Andrzej Wajda, whose war trilogy of *A Generation* (1954), *Kanal* (1956) and *Ashes and Diamonds* (1958) played regularly at The Scala during the decade, alongside subsequently neglected works by such compatriots as Jerzy Kawalerowicz, Andrzej Munk, and Jerzy Skolimowski. The latter was markedly influenced by Godard, but elsewhere behind the Iron Curtain, Milós Forman sought inspiration in Free Cinema for such droll social satires as *A Blonde in Love* (1965). By contrast, many of his peers in the Czech Film Miracle exploited the tenets of Kremlin-imposed Socialist Realism to comment upon the contemporary scene. in such wartime dramas as Ján Kadár and Elmar Klos's Oscar winner, *The Shop on the High Street*, which reached The Scala in October 1965.

Soviet cinema also produced several notable pictures about the Great Patriotic War, while the Hungarian filmmaker Miklós Jancsó delved further back into his own country's past in *The Red and the White* (1967),

which showcased his trademark long shots and long takes. An unnamed Central European country provided the setting for Ingmar Bergman's *The Silence* (1963), which completed the 'trilogy of faith' that had started with *Through a Glass Darkly* (1961) and *Winter Light* (1962). The Swede was a Scala darling at this time, along with Luis Buñuel, Jean Renoir, Akira Kurosawa, and Alfred Hitchcock. However, there was also a demand for Hollywood and European revivals, as, in this pre-video era, the cinema was often the only place to see classics that were rarely (if at all) shown on television. Such progressive programming ensured, therefore, that the days of Bs and mainstream mediocrities were gone forever.

Alfred Hitchcock.

Instead, avant-garde offerings like Adolfas Mekas's *Hallelujah the Hills* (1963) and William Klein's *Who Are You, Polly Magoo?* (1966) screened alongside documentaries reflecting the decade's radical political realities, such as Peter Watkins's *The War Game* (1965), an Oscar winner that had been commissioned and then banned by the BBC, and *Far From Vietnam* (1967), which contained contributions from some of Europe's leading *auteurs*. The first inklings of Das Neue Kino also appeared in the late 1960s, as Alexander Kluge and Volker Schlöndorff paved the way for the prolific and tragically short-lived Rainer Werner Fassbinder, as well as more enduring contemporaries like Margarethe von Trotta, Werner Herzog, and Wim Wenders. But the 1970s saw The Scala pass into new hands, change its name to Studio 1 & 2, and descend into what many consider to be its darkest days.

In June 1970, the Poyntz family ceded control of the cinema it had run with such distinction for 40 years to the Leeds-based Star Associated Holdings, whose primary business was bingo. Following a screening of Stanley Kubrick's *Spartacus* (1960) on 24 October 1970, The Scala closed its doors. They opened on the new venue with Charles Jarrott's Tudor drama *Anne of the Thousand Days* (1969) and Joseph L. Mankiewicz's comedy Western, *There Was a Crooked Man...* (1970), on 28 December. The date was apposite, as it marked the 75th anniversary of the first screening ever given to a paying audience by Louis and Auguste Lumière at the Salon Indien in

Exeter College alumnus Richard Burton starred in Anne of the Thousand Days.

the Grand Café on the Boulevard des Capucines in Paris in 1895. Any sense of this being a new dawn on Walton Street slowly dissipated as the decade progressed and it was extinguished altogether when Studio 2 was turned into the private cinema club, Studio X, in July 1976.

Austrian Franz Antel's *The Sweet Sins of Sexy Susan* (1967) had provided a hint of things to come in September 1970. But, while softcore Euro porn with titles like *Sex Is Not For Virgins* (Hans Billian, 1970), *Danish Dentist on the Job* (John Tilbard, 1971), and *Clockwork Banana* (Jean-François Davy, 1973) became a Studio staple, it also showcased directors who have since been accorded a certain cult cachet, including Pole Walerian Borowczyk, Frenchman Just Jaeckin, and Swedes Gustav

Wiklund and Torgny Wickman. American sexploitation specialists like Russ Meyer, Radley Metzger, Joseph W. Sarno, and Doris Wishman also had their adherents, while X-rated pictures like Vilgot Sjöman's *I Am Curious (Yellow)* (1967), Dušan Makavejev's *W.R.: Mysteries of the Organism* (1971), and Bernardo Bertolucci's *Last Tango in Paris* (1972) were revived regularly in future Phoenix programmes.

Notable by their absence, however, were harder core American items like Gerard Damiano's *Deep Throat* (1972), which sparked a brief vogue for date porn. Similarly, despite the scheduling of lowbrow comedies like Wolf Rilla's *Secrets of a Door-to-Door Salesman* (1973) and Jim Atkinson's *Can You Keep It Up for a Week?* (1975), there was a shortage of cheap and cheekily cheerful British smut headlined by such leading stars as Robin Askwith, Fiona Richmond, and Mary Millington. Often no more saucy than a Donald McGill postcard, these romps were only marginally ruder than movies spun off from TV sitcoms, like Harry Booth's *On the Buses* (1971).

The same year also saw the release of Ian McNaughton's *And Now for Something Completely Different* (1971), a compilation of sketches from the cult show *Monty Python's Flying Circus* that pushed British big screen comedy in an entirely new direction. Despite the continuing popularity of the polished pictures produced by Hammer, Amicus, and Tigon, British horror was also changing, as it fell under the influence of the violent Euro erotica being produced by the likes of Mario Bava and Jesús Franco, which often played at Studio 1 & 2 alongside such family favourites as Ken Hughes's *Chitty Chitty Bang Bang* (1968) and Lionel Jeffries's *The Railway Children* (1970).

The most shocking British films of the period were Stanley Kubrick's *A Clockwork Orange* and Ken Russell's *The Devils* (both 1971), which screened in October 1973 and March 1974 respectively (the latter having first endured a run-in with the British Board of Film Censors). In these years, a new brand of American cinema also reached Oxford, following the scrapping of the infamous Production Code in 1968. Finally able to tackle serious themes in an adult manner, New Hollywood filmmakers like Robert Altman, William Friedkin, and Hal Ashby were soon joined by such 'movie brats' as Francis Ford Coppola, Martin Scorsese, and Brian De Palma, who continued the trend of exposing national insecurities in the Watergate era started by such pictures as Roman

Polanski's *Chinatown* (1975) and Alan J. Pakula's *All the President's Men* (1976). However, few blockbusters by the likes of George Lucas and Steven Spielberg found their way to Walton Street. Blaxploitation similarly went elsewhere, although Ossie Davis did blaze a trail for African-American directors with *Cotton Comes to Harlem* (1970). Meanwhile, American underground filmmaking was represented most frequently by Andy Warhol and Paul Morrissey.

Despite a now-popular conception, good cinema did not disappear entirely during the Studio 1 & 2 phase. However, from the moment Charles and Kitty Cooper of Contemporary Films became the proprietors of the rebranded Phoenix Cinema on 17 July 1977, the calibre of the programming improved appreciably. Within the first couple of months, Ousmane Sembene became the venue's first sub-Saharan filmmaker with the scathing post-colonial satire *Xala* (1975), while Dariush Mehrjui anticipated the post-revolutionary Iranian New Wave with the allegorical drama, *The Cycle* (1978). New Queer Cinema also arrived in the form of Derek Jarman's *Sebastiane* (1976), a fetishised retelling of the life of a Christian martyr that was the first feature made in Latin, while welcome room was found for genuine cult classics like Chilean Alejandro Jodorowsky's trippy Western *El Topo* (1970), Belgian Harry Kümel's eerie Greek mythology saga *Malpertuis* (1971), and Italian Marco Ferreri's outrageous bourgeois satire, *La Grande bouffe* (1973).

A Yank at Oxford (1938) made its belated debut at The Phoenix in 1980.

Faced with potent competition from The Penultimate Picture Palace, The Phoenix responded with a series of themed weeks that ran sporadically throughout the 1980s. Shakespeare, literature, and opera were perennial themes, although Russian, Indian and Irish films were also showcased. Taken together with the late-night, Saturday matinee and Sunday lunchtime shows, these events significantly increased the number of pictures on offer each month. Indeed, by shuttling between Jeune and

Walton streets, it was possible to receive an unrivalled cinematic education in the early 1980s, which was soon supplemented by the advent of home video.

A conscious effort was made to lure back student cineastes and a balance was struck between subtitled films and quality American features from the likes of Woody Allen, Bob Rafelson, John Waters, and Terrence Malick. As a consequence, certain favourites began to recur on the printed monthly bulletin, among them Donald Cammell and Nicolas Roeg's Swinging London treatise *Performance* (1970), Ralph Bakshi's raunchy animation *Fritz the Cat* (1972), David Lynch's surreal debut *Eraserhead* (1977), Alex Cox's punk sci-fi comedy *Repo Man* (1984), Terry Gilliam's dystopian fantasy *Brazil* (1985), the 'cinéma de look' pairing of Luc Besson's *Subway* (1985) and Jean-Jacques Beineix's *Betty Blue* (1986), Bruce Robinson's laddish lost weekend *Withnail & I* (1987), and Giuseppe Tornatore's irresistibly romantic *Cinema Paradiso* (1988). There were also occasional epic presentations, such as Edgar Reitz's 924-minute *Heimat: A Chronicle of Germany* (1984) in July 1985 and Claude Lanzmann's 565-minute Holocaust documentary, *Shoah* (1985), in March 1987.

However, these were tough times for art-house cinemas and The Phoenix nearly became part of Menahem Golan and Yoram Globus's Cannon empire in 1984. Adventurous repertory programming was becoming an expensive luxury and a greater reliance on nationwide release schedules became apparent when, five years later, Tony Jones and Lyn Goleby secured the venue's independence under the umbrella of the newly formed City Screen. The Phoenix now began to attract some big names to introduce their films, among them Robert Altman, Danny Boyle, Jack Cardiff, Stephen Daldry, Miloš Forman, William Friedkin, James Ivory and Ismail Merchant, Patrick Keiller, Krzystof Kieslowski, Mike Leigh, Alan Parker, and Whit Stillman.

Mike Leigh at The Phoenix.
Courtesy of Martin Jennings-Wright.

Yet, while a combination of nationwide changes affecting the art-house sector in the early 1990s and a shift towards central programming later in the decade impacted undeniably upon the cinema's personality, it was still able to present features emanating from the Australian New Wave, the rise of the American independents, the emergence of the Chinese Fifth Generation, the 1980s heritage boom, the Dogma 95 manifesto, mumblecore, and the millennial new waves from Eastern Europe, Asia, Africa, and Latin America.

It may seem a little brusque to end a chapter with so many fine filmmakers still waiting in the wings, among them Peter Greenaway, David Cronenberg, Atom Egoyan, Steven Soderbergh, Joel and Ethan Coen, Spike Lee, Istvan Szábo, Raúl Ruiz, Pedro Almodóvar, Aki Kaurismäki, Ang Lee, Quentin Tarantino, Wong Kar-wai, Abbas Kiarostami, Jean-Pierre Jeunet, Sally Potter, Jane Campion, Claire Denis, Sofia Coppola, Baz Luhrmann, Michael Winterbottom, Gus Van Sant, Richard Linklater, Michael Moore, Paul Thomas Anderson, Michael Haneke, Jean-Pierre and Luc Dardenne, François Ozon, Elia Suleiman, Hayao Miyazaki, Aleksandr Sokurov, and Béla Tarr. No apology is made for including such a long list, as instant memories will be evoked by the mere mention of those who have entertained Phoenix audiences over the past 25 years. Yet there was less serendipity about their arrival on Walton Street, as every other Picturehouse had also welcomed them. This is not intended as a criticism. Oxford is very fortunate to have a cinema offering such quality and diversity and one hopes that Cineworld, which assumed control of the parent company in December 2012, will uphold the proud traditions.

'A Place Like Home' Memories of Cinemagoing at The Phoenix Picturehouse

by Daniela Treveri Gennari

Memory reclamation has gained recent popularity in Film Studies, after being neglected for many years in favour of textual and contextual analysis, and investigations into the industrial history of production, distribution, and exhibition. A new emphasis on the protagonists of cinemagoing (its audiences) has given cinema history new focuses and dimensions.

There are now many studies featuring memory work as a crucial tool for analysing the cinemagoing experience. In particular, Jackie Stacey's *Star Gazing: Hollywood Cinema and Female Spectatorship* (1994), and Annette Kuhn's investigation into British audiences in the 1930s, *An Everyday Magic: Cinema and Cultural Memory* (2002), have contributed greatly to the development of this field, which has recently generated widespread research both in Europe and in the United States.[1] Some scholars have concentrated on relatively wide geographical areas (such as a country), others on individual cities, and a handful on specific cinemas.[2]

Cinema buildings are often the element of film consumption that audiences remember the most vividly. While memories of film narratives, for instance, are often very patchy and erratic, spectators seem to have fewer difficulties with what Kuhn calls 'topographical remembering': identifying cinemas they visited 50 years earlier, describing their façades and interiors in great detail, and bringing to life the special atmosphere associated with those venues.[3]

Although several academic works concentrate on cinemas as social spaces and as focal points for memories, there remains, as scholar Glen McIver notes, a paucity of "the kind of in-depth case study (a particular cinema in a particular city) which might allow us to examine more closely the ways in which a cinema has worked in relation to people's everyday lives in the longer term."[4] (This is an imbalance he has attempted to redress through his own study of audience memories of Liverpool's Rialto cinema.) More research is needed to comprehend fully the extent to which a specific cinema may have influenced people's daily experience and contributed to a local community.

This chapter examines the role played by The Phoenix in the memories of its audiences. Although based on Kuhn's methodology for memory work in relation to cinemagoing remembrances, its empirical scope differs. Whereas Kuhn's work concentrated on memories of cinemagoing in 1930s Britain, our project has a more limited geographical location (The Phoenix in Oxford). Conversely, it has far greater historical range, as we investigate how customer memories have evolved from the 1950s to the present day. This combination of sharp topographical focus and longitudinal magnitude is unusual in this field of research, and helps to paint a picture of the importance of cinemagoing within a local community across a period of over 60 years.

This approach has limitations, of course. The memories gathered here can only provide readers with a local dimension (one which, as will be discussed later, was in many ways exceptional). Moreover, as the survey features recollections spanning more than 60 years, it can only offer a limited insight into any specific period. What it does, however, is portray a combination of local history and cinema history through the voices of the audiences. This is what film scholar Richard Maltby defines as "writing cinema history from below." It is a history "concerned not with the kings and queens of Hollywood but with their audiences and with the roles that these performances of celebrity played in the ordinary imaginations of those audiences."[5] It fosters an understanding of cinema as a social space: one which Christine Geraghty describes as being "constructed not so much through audience numbers or bricks, mortar and capital but through the physical experience of being part of a mass audience in a space specifically designed for watching films."[6]

Cinemagoing in Oxford

As a renowned international centre of academia, Oxford has attracted students from all over the world since the 11th century. Students live in the city on a temporary basis, and become the main users of many city goods and services. At the same time, its industrial framework of car manufacturing, science and technology businesses, as well as publishing companies, university education, and tourism has allowed the city to develop and provide a diverse economy to sustain its 151,900 inhabitants.[7]

Cultural life in the city has always been based on traditional arts, such as music, theatre, and literature, which are closely linked to the university world. One might argue that cinema has been comparatively neglected, and regarded a 'second-class citizen' among the arts. For instance, Film Studies was not offered as a single-honours degree subject until 2005 (at Oxford Brookes), and the city still hosts only one major film festival (the annual documentary event, OxDox). It is, nevertheless, well provided with cinema screens, and its current screen density (20 for 151,900 inhabitants) is significantly higher than the UK average of 6.1 screens per 100,000 people.[8]

Oxford's five cinemas (The Phoenix, The Ultimate Picture Palace, Odeon George Street, Odeon Magdalen Street, and Vue) have differential appeal on several levels. For one thing, many spectators make a clear distinction between the programming of blockbusters and of arthouse and international productions (a dichotomy very evident in the comments of the audiences interviewed for this project). For another, the city's status as an internationally diverse but transient location has had a profound impact on the development and significance of 'local belonging'—a feeling often associated with a venue such as a local cinema. (Many students remain in Oxford only for the duration of their studies and, during that period, are often resident in the city only during termtime, which is less than half the year.)

When analysing the data collected from Phoenix customers regarding their cinemagoing habits and experiences, both the local and global dimensions of the city will be taken into account, since both are crucial to understanding the role played by this venue within the wider history of Oxford. This approach is informed by several publications by sociologists Michael Savage, Gaynor Bagnall, and Brian Longhurst, in which they consider "the contemporary significance of local belonging [which] encapsulates [Pierre] Bourdieu's interest in how people may feel comfortable or not in any one place, relating this to the habitus and capital of its residents."[9] Their concept of 'elective belonging' (an "attachment of people to places where they have decided to live") has proved helpful when analysing the close relationship between The Phoenix Picturehouse and its audiences.[10]

The Phoenix audience

Our ethnohistorical project started in 2011. The intention was to gather memories from staff and customers at The Phoenix Picturehouse in order to construct a new history of the cinema through the voices of the interpreters of that history. Participants were recruited in a number of ways: at The Phoenix itself (by staff and volunteers), via the cinema's customer email list, through publicity in the local press, and by word of mouth. Alongside some purely qualitative forms of feedback (such as letters and interviews), 126 questionnaires were collected between January and December 2012. The questionnaire was designed to gather both quantitative and qualitative data, and the responses to it form the basis of the study presented in this chapter.[11]

The demographic breakdown of respondents skewed towards women aged 60 or above. Of those providing gender and age information, 64% were women, and 59% were over 60 at the end of 2012. This reflects a British cinemagoing pattern that dates at least as far back as the 1920s. (In the twenties, between 60% and 75% of British cinema audiences were women, and this bias continued through the 1940s and 1950s.[12] By the 2010s, the female market share had fallen to 49%, but, in the over-45 age group, women retain a majority that accords with the age distribution of survey respondents.[13]) Ages ranged from 16 to 90, with an average age of 58, and with the largest group (35%) born in the 1940s.[14] The bias towards older age groups is in line with both the overall Phoenix audience and those of UK art houses in general (compared to multiplex cinemas).[15]

The distribution of preferred cinemagoing partners reflects well-established patterns already commented on by scholars of British cinema.[16] Our respondents enjoy attending screenings with their spouse or partner (56%), friends (44%), and alone (31%), while a smaller number like to attend as a family (25%). The relatively low attendance by family groups may be partially determined by the high level of transience within Oxford's population, but also by the fact that the Phoenix programming is far less child-orientated than is that of the local multiplex cinemas. These viewing preferences are often elaborated in the freeform comments provided by questionnaire respondents.

Another finding from the data is that the majority of respondents began attending The Phoenix relatively recently, although many now characterise themselves as 'loyal' or 'regular' customers. The results show the largest group first attending between 2000 and 2012 (35%), with a fairly linear pattern of chronological decline: 1990s (21%), 1980s (17%), 1970s (7%), 1960s (14%), 1950s (7%). This doubtless reflects the transience of Oxford's population; questionnaires were collected from current customers (to the exclusion of lapsed attendees, who may have moved away from the area).

Very few survey respondents had collected and retained memorabilia from The Phoenix. (The exceptions were two who had kept old programmes and/or tickets, and one who had photos of a birthday party held there.) This might be interpreted in several ways. One is as another sign of Oxford's transitory dimension; a second is as a way to identify cinemagoing as a common practice that people don't feel the need to record through photos or objects; a third is as evidence of a widespread contemporary attitude towards memory preservation and visual images. The last of these relates to a shifting model of articulating the national past, identified by the German film scholar Thomas Elsaesser in his work on contemporary European cinema.[17]

Elsaesser argues that together with "incessant memory work done by television, through its documentary output [...], media memory is now is one of the major ways in which the nation is 'constructed,' but also spontaneously 're-lived.'" He describes television as conducting 'bottom-up' work drawn from "eyewitness accounts, personal reminiscences, family photos, home movies and other forms of period memorabilia accessible to all."[18] This full accessibility may have reduced individual desire to collect and preserve those memories now instantly accessible on television screens and online.

A sense of belonging

Christine Geraghty's study of post-war cinemagoing in Britain led her to conclude that "gazing at the screen was only one of a number of things which could be done in the cinema and it is the way in which the audiences experienced and thought about the cinematic space which interests me here."[19] Analysing freeform comments about memories of going to The Phoenix inspires exactly the same conclusion and sentiment.

Although the memories described are not always entirely accurate (as is often the case with autobiographical memories; film titles are forgotten, and a non-existent balcony remembered), they remain highly significant because they are not invented but "created at retrieval."[20] Thus, they represent an essential component in any attempt to reconstruct the historical relationship between the cinema and its patrons.

Cinema represents for its audiences a multi-space. This is a space distant from home, and yet as close to home as it could be; it is also a space representing entry into new worlds.[21] Annette Kuhn argues that for British audiences in the 1930s, cinemas represented "the very earliest ventures into the world beyond the home, close to home, almost an extension of home, and yet not home."[22] For Phoenix customers of various generations, this remains one of the most heartfelt elements of their cinemagoing memories, as the following comments illustrate.

Jeannie Bincliffe says The Phoenix "has an 'at home' feel. I love the cute bar [and] enjoy taking a cup of wine into the film." Similarly, this public space is described as having a "nice homely feel" (Theodora Hunter), feeling like "being at home" (anonymous), and even having a "lovely living room atmosphere" (Frankie McGauran). It is the only cinema that Lesley feels happy to visit alone (which implies associations with safety and homeliness), while Rita Reale, who moved to Oxford from London, describes what it meant to have found "a familiar friend in a new city."

Anton's description of his attachment to the cinema evokes several aspects of the phenomenon of 'elective belonging' cited earlier:

I arrived in Oxford totally lost and out of place, and only really felt that I had found a home after discovering The Phoenix. It became my refuge, my procrastination zone, and my pleasure dome during two degrees at Oxford (more or less 1989-2000), and has contributed significantly over the years to my repertoire of movie knowledge (I've since become a film critic). And now that I have children, Kids' Club was a Saturday staple for several years. I remember catching a late-night screening of Tetsuo II: Body Hammer *[Shin'ya Tsukamoto, Japan, 1992] there, and being gratified that Oxford catered to grindhouse as well as art-house tastes. I also really enjoyed the horror all-nighter in 2002.*

His feelings of alienation were defused by his discovery of the cinema, which not only became his place of refuge and retreat, but also provided a space for family bonding and a path for his future career. Anton's comments (like the others above) suggest that the concept of 'elective belonging' as an attachment formed to a chosen place of residence can fruitfully be extended to include a specific location that is identified as a home away from home. Savage, Bagnall, and Longhurst argue that "elective belonging is a way of dealing, at the personal level, with people's relative fixity in local routines of work, household relationships, and leisure on the one hand, and the mobility of their cultural imaginations on the other."[23] Developing a close personal (and personally publicised) tie to a cinema such as The Phoenix can help fulfil the desire many people harbour to "announce their identities" to their peers.[24]

The Phoenix Picturehouse represents, in a sense, a "chosen residential location" to which individuals have assigned their own biography, articulated through "a sense of spatial attachment, social position, and forms of connectivity to other places."[25] This sense of belonging is formulated through the cinemagoers' memories in several ways. The Phoenix Picturehouse represents a home from home for a transient population, for newcomers into the city, and even for established residents such as JoJo Goodfellow, for whom visiting is "a family affair—and one that always sparks discussion."

This sense of familiarity and belonging has, in various ways, encouraged many audience members to feel comfortable with direct participation in the programming process. Monica Payne recounts her "best ever memory" of The Phoenix:

> *When my children were small we used to bring them to Kids' Club on a Sat-*
> *urday afternoon. On one occasion my husband and I wanted to see a film next*
> *door but it finished after Kids' Club. No problem. They put on an extra cartoon*
> *for kids so we would be ready and waiting for them after our film.*

This account of her unusual experience illustrates how customers' feelings of affinity with the cinema (which extend far beyond self-identity as mere spectators) have helped to dissolve traditional boundaries between the business operation and its patrons.

Such feelings of belonging are closely connected with both the cinema environment and the range of films on offer. As well as feeling personally 'at home' in the physical space of the building, many audience members consider The Phoenix the natural home for certain types of film, which they regard as their ideal cohabitants. Arthur's comments illustrate this notion:

> *It represents a more special experience than the standard multiplex, some-*
> *thing more personal than a typical conveyor-belt cinema. It shows that the inde-*
> *pendent / cult / downright strange movies still have a place to call home, and that*
> *should never change. David Lynch's* Lost Highway *in 1997. The Phoenix was*
> *the perfect setting to see this masterpiece (a small, dark cinema, very 'Lynch'),*
> *the film seemed to 'belong' there. I went along with a friend, and we spent the*
> *next week discussing our theories of what the hell it was we had seen and "what it*
> *all meant," and we were so mesmerised by it the first time, we had to go back and*
> *watch it again… and it was just as stunning the second time. It was undoubtedly*
> *the most powerful cinema experience I've ever had, and I think the cinema in*
> *which we saw it played a huge part in that experience.*

His detailed account makes palpable his own feelings of belonging, and also gives an insight into The Phoenix's unique identity—one that emerges from, and is perpetuated by, the memories of its audiences. His conviction that his experience of an exceptional film was enhanced by the location in which it was viewed partakes of a recurrent theme in the memories collected.

Experiences of cinemagoing are also associated with the marking of important moments in people's lives. Birthday parties; courtship rituals; the first cinema visit with a spouse—these are all moments audiences remember far more vividly than film titles or plots. Roy Kennedy comments on how nice it was to attend a "small, intimate cinema" to celebrate a family birthday. Steve Rolfe remembers marking his own 40th birthday with a private screening of *It's a Wonderful Life* (Frank Capra, US, 1946) in a venue that he loved for its "handmade" feel. It was, he says, "a wonderful evening." Catherine Hilliard still recalls that on her first date with her husband, back in 1963, they watched *The Trouble with Harry* (Alfred Hitchcock, US, 1955).

Kathy describes more fully the magnitude of what The Phoenix has come to represent for her and her husband.

In chatting to my husband as I write this, we realise that The Phoenix has always been a part of our relationship as, when we met 20 years ago, it was the place we shared our love of foreign and art-house film—and are still doing this now! The first film we watched that really made a mark was Orlando *[Sally Potter, UK, 1992]... and we still talk about that now. I remember coming out and rushing into Freud's for a late-night hot chocolate, brimming over with thoughts about the film and getting his 'take' on it! Every time we go now, I guess it always feels very special—partly because it was central to the early years of our relationship, and where a good proportion of 'dates' took place!*

Her sense of belonging remains undiminished by the various changes that have taken place over the past 20 years.

Well, the arrival of popcorn for starters! But we forgive them for that. The bar upstairs is a welcome addition too. We also like the live screenings of theatre, operas and ballet. I went with my son to see the first of these, Phèdre, *which was particularly special. The push towards some mainstream blockbuster films stacks up commercially, so I can see why they do that. However, I feel they continue to retain their authenticity as a little independent cinema. I just hope they hang on to this with the Cineworld buyout.*

As well as showing how closely The Phoenix is associated with landmark moments in Kathy's past, her account illustrates its ongoing place in her family life. Moreover, as the cinema has played such a big role in Kathy's relationship with her husband across a 20-year period, she feels, like many Phoenix regulars, entitled to comment on various aspects of its development. Changes to the kinds of films and food provided, the introduction of satellite events, and Cineworld's recent acquisition of the Picturehouse group, are all issues she feels comfortable discussing as belonging to her own life as much as the cinema's.

Other audience members feel, like Kathy, that they have earned the authority to pass comment on changes at The Phoenix, and single out specific developments, which they usually characterise as positive or negative. Their remarks, like so many others in this survey, often arise from an apparent sense of belonging. Several voice their opinions of changes to the facilities, which have, Scott Ellis believes, "improved a lot since the 1990s." Thiru cites "improvements to the toilets and bar area" during the same period, while Diana S. agrees "the bar has changed—for the good," but suggests that "toilets could do with re-vamping." Theodora Hunter, who remembers the bar from the start, thinks it not only looks better now, but that it also serves a better choice of wines, while Claire and Birnie appreciate the addition of the bar as it is "good for rendezvous with friends."

Many long-standing customers have shared memories of how different The Phoenix was in the past. First-hand recollections of how it used to be provide an indispensable resource for researchers hoping to capture the atmosphere of its bygone days. For instance, the frequent and fond recall of the pre-1970 double seating in the back row emphasises the importance of the cinemagoing experience in the courting process.[26] Susanna Pressel remembers it as being "very romantic—and a little bit embarrassing at first." Margaret and Harry Charlton recall that in their university days they would arrive early in the hope of securing a double seat. When commenting on her fondest memories of The Phoenix, Dianna Marsh avers that, even today, her 75-year-old husband will only go with her if they can have a back row seat.

Despite the popularity of the double seats, another recurrent theme is the erstwhile deficiencies of the cinema as a physical space. Sue Bateman remembers getting bitten by fleas in the 1960s, an anonymous respondent recalls a visit in 1957 when "I sat by an old radiator emitting an unbearable amount of steaming heat!" and Mike H. remembers "the horrendously uncomfortable early seats, the horrible smell of popcorn, and the somewhat sweaty smell of the 11.00 p.m. shows." A refurbished lobby, more comfortable seats, better facilities for the disabled, and other improvements to the building have all inspired favourable comments about the current ambience.

Memories of The Phoenix are often marked by a potent sense of nostalgia (which is quite usual in this kind of retrospection), and which stretches to an apparent affection for the cinema's historical shortcomings as well as its strengths. Elisabeth Salisbury's encounter with a rat in the late 1950s did not prevent her from becoming one of the venue's most loyal and long-term customers; after moving away from the area, she spent 38 years travelling from Reading in order to continue watching films at The Phoenix. This level of commitment indicates that, for her, it has always been more than just a cinema.

Others have commented on the cinema's local role, and the extent to which The Phoenix "is now part of the community" (Susanna Pressel), "a great asset to the community" (anonymous), and a "key element in [the] cultural life of North Oxford" (anonymous). This impression appears to work on two levels. On the one hand, it is regarded as contributing to the general facilities of the Jericho area; Susanna Pressel writes, "as a local councillor, I particularly appreciate the way you cater for older residents." On the other hand, it acts as the hub of a more specific, self-selected community of cineastes.

This brings us back to the sense of elective belonging that emerges from the memories and comments of many Phoenix audience members. Mrs. Biggar remarks, "I like the cinema because intelligent film people come here. We like to sit and watch the credits to see who has been involved, and we like that other people do that too at this cinema— not like The Odeon." Val says she and her partner "have become total converts to the Phoenix ethos and come often." Indeed, not only is The Phoenix the first choice for many customers; for some it is the only choice. For Anais, it is "the only cinema we will come to—for its special atmosphere and the quality of the programming." Another (anonymous) respondent concurs: "it is the only cinema I go to in Oxford—if the film is not on at PH I don't go!"

One of the topics that crops up most often in the questionnaire responses is the film programming. Phoenix customers tend to fit a profile that John Sedgwick, a professor of film economics, labels "selective filmgoers." In his research into film consumer decision-making, Sedgwick identifies a group of spectators whose choices arise from a close attention to a film's specific qualities, and who don't always follow word of mouth. He contrasts them with other groups, "including those who consumed films on a purely habitual basis, those attracted by the ambience of the film-going experience, rather than the particular film being shown, and those who attended the cinema with companions who chose the film to be viewed."[27]

Although Phoenix customers report various motivations for their attendance and film choices, their memories and comments show a significant leaning towards foreign films, which feature regularly in the list of memorable films cited. Alongside "foreign films" in general, French, German, Italian, Spanish, and South American cinemas have all been singled out for praise in terms of their collective outputs. Films from France, Sweden and the Soviet Union (as well as from the UK) received the most citations from audience members who started attending in the 1950s and 1960s (*The Seventh Seal* getting the most mentions). There is a notable increase in the number of American films (a mix of mainstream, independent, and classic) mentioned by newer attendees, but films made in more recent years also hail from a wider range of locations. As well as the aforementioned countries, these include Austria, Canada, Denmark, Ireland, Japan, Lebanon, Mongolia, New Zealand, and Palestine.

This conforms to a well-known pattern dating back to the 1950s, when "the established middle class rejected Hollywood and espoused European 'quality films.'"[28] Films such as *Orphée* and *The Wages of Fear* made a great impression on audiences, especially during the 1950s and 1960s when they were less readily available in cinemas outside London than they are now. Rosemary Pountney recalls that before moving to Oxford in 1965 "I had never lived in a city where foreign films were shown and often went to The Scala at least twice a week [...] I remember being especially struck by *Wild Strawberries* and *The Seventh Seal*— where the final scene remains vivid in my memory."

Even among viewers who discovered foreign films in later years, considerable passion is evident. Sara (who started attending in the 1980s) remembers that "as a teenager, moody French films had a big impact on me!" Jeffery Miller (a Phoenix customer since the early 1990s) says, "the best memories are of watching foreign films [...] The French/Spanish etc. films are almost always an enigma waiting to be revealed."

Will observes that, "For a long time The Phoenix has been pretty much the only place in Oxford you could see old films, or foreign-language films without having to go to London or the UPP off the Cowley Road." Moreover, what helps bring these films alive from an audience point of view is the programming of events, Q&As, special editions, and director's cuts that are rarely, if ever, available in other cinemas. Barbara enjoyed a French cinema season with talks beforehand; Will's fondest memory is of watching *Blade Runner* for the first time on the big screen, as it has been his favourite film for years:

This was a quite worn-looking director's cut of the film, before they digitally remastered it, but it still looked amazing. I went to see DR Hood's Wreckers *[UK, 2011] at The Phoenix and stayed for the Q&A session with the director after the film, which was really interesting. I found out a bit about the process of developing an idea into a screenplay and then turning that into a script, along with what it was like to actually make the film.*

By scheduling special events tailor-made for its audiences, The Phoenix has created a community of regular spectators who can be defined as selective (according to John Sedgwick's conception) but who also put trust in the Phoenix programming choices, because a close relationship with the cinema has been developed over time. Such trust is amply illustrated by a comment from Jeffrey Miller: "we both remember the Spanish *Red Squirrel* [Julio Medem, 1993] of years ago. Not many films resonate as much as those unexpected surprises."

Whenever patrons believe this trust has not been fulfilled, or that the cinema is moving in an unexpected direction, difficulties emerge. For this reason, several customers feel entitled to express negative judgements about recent programming changes. Sara thinks there are "more annoying adverts now," as well as "less world cinema," and advises the Phoenix management that it "doesn't seem necessary to programme mainstream films that are also showing at Odeon and Vue." Catherine Hilliard believes "the programming went through a boring patch some years ago when it was showing too many mainstream releases. I think there are still too many of these, but the art-house proportion has increased," although she would still like to see more German films. Michael became so concerned about the absence of world cinema titles from the schedule that he created a blog page to raise awareness of the issue.

I get the impression that the kind of films I want to see (mainly Spanish and French-language films, also Arabic, German, rest of the world) are gradually disappearing from the programme, as quite a few of them no longer get UK releases. Some, including recent releases Where Do We Go Now? *[Nadine Labaki, France/Lebanon, 2011] and* 7 Days in Havana *[Various, France/ Spain, 2012] get only shown once or twice. When [Julio] Medem's* Room in Rome *[Spain, 2010] failed to show up I started a list of films not shown in the UK, which has grown quite long, unfortunately.*[29]

Such an active interest in programming shows another facet of the sense of belonging so many Phoenix customers evidently feel. Discussing which films should be screened is another way of engaging with a community whose members do not see themselves as passive viewers, and who show interest in every aspect of the business. This is why Kathy, for instance, expresses anxiety about how the sale to Cineworld might affect the cinema's future.

This level of audience participation (which goes far beyond such communal experiences as applause at the end of a film—a moment Ellie remembers vividly) cannot be reduced to a tendency to find fault. Their remarks signal a positive desire to take ownership of a space where the cosy atmosphere, and the pleasures of choosing from a range of world cinema titles, makes the experience of attending The Phoenix Picturehouse far more than just entertainment.

Conclusions

How typical is the cinemagoing experience at The Phoenix? Does the Phoenix audience differ from the general cinema audience in contemporary Britain? Is its audience typical within a broader context of the British film industry? Cinema historian Nicholas Hiley's suspicion that it is difficult (if not impossible) to identify a typical audience, a typical performance, or a typical venue is certainly to be borne in mind in this small study.[30] However, what this project has shown is similarities with other research findings, alongside certain differences that seem to relate to particular features of Oxford as a city and, even more strongly, with The Phoenix as a specific venue.

Localism and transience, town and gown, are expressed through personal memories that participate in the construction of a broader social history of the city. Moreover, life landmarks (whether related to family, career, study, or leisure) are closely associated with memories of cinemagoing—an activity of great importance in many people's lives.

Annette Kuhn's argument that past visits to the cinema tend to be "remembered as both daring and safe" accords well with the experiences described by Phoenix audiences.[31] Their collective memories demonstrate its function as a non-domestic space where patrons feel comfortable and at home, but which also permits experimentation in the choice of films viewed. As Glen McIver suggests, it is "important to recognise the interplay between the cultural offer" embodied in the site and "the way in which this [is] intertwined with people's own actions, their social performances, within the site."[32] In helping to develop an appreciation of just how far the interweaving of cinemagoing memories with broader personal narratives contributes to the development of both social and cultural heritage, the case of The Phoenix provides a fascinating example of how location, space, and programming combine to shape the special relationship between a cinema and its audience.

Celebrating The Phoenix

by Phoenix Customers

In concluding our celebration of 100 years of The Phoenix, it seems only right to give the final word to its customers, both old and new, without whom neither the cinema nor this book would exist. The reminiscences and observations reproduced below are deeply personal, but speak also of common experience. Although we're disappointed that space has not allowed us to reproduce each and every one of the letters, emails, and questionnaires submitted, we think (and certainly hope) this small sample goes some way towards capturing the spirit of this much-loved local institution, and the ways people feel about it.

For many local residents, The Phoenix is a comfortable home from home, and also serves as a space in which to pursue romance, bond with family members, or socialise with friends, while also offering a gratifying dose of nostalgia to regular visitors from further afield. Films seen at The Phoenix (or The Scala, in earlier days) have been an important part of the growing-up process for children and undergraduates alike, and are widely credited with expanding personal horizons. The opportunity to experience a vast array of international film productions, both classic and contemporary, is celebrated as an escape from the routines of everyday life, as well as a chance to absorb new critical perspectives that can help us negotiate the world in which we live.

Through the course of the past century, the cinema on Walton Street has been many things to many people, and their viewing choices have shaped all that The Phoenix has been and is today. We'd like to say a great big 'thank you' to all Scala, Studio, and Phoenix customers, and especially to all those who have helped with this book project. Here's to the next 100 years!

Alexa: *Going to The Phoenix contributed a lot to make me love living in Oxford. I moved to England about a year ago. On my second night in England I came to The Phoenix to watch* Never Let Me Go *[Mark Romanek, UK/US, 2010] with my husband. It was a wonderful night.*

Dianna Marsh: *I moved to Oxford in 1981 from the North of England and knew no one. The Phoenix has always been warm and welcoming. To me it* IS *Oxford.*

Rita Reale: *We moved from East London to Jericho in 2008. In London we either went to The Picturehouse in Stratford or The Rio in Dalston. The Phoenix in Jericho was like a familiar friend in a new city when we first got to Oxford. I love going to The Phoenix Cinema (sometimes with our ten-year-old daughter who is an avid cinema fan; sometimes with my partner) so that we can spend some rare quality time together and disappear temporarily from our quotidian lives into a land of fantasy, escape and entertainment of film and sometimes live opera. I also like the friendly staff, who see us kindly into the cinema experience with a friendly smile or a few warm words. And then there is the wonderful bar upstairs where I sometimes sit—simply just to be, and to again feel far away from daily worries. I realise now that The Phoenix is for me a place of necessary sanctuary.*

Robin Jacoby: *I first came to The Scala as an undergraduate in 1961. I saw all sorts of memorable films here, including the best I have ever seen:* Black Orpheus *[Marcel Camus, Brazil, 1959]. I spent more happy hours here as a student than anywhere else in Oxford.*

Kyna Morgan: *I first visited England as a teenager and saw my first film at The Phoenix:* The Madness of King George *[Nicholas Hytner, UK, 1994], which was a good film, although I longed to go see my idol Gus Van Sant's* My Own Private Idaho *[US, 1991], as the cinema was screening the film in hon-*

our of the late River Phoenix who passed away a few months before. I attended a doc fest there a few years back, saw [Ken] Loach's The Wind that Shakes the Barley *[Ireland/UK, 2006] with my mother, and remember going with a friend and squeezing into a fully packed house during a screening of* The Seventh Seal *right after the news of Ingmar Bergman's death. It's such a great theatre, and has now become even greater for me personally considering its long history! I haven't been to Oxford in a few years, but whenever I visit, I always go for at least one show at The Phoenix in Jericho.*

Karin André: *Always a great atmosphere: arty, world cinema, fabulous cosy bar, and friendly staff. Why would you go anywhere else? As a member, I have been to free previews on Sunday mornings—perfect Sun a.m. time! I LOVE The Phoenix.*

Anon: *My earliest memory [of this cinema] is coming to The Scala to see* Last Year at Marienbad *[Alain Resnais, France/Italy, 1961] in the late sixties and being completely baffled! My husband jokes that it is the close proximity of my house to The Phoenix that persuaded him to propose to me!*

Patrick Moles: *My first memory of The Phoenix in 1970 is of trying to meet two girls there that I knew, to see* Anne of the Thousand Days *[Charles Jarrott, US, 1969], and being solemnly shown to a seat one row back from them in an almost empty cinema by a female usherette with a torch. I tried to take my wife to The Phoenix on our first date in 1972 to see* Butch Cassidy and the Sundance Kid *[George Roy Hill, US, 1969] but found a long queue and a full house and so had to go to the ABC in Gloucester Green to see* Asylum *[Roy Ward Baker, UK, 1972] and Steven Spielberg's* Duel *[US, 1971] instead.*

Marriage and a young family reduced my visits in subsequent years but I still visit occasionally and in recent years have viewed Downfall *[Oliver Hirschbiegel, Germany, 2004] as well as* Che Part One *and* Che Part Two *[Steven Soderbergh, France/Spain/US, 2008] which I found very moving. I also enjoyed a re-showing of* Army of Shadows *[Jean-Pierre Melville, France/Italy, 1969] a couple of years ago, which is a good example of French tongue in cheek black humour and a good tribute to the World War Two role of La Resistance.*

Martin Jennings: *In 1977, while I was a student at the university, I took a part-time job behind the counter selling sweets, drinks and hot dogs. I remember that, when cashing up at the end of the evening, I could never balance the till. When I'd made extra cash I ate my way through the difference, but was always having my pay docked when I made a loss. Having finished my shift, I could go and watch the play-through of the next day's films alone in the auditorium. These were always in reels and were played in no particular order. I remember being rather baffled by* The Canterbury Tales *[Pier Paolo Pasolini, Italy/France, 1972] after watching the final reel, followed by the middle reel, followed by the beginning.*

I returned to Oxford in the 1980s and brought up a family here. Taking my children to cinemas in the centre of town, with their wallet-busting prices for popcorn and water, and their tacky-underfoot auditoria, is invariably a rebarbative experience wholly in contrast to the dependable pleasures of being at The Phoenix. I've enjoyed three decades of film here. I love The Phoenix. Long may it thrive.

Adder: *The first time I came here was with a friend, John. We were undergraduates at Oxford, and he had fallen in love with Olivia Hussey as Juliet in [Franco] Zeffirelli's* Romeo and Juliet *[UK/Italy, 1968]. He came every night and sobbed and wept and swooned and lamented for weeks afterwards. I told him to grow up, and when he finally did he became a hugely successful and uncompromising capitalist in the Thatcher era. He married someone lovely and very unlike Olivia Hussey, and lives in a huge house in Dorset. He grows asparagus and recently fell off his horse again. He retains no amorous feelings for Juliet, or Shakespeare. I love him dearly.*

Denis Kane: *I first went to The Phoenix when it was The Scala and I was eight years old. I then went nearly every week from eight years to about sixteen years of age. Watching movies from John Wayne movies to Polanski and Bergman had a great impact on my cultural and visual sense.*

Jane Lavender Brown: *Well, The Phoenix just gets better. There is real effort to work out what various audiences' needs are. My need to avoid blockbusters and to see interesting non-mainstream films is amply met. I can't keep up with all that's on offer. I love the variety. Someone is working very hard behind the scenes to get good films.*

Philip Pullman: *I have been going to the Phoenix regularly for several years on Sunday evenings in the company of some friends—we call ourselves jokingly 'the film club.'*

But I remember the cinema from much further back than that. I saw The Blair Witch Project *[Daniel Myrick and Eduardo Sánchez, US, 1999] there and came out blinking and feeling nauseous, because of all the shaky handheld camera work. (I had the same experience with the 'film club' when we saw* The Hurt Locker *[Kathryn Bigelow, US, 2008].) When I was an undergraduate over forty years ago I am almost certain it was at the Phoenix that I saw the Japanese film* Hara-Kiri *[Masaki Kobayashi, 1962], and came out disgusted and horrified. Our 'film club' comes to see whatever is on, and sometimes we come with excitement and pleasure (as we did recently with* The Artist *[Michel Hazanavicius, France, 2011]) and sometimes with reluctance, when we are almost certain we don't want to see the film, but we feel we should keep up the habit. And we are often surprised and delighted with something that we'd never have chosen to go to normally, such as Paddy Considine's* Tyrannosaur *[UK, 2011] last year, which we all thought a magnificent film. So was Steven Fechter's* The Woodsman *[Nicole Kassell, US, 2004]. And we hugely enjoyed the documentary about the ukulele which was on more recently [*The Mighty Uke *(Tony Coleman, Canada, 2010)]—another film we'd have been most unlikely to choose to go and see, and which turned out to be delightful.*

A Mackrell: *Coming to visit The Phoenix plays an important role in my life. A number of movies have made a big impact on me and my life. There are so many, and I have learnt so many life lessons from movies here, from* Life in a Day *[Various: US/UK, 2011], reminding me that we all have the same joy, pain and similar life experiences the world over, to* Little White Lies *[Guillaume Canet, France, 2010], which was a multi-relationship roller-coaster that took me through ALL the emotions! Coming to watch movies here restores and reminds me of the beauty of life and the faith in humankind! Thank you!*

Anon: *All really good films provide a fresh perspective on old themes or introduce new ones (same as good books): metaphor, myth, fable, parody, etc. They add to the narrative of all the themes of life, and aid navigation through it. I love this place.*

William Goodfellow: *The friendly atmosphere hasn't changed at all since I started visiting. The films that have had the most profound impact on me are the European ones—for example,* Let the Right One In *[Tomas Alfredson, Sweden, 2008]* and The Girl with the Dragon Tattoo *[Niels Arden Oplev, Sweden, 2009]. I also enjoy documentaries such as* Bombay Beach *[Alma Har'el, US, 2011],* Into the Abyss *[Werner Herzog, US, 2001], and* Exit Through the Gift Shop *[Banksy, US/UK, 2010]. Coming to the cinema is a great way to relieve the stress of the week and to forget about schoolwork.*

Anon: *My father parted from my mother when I was aged eight, and fled to the suburban comfort of the Rutherway estate, newly built on the grave of Lucy's Ironworks. Every weekend, my sister and I were handed over, like prisoners at Checkpoint Charlie, and my dad was left with the dilemma of how to entertain the two blighters he thought he'd got away from. The answer was almost always cinema.*

The led to my first experience of The Phoenix when I was twelve, on a wet Sunday afternoon in 2002. My dad had booked us to see Nicholas Nickleby *[Douglas McGrath, UK/US, 2002] (starring Charlie Hunnam, Anne Hathaway and Christopher Plummer). I threw a wobbly because I wanted to see* Spider-Man *[Sam Raimi, US, 2002] at the George Street Odeon instead, and my sister would rather be anywhere else. I remember very little about what I thought of the cinema; I just remember the movie stank. We shuffled out afterwards, back into the Walton Street gloom, and feigned interest in what we had just seen to appease my dad.*

Eight years pass before I darken the cinema doors again. In the summer of 2009, I am now working for the blasted George Street Odeon, the cathedral where I once worshipped false idols, except now I am its slave—cleaning the nozzles of the fizzy pop dispensers; stopping teens from fornicating on the back row of Hannah Montana *[Peter Chelsom, US, 2009]; and most of all taking complaints from customers about how thoroughly migraine inducing the 3D is. I still liked watching films, but I'd be damned if I'd do it at the place where I had to work a double shift during the first week of* Harry Potter and the Half-Blood Prince *[David Yates, UK/US, 2009].*

Thus, I found my love of The Phoenix when I went to see Andrea Arnold's dark and streetwise masterpiece Fish Tank *[UK, 2009]. I had read about the film's lead Katie Jarvis having no prior acting experience, and being cast purely off when one of the casting directors saw her arguing with her boyfriend in a train station. I had to see this for myself. Not only did I love the film (Michael Fassbender's best performance to date), but I loved this other world that lay upon* my doorstep: the welcoming staff; the comfortable, evenly spaced seats; the fact I could buy a beer with my salted popcorn (a god-created combination) and both served in sensible portions.

Since Fish Tank, *the glories I have lived in The Phoenix have been many. Being the only person in a screening of* Where the Wild Things Are *[Spike Jonze, US, 2009]; falling in love with Carey Mulligan in* An Education *[Lone Scherfig, UK, 2009]; and being reduced to a quivering wreck by Phillippe Lioret's immigration drama* Welcome *[France, 2009], to name but several. The Phoenix taught me to fall in love with film again, and for that I am eternally in the big blue building's debt. Thank you.*

The Phoenix in 2012. Photograph by Sam Clements.

Notes

Introduction

1. All customer comments and recollections are drawn from questionnaire responses or letters and emails to the project team, unless otherwise noted.
2. *Sydney Morning Herald*, "Graham Greene was Wrong about Shirley Temple, 9," 13 January 1982, 5.

Chapter One

1. St John's College Oxford, "History of St John's," www.sjc.ox.ac.uk/390/History-of-St-John%27s.html (accessed 15 April 2012).
2. Malcolm Graham, "The Suburbs of Victorian Oxford: Growth in a Pre-Industrial City" (PhD diss., University of Leicester, 1985), https://lra.le.ac.uk/jspui/bitstream/2381/8427/3/1985Grahammphd.pdf.txt (accessed 27 October 2012).
3. St John's College Lease Ledger, file EST I.A.30, St John's College Archive, Oxford.
4. Oxford City Council, *Jericho Conservation Area Designation Study* (Oxford: Oxford City Council, 2010), 24.
5. St John's College Lease Ledger.
6. St John's College Lease Ledger.
7. St John's College Lease Ledger.
8. *Touch Local*, "M. J. Soden & Son," www.touchoxford.com/business/list/bid/1327958 (accessed 27 October 2012).
9. Paul J. Marriott, *Early Oxford Picture Palaces* (Oxford: Paul J. Marriott, 1978), 20; St. John's College Lease Ledger.

10.   Marriott, *Early Oxford Picture Palaces*, 20.

11.   St John's College Lease Ledger.

12.   *London Gazette*, 21 July 1882, 3443; *London Gazette*, 30 April 1929, 2891.

13.   *London Gazette*, 10 December 1909, 9452; *London Gazette*, 11 July 1919, 8890; Hubert Lionel Wood, *The Changing Scene* (2002), www.bodley. ox.ac.uk/external/hlw/hlw04.htm (accessed 27 October 2012).

14.   *Oxford Times*, "Fatal Accident in Wychwood Forest," 29 March 1902, 8.

15.   Marriott, *Early Oxford Picture Palaces*, 20.

16.   St John's College Lease Ledger; Licenses 22 May 1920 and 30 July 1920, file EST I.A.30, St John's College Archive.

17.   *Wikipedia*, "Cyril Beeson," http://en.wikipedia.org/wiki/Cyril_Beeson (accessed 23 March 2013).

18.   *St John's College Notes*, 1947, 5.

19.   Marriott, *Early Oxford Picture Palaces*, 20.

20.   Mortgage document, 1 July 1925, Oxfordshire History Centre.

21.   Linn Harmer, email to Deborah Allison, 22 April 2012.

22.   David Parkinson, *Oxford at the Movies* (P.Inks Books, 2003), 76.

23.   *Oxford Journal Illustrated*, "Oxford's Latest Picture Palace," 12 February 1913.

24.   Syd Taylor, "My Interest in Cinema," n.d., Taylor Family private collection.

25.   *Oxford Times*, 22 March 1913.

26.   Brian Hornsey, *Ninety Years of Cinema in Oxford* (Mercia Cinema Society, 1995), 21.

27.   Syd Taylor, letter to Michael Maguire, 3 May 1995, Taylor Family private collection.

28.   *Oxford Times*, 31 May 1913, 16.

29.   Marriott, *Early Oxford Picture Palaces*, 20.

30.   Taylor, letter to Maguire.

31.   Syd Taylor, letter to Mr. Hughes, 19 May 1993, Taylor Family private collection.

32.   Taylor, "My Interest in Cinema."

33.   Syd Taylor, letter to Mr. and Mrs. Holloway, 25 October 1976, Taylor Family private collection. Circumstantial evidence leads us to speculate that the Bull to whom Taylor refers may be Reginald Fred Bull, born in Banbury in 1893.

34.   Taylor, letter to Holloways.

35. Taylor, "My Interest in Cinema." As *The Scarlet Runner* was not released in the USA until October 1916, it is unlikely to have appeared at the North Oxford Kinema before that date. It therefore seems probable that Mr. Taylor's visits began a year or so later than he believed, or that he watched it some time after his first visit.

36. Syd Taylor, letter to Ena Baga, 31 October 1983, Taylor Family private collection.

37. Taylor, letter to Holloways. A recording of 'The Winning Fight,' written by Abe Holzmann in 1911, can be listened to at www.youtube.com/watch?v=Eiw5Le_RD70 (accessed 23 March 2013).

38. Taylor, letter to Holloways.

39. Taylor, "My Interest in Cinema."

40. Syd Taylor, letter to Mr. Chapman, n.d., Taylor Family private collection.

41. Taylor, "My Interest in Cinema."

42. Taylor, letter to Chapman.

43. Taylor, "My Interest in Cinema."

44. Marriott, *Early Oxford Picture Palaces*, 23.

45. Syd Taylor, letter to Mr. and Mrs. Fisher, 8 July 1980, Taylor Family private collection.

46. Taylor, "My Interest in Cinema."

47. Taylor, letter to Fishers.

48. Hiu M. Chan, *100 Years at the Phoenix: Archive of an Oxford Cinema 1913-2013* (Oxford: Oxfordfolio, 2013), 12-13.

49. David Parker, email to Deborah Allison, 21 March 2012.

50. Julie Parker, email to Ian Meyrick, 22 April 2008.

51. David Parker, email to Deborah Allison, 5 August 2013.

52. Taylor, "My Interest in Cinema."

53. St John's College Lease Ledger.

54. John R. Poole, *A Coronation and a Century* (1937), 3, 5-8.

55. All quotations from Genevieve Poole are drawn from emails to Deborah Allison, 25 February-22 August 2013.

56. Hudson John Powell, *Poole's Myriorama* (Bradford on Avon: ELSP, 2002), 123-24, 139-40.

57. Scala, advertisement, *Oxford Times*, 23 April 1920, 5.

58. Scala, advertisement, *Oxford Times*, 8 June 1923, 4; *Oxford Times*, 25 May 1923, 4.

59. *Kinematograph Year Book* 1923 (London: Kinematograph Publications, n.d.), 388.

60. Poole, *A Coronation*, 15.

61. *Oxford Times*, "North Oxford Scala," 23 April 1930, 16.

62. Taylor, "My Interest in Cinema."

63. Scala, advertisement, *Oxford Times*, 23 April 1920, 5.

64. Scala, advertisement, *Oxford Times*, 16 April 1920, 5.

65. Scott Eyman, *Lion of Hollywood: The Life and Legend of Louis B. Mayer* (New York: Simon & Schuster, 2005), 52.

66. Taylor, "My Interest in Cinema."

67. Jeremy Leon Stein, "Ideology and the Telephone: The Social Reception of a Technology, London 1867-1920" (PhD diss., University College London, 1996), 150.

68. Powell, *Poole's Myriorama*, 146. The date of ownership transfer is uncertain, but changes in the style of cinema advertisements in *The Oxford Times* suggest it to have been during or after June 1923.

69. *London Gazette*, 21 April 1925, 2734.

70. Taylor, "My Interest in Cinema."

71. Taylor, letter to Maguire.

72. *London Gazette*, 21 April 1925, 2734; *London Gazette*, 28 April 1925, 2898.

73. New Scala, advertisement, *Oxford Times*, 11 September 1925, 5.

74. Brass Plaque for Ben Jay Head Office, Peter Jay private collection.

75. Peter Jay, "Jaywalking" (extract from manuscript of forthcoming book).

76. Stephen Peart, *The Picturehouse in East Anglia* (Lavenham: Terence Dalton, 1980), 74.

77. Jay, "Jaywalking."

78. New Scala, advertisement, *Oxford Times*, 11 September 1925, 5.

79. All quotations from Martin Selwood are drawn from an interview by Deborah Allison, 26 September 2012.

80. Anthony Wood, "Dim the Lights and Let's Run the Old Reels," *Oxford Mail*, 26 October 1977.

81. Taylor, "My Interest in Cinema."

82. Wood, "Dim the Lights."

83. Taylor, "My Interest in Cinema."

84. Taylor, letter to Chapman.

85. Wood, "Dim the Lights."

86. Taylor, letter to Baga, 31 October 1983.

87. Marriott, *Early Oxford Picture Palaces*, 23. This 'quotation' appears to have been constructed from bullet points appended to Taylor, "My Interest in Cinema."

88. Wood, "Dim the Lights."

89. Taylor, letter to Chapman.

90. Marriott, *Early Oxford Picture Palaces*, 23-24.
91. Taylor, letter to Chapman.
92. Wood, "Dim the Lights."
93. Taylor, "My Interest in Cinema."
94. *Kinematograph Year Book* 1928 (London: Kinematograph publications, n.d.), 450.
95. Taylor, "My Interest in Cinema."
96. Scala, advertisement, *Oxford Times*, 6 January 1928, 3.
97. Scala, advertisement, *Oxford Times*, 25 October 1929, 5.
98. St John's College Lease Ledger.

Chapter Two

1. Peter Cowie (ed.), *The International Film Guide 1966* (London: Tantivy Press, 1965), 269.
2. All quotations from Martin Selwood are drawn from an interview by Deborah Allison, 26 September 2012.
3. Ann Cole, Phoenix Centenary reminiscence group led by Colin Clarke at Oxford Brookes University, 5 September 2012, and interview by Deborah Allison, 30 June 2013.
4. *Times* (London), 28 May, 1930, 5.
5. Anthony Wood, "Dim the Lights and Let's Run the Old Reels," *Oxford Mail*, 26 October 1977.
6. Roger Manvell, *Film* (Penguin: Harmondsworth 1944), 199.
7. All quotations from Oxford Film Society ephemera are drawn from materials held in the Oxford Film Society Collection, British Film Institute Special Collections, London (unless specified otherwise).
8. Scala, Hilary Term programme 1937, Ian Meyrick private collection.
9. Scala, Hilary Term programme 1938, Ian Meyrick private collection.
10. Hans-Michael Bock and Tim Bergfelder (eds.), *The Concise Cinegraph: Encyclopedia of German Cinema* (New York: Berghahn Books, 2009), 460.
11. *Jewish Chronicle*, 15 December 1939, 22.
12. *Jewish Chronicle*, 16 January 1942, 22.
13. A 1939 letterhead lists E. F. Bowtell as Secretary to The Scala. John Poyntz, letter to Ronald Hart-Synnot, n.d. [October 1939], file EST I.N.B.7, St John's College Archive.
14. Timothy Gee, email to Phoenix Memories, 12 September 2012, and interview by Deborah Allison, 31 December 2012.

15. E. A. Roberts, letter to Ronald Hart-Synnot, 9 January 1933, file EST I.N.B.7, St John's College Archive.

16. Ronald Hart-Synnot, letter to E. A. Roberts, 10 January 1933, file EST I.N.B.7, St John's College Archive.

17. E. A. Roberts, letter to Ronald Hart-Synnot, 11 January 1933; Ronald Hart-Synnot, letter to E. A. Roberts, 18 January 1933, both file EST I.N.B.7, St John's College Archive.

18. Ronald Hart-Synnot, "Notes of Interview with Mr. Poyntz 8.10.1934. re Scala Cinema. Walton Street," file EST I.N.B.7, St John's College Archive. The £50,000 figure cited seems remarkably high, and we wonder whether it should read £5,000.

19. Frank Matcham Society, "Frank Matcham 1854-1920," www.frankmatchamsociety.org.uk/matcham.html (accessed 29 March 2013).

20. Oxford Playhouse, "Oxford Playhouse: An Introduction," www.oxfordplayhouse.com/anniversary/ourhistory.html (accessed 29 March 2013).

21. Frederick Chancellor, letter to John Poyntz, 16 June 1939, file EST I.N.B.7, St John's College Archive.

22. Ronald Hart-Synnot, letter to John R. Poyntz, 30 June 1939, file EST I.N.B.7, St John's College Archive.

23. Office of Morrell, Peel & Gamlen, letter to Ronald Hart-Synnot, file EST I.N.B.7, St John's College Archive.

24. Ronald Hart-Synnot, letter to John R. Poyntz, 25 September 1939, file EST I.N.B.7, St John's College Archive.

25. John Poyntz, letter to Ronald Hart-Synnot, n.d, file EST I.N.B.7, St John's College Archive.

26. Stephanie Jenkins, email to Rootsweb online forum, http://archiver.rootsweb.ancestry.com/th/read/OXFORDSHIRE/2002-10/1033590951 (accessed 29 March 2013); Ian Meyrick, *Oxfordshire Cinemas* (Stroud: Tempus Publishing, 2007), p.102.

27. Charlotte Breeze, *Hutch* (London: Bloomsbury, 1999), 162.

28. Scala, advertisement, *Oxford Times*, 13 October 1939.

29. Cole, Centenary reminiscence group, and interview by Allison.

30. Jim Wright, Centenary reminiscence group, and interview by Deborah Allison, 2 August 2012.

31. Jim Tallett, Centenary reminiscence group.

32. Richard Asser, "Cheek to Cheek – Letter," *Times* (London), 21 November 1996, 23.

33. Gee, email to Phoenix Memories, and interview by Allison.

34. June Parker, Centenary reminiscence group.

35. Wright, Tallett, and Cole, Centenary reminiscence group.

36. Gee, interview by Allison.

37. *London Gazette*, 5 March, 1963, 2077; Wales Census (1911), http://search. ancestry.co.uk/cgi-bin/sse.dll?gl=35&gsfn=John&gsln= Pontichill&gss=angs-d (accessed 6 January 2013); London Gazette, 5 March 1965, 2368.

38. *London Gazette*, 8 April 1966, 4188.

39. *London Gazette*, 18 February 1969, 1857.

40. Wright, interview by Allison.

41. Ian Meyrick, interview by Deborah Allison, 30 June 2013.

42. *Oxford Mail*, "Carry On, Scala," 24 June 1970.

43. Michael Robinson, interview by Deborah Allison, 3 March 2013.

44. Judy Brown, interview by Deborah Allison, 24 February 2013.

Chapter Three

1. Ian Meyrick, interview by Deborah Allison, 30 June 2013.

2. Brian Hornsey, *Star Cinemas: Britain's Leading Independent Cinema Circuit* (Stamford, Lincs.: Fuchsiaprint, 2002), 2, 9, 4.

3. *Daily Express*, "Man with Faith Puts in £300,000," 30 July 1958, 5.

4. Francis Boyd, "Verdict on the Bingo Age," Guardian (London), 19 December 1962, http://century.guardian.co.uk/1960-1969/ Story/0,,105545,00.html (accessed 19 January 2013).

5. Boyd, "Verdict on the Bingo Age."

6. Hornsey, *Star Cinemas*, 4, 6.

7. Star Associated Holdings Ltd., "Managerial Opportunities," *Daily Express*, 31 November 1964, 8.

8. *Financial Times*, "ABC Dropping Bingo to Expand its Cinema Chain," *Financial Times*, 13 May 1969, 10.

9. Peter Waymark, "Cinema: Back in Twos and Threes," *Times*, 19 December 1970, 10.

10. Hornsey, *Star Cinemas*, 7.

11. Meyrick, interview by Allison.

12. Star Group of Companies, "Studio 1 & 2," *Oxford Times*, 1 January 1971.

13. Ron Nicholson, email to Deborah Allison, 9 May 2012.

14. Alan North, email to Deborah Allison, 16 May 2012.

15. All quotations from Mike Vickers are drawn from an interview by Deborah Allison, 26 September 2012.

16. All quotations from Bob Ord are drawn from his series of emails to Phoenix Memories and Deborah Allison, 29 February-27 April 2012.

17. *Oxford Mail*, "All You Need," 15 October 1975.

18. Peter Bradley, "Studios One and Two," *Oxford Times*, 9 July 1976.

19. *Times* (London), "Brothers are Jailed for Income Tax Fraud," 26 July 1975, 4.

20. *Times* (London), "Law on Bingo was 'Disregarded'," 30 August 1961, 5.

21. *Times* (London), "EMI Bingo Expansion," 11 February 1975, 18.

22. *London Gazette*, 11 March 1975, 3338.

23. *London Gazette*, 11 July 1975, 8941.

Chapter Four

1. Contemporary Films, "Company Profile," www.contemporaryfilms.com/profile/profile.html (accessed 29 March 2013).

2. Charles Cooper, "Friends of The Phoenix," (draft of speech delivered at Phoenix Cinema on 28 April 1985), Kitty Cooper private collection.

3. All quotations from Kitty Cooper are drawn from interviews by Deborah Allison, 24 January and 11 May 2012.

4. Ivor F. Martin FSVA, "Opinion and Report: Studio Cinema Complex, Walton Street, Oxford, " 14 October 1976, Kitty Cooper private collection.

5 All quotations from David Powell are drawn from an interview by Deborah Allison, 15 May 2012.

6. Hiu M. Chan, *100 Years at the Phoenix: Archive of an Oxford Cinema 1913-2013* (Oxford: Oxfordfolio, 2013).

7. Dave Richardson, "Club Still Rules, OK, at Phoenix," *Oxford Star*, 27 November 1980.

8. Richardson, "Club Still Rules."

9. Cinema Exhibitors' Association, "UK Cinema – Annual Admissions 1935-2012," www.cinemauk.org.uk/facts-and-figures/admissions/annual-uk-cinema-admissions-1935-2012 (accessed 14 April 2013).

10. David Docherty, David Morrison, and Michael Tracey, *The Last Picture Show? Britain's Changing Film Audiences* (London: BFI, 1987), 38, 62.

11. Docherty, Morrison, and Tracey, *The Last Picture Show?* 55.

12. David Abbott, "A Graphical History of Current UK Cinema Circuits," 2006, www.cinematopia.co.uk/circuits/circuits_20061008.pdf (accessed 14 April 2013).

13. All quotations from Tony Jones are drawn from an interview by Deborah Allison, 31 July 2012 (unless specified otherwise).

14. David Boyle, "Cinema To Be Sold," *Oxford Star*, 11 October 1984, 3.

15. John Macgrath, "Busker Bids to Buy up Cinema, " *Oxford Star*, 6 December 1984.

16. Jonathan Flint, interview by Hiu M. Chan, August 2012.

17. *Oxford Star*, "Phoenix Reborn!" 28 February 1985.

18. All quotations from John Hughes are drawn from an interview by Deborah Allison, 4 December 2012.

19. *Oxford Star*, "Cinema Saved," 13 December 1984, 9.

20. *Oxford Star*, "Cinema Saved," 9; Phoenix Cinema, Friends of the Phoenix application form (1985), private collection.

21. Phoenix Cinema, Friends of the Phoenix application form (1985), private collection.

22. Phoenix Cinema, Friends application form; Charles Cooper, "Friends of The Phoenix."

Chapter Five

1. All quotations from Lyn Goleby are drawn from an interview by Deborah Allison, 29 February 2012.

2. All quotations from Tony Jones are drawn from an interview by Deborah Allison, 31 July 2012.

3. All quotations from Alastair Oatey are drawn from an interview by Deborah Allison, 13 July 2012.

4. All quotations from John Hughes are drawn from an interview by Deborah Allison, 4 December 2012.

5. Sharon Woodward, email to Phoenix Memories, 17 June 2012.

6. Suzy Sheriff, email to Deborah Allison, 28 February 2012.

7. Phoenix Picturehouse, "The Phoenix Picturehouse Junior Friends' Club June 1996 – April 1997," 1997, Picturehouse Cinemas private collection.

8. Ian Christie, "The Phoenix Cinema and Film Studies at Oxford University," 6 November 1998, Picturehouse Cinemas private collection.

9. All quotations from Clare Binns are drawn from an interview by Deborah Allison, 7 June 2013.

10. All quotations from Mike Warner are drawn from an interview by Hiu M. Chan, 6 February 2012.

11. All quotations from Marc Allenby are drawn from an interview by Deborah Allison, 17 July 2012.

12.   Peter Schofield, "The Met in HD: Phoenix Picturehouse," *Peter Schofield's Reviews* (online blog), http://peterschofieldsreviews.weebly.com/the-met-in-hd.html (accessed 7 July 2013).

13.   Schofield, "The Met in HD: Phoenix Picturehouse."

14.   Cineworld, "Cineworld Group plc Announces Acquisition of Picturehouse," news release, 6 December 2012.

15.   All quotations from Steve Wiener are drawn from an interview by Deborah Allison, 20 June 2013.

16.   Picturehouse Cinemas, "Business as Usual," www.picturehouses.co.uk/businessasusual (accessed 7 July 2013).

17.   Phoenix Picturehouse (PhoenixPH), Twitter feed, 6 December 2012, https://twitter.com/PhoenixPH (accessed 7 July 2013).

18.   Fran Bardsley, "Cinema Proposal is a Reel Love Story," *Oxford Mail*, 1 February 2012. Richard Smith's video proposal can be watched at www.youtube.com/watch?v=Z8a0dok1U54 (accessed 7 July 2013).

'A Place Like Home'

1.   Jackie Stacey, *Star Gazing: Hollywood Cinema and Female Spectatorship* (London: Routledge, 1994); Annette Kuhn, *An Everyday Magic: Cinema and Cultural Memory* (London: I. B. Tauris, 2002). See also Robert C. Allen, "From Exhibition to Reception: Reflections on the Audience in Film History," *Screen* 31, no. 4 (Winter 1990), 347-56; Daniël Biltereyst, Philippe Meers and Liesbeth Van de Vijver, "Social Class, Experiences of Distinction and Cinema in Postwar Ghent," in *Explorations in New Cinema History: Approaches and Case Studies*, ed. Richard Maltby, Daniël Biltereyst and Phillipe Meers (Malden: Wiley-Blackwell, 2011), 101-24; Marc Jancovich and Lucy Faire with Sarah Stubbings, *The Place of the Audience: Cultural Geographies of Film Consumption* (London: BFI, 2003); Jo Labanyi, "Cinema and the Mediation of Everyday Life in 1940s and 1950s Spain," *New Readings* 8 (2007), 539-53.

2.   For an example of a national study see Peter Miskell, *A Social History of the Cinema in Wales 1918-1951: Pulpits, Coal Pits and Fleapits* (Cardiff: University of Wales Press, 2006). For examples of city studies see Terry Lindvall, "Sundays in Norfolk: Towards a Protestant Utopia Through Film Exhibition in Norfolk, Virginia, 1910-1020" in *Going to the Movies: Hollywood and the Social Experience of Cinema*, ed. Richard Maltby, Melvyn Stokes and Robert C. Allen (Exeter: University of Exeter Press, 2007; Margaret O'Brien and Allen Eyles, eds., *Enter the Dream-House: Memories*

of Cinemas in South London from the Twenties to the Sixties (London: BFI, 1993); Helen Richards, "'Something To Look Forward To': Memory Work on the Treasured Memories of Cinema Going in Bridgend, South Wales," *Scope*, November 2004, www.scope.nottingham.ac.uk/article. php?issue=nov2004&id=253&section=article; John Sedgwick and Michael Pokorny, "Film Consumer Decision-Making: The Philadelphia Story, 1935-36," *Journal of Consumer Culture* 12, no. 3 (November 2012), 323-46; Joanne Lacey, "Seeing Through Happiness: Hollywood Musicals and the Construction of the American Dream in Liverpool in the 1950s," *Journal of Popular British Cinema* 2 (1999), 54-65; Daniël Biltereyst, Kathleen Lotze and Philippe Meers, "Triangulation in Historical Audience Research: Reflections and Experiences from a Multi-Methodological Research Project on Cinema Audiences in Flanders," *Participations* 9, no. 2 (November 2012), 690-715, www.participations.org/Volume%209/Issue%202/ 37%20Biltereyst_Lotze_Meers.pdf. For an example of a specific cinema study see Glen McIver: "Liverpool's Rialto: Remembering the Romance," *Participations* 6, no. 2 (November 2009), 199-218, www.participations. org/Volume%206/Issue%202/special/mciver.htm (all online articles accessed 22 June 2013).

3. Kuhn, *An Everyday Magic*, 28.
4. McIver: "Liverpool's Rialto."
5. Richard Maltby, "On the Process of Writing Cinema History from Below," *Tijdschrift voor Mediageschiedenis* 9, no. 2 (2006), 85.
6. Christine Geraghty, "Cinema as a Social Space: Understanding Cinema-Going in Britain, 1947-63," *Framework* 42 (2000), www.frameworkonline. com/Issue42/42cg.html (accessed 22 June 2013).
7. Oxford City Council, "Population Statistics," www.oxford.gov.uk/ PageRender/decC/Population_statistics_occw.htm (accessed 22 June 2013).
8. British Film Institute, *Statistical Yearbook 2012* (London: BFI, 2012), 97.
9. Mike Savage, Gaynor Bagnall, and Brian J. Longhurst, *Globalization and Belonging* (London: Sage, 2005), 11.
10. Savage, Bagnall, and Longhurst, *Globalization*, 53. See also Brian Longhurst, *Cultural Change and Ordinary Life* (Maidenhead: Open University Press, 2007).
11. The questionnaires included these core questions: 1) When did you start visiting The Phoenix? 2) With whom do you normally come to The Phoenix? 3) Please tell us your memories of The Phoenix. (For instance: Has the building, programming, or atmosphere changed much since your

first visit? Have any particular films or events made a profound impact on you, and why? What role does coming to the cinema play in your life?). Year of birth was an optional question.

12. Nicholas Hiley, "'Let's Go to the Pictures': The British Cinema Audience in the 1920s and 1930s," *Journal of Popular British Cinema* 2 (1999), 47; Sarah Street, *British Cinema in Documents* (London: Routledge, 2000), 124; Stacey, *Star Gazing*, 83.

13. Cinema Exhibitors' Association, "Audience by Age and Gender," www.cinemauk.org.uk/facts-and-figures/uk-cinema-audience-analysis/uk-cinema-audience-by-age-and-gender (accessed 22 June 2013).

14. Birth dates of respondents (where given) is as follows: 1920s: 1%; 1930s: 15%; 1940s: 35%; 1950s: 15%; 1960s: 16%; 1970s: 8%; 1980s: 6%; 1990s: 4%.

15. Pearl & Dean, "Audience Profile," http://business.pearlanddean.com/audience_profile (accessed 26 August 2013).

16. See, for instance, Annette Kuhn, "'I Wanted Life to be Romantic, and I Wanted to be Thin': Girls Growing Up with Cinema in the 1930s," in *Reclaiming the Archive: Feminism and Film History*, ed. Vicki Callahan (Detroit: Wayne State University Press, 2010), 58-73; Christine Geraghty, *British Cinema in the Fifties: Gender, Genre and the 'New Look'* (London: Routledge, 2000).

17. Thomas Elsaesser, *European Cinema: Face to Face with Hollywood* (Amsterdam: Amsterdam University Press, 2005), 74-75.

18. Elsaesser, *European Cinema*, 75.

19. Geraghty, "Cinema as a Social Space."

20. David C. Rubin, ed., *Remembering Our Past: Studies in Autobiographical Memory* (Cambridge: Cambridge University Press, 1999), 4.

21. Kuhn, *An Everyday Magic*, 146.

22. Kuhn, *An Everyday Magic*, 36.

23. Savage, Bagnall, and Longhurst, *Globalization*, 208.

24. Savage, Bagnall, and Longhurst, *Globalization*, 207.

25. Savage, Bagnall, and Longhurst, *Globalization*, 29, 27.

26. See also Kuhn, *An Everyday Magic*, 145.

27. Sedgwick and Pokorny, "Film Consumer Decision-Making," 329.

28. Sue Harper and Vincent Porter, "Cinema Audience Tastes is 1950s Britain," *Journal of Popular British Cinema* 2 (1999), 69.

29. Michael, "Movies We're Not Allowed to See," *Prose and Passion* (online blog), 19 September 2010, http://proseandpassion.blogspot.co.uk/2010/09/movies-were-not-allowed-to-see.html (accessed 22 June 2013).

30. Hiley, "'Let's Go to the Pictures,'" 39.
31. Kuhn, *An Everyday Magic*, 36.
32. McIver, "Liverpool's Rialto."

About the Authors

Deborah Allison, leader of the Phoenix Centenary Project, has worked in the cinema industry since 1990, and has been a programmer for Picturehouse Cinemas since 2005. She holds a doctorate in Film Studies from the University of East Anglia, and is an associate research fellow at De Montfort University's Cinema and Television History Research Centre. Her writing has appeared in more than a dozen books and journals, including *Film International*, *Film Quarterly*, *Senses of Cinema*, *Screen*, *Scope*, and *The Schirmer Encyclopaedia of Film*. Her monograph *The Cinema of Michael Winterbottom* was published by Lexington Books in 2012.

Hiu M. Chan is a PhD candidate in Film and Cultural Studies at Cardiff University. She worked at The Phoenix Picturehouse from 2008 before moving to Cardiff in September 2013. As part of the Phoenix Centenary Project, she compiled a film archive with the assistance of students Sean Kelly and Leyla Richardson. The archive is currently being displayed in the cinema's bar. Her research interests are many, but mainly focus on Chinese cinema, jazz in movies, film history and film theory. She is the guest editor of the *Soundtrack* journal special issue 'Jazz and Cinema.' Meanwhile, she carries multiple identities while being a full-time dreamer.

Daniela Treveri Gennari is Reader in Film Studies at Oxford Brookes University. Her research has been published in several journals and edited volumes as well as in her monograph *Post-War Italian Cinema: American*

Intervention, Vatican Interests (New York: Routledge, 2008). Daniela is currently leading a major AHRC-funded project, *In Search of Italian Cinema Audiences in the 1950s: Gender, Genre and National Identity*, in collaboration with the Universities of Bristol and Exeter. She has recently been working on a project on spectatorship in post-war Rome as part of her successful British Academy Mid-Career Fellowship.

David Parkinson is a film critic and historian. In addition to being a contributing editor at *Empire*, he also reviews for *Radio Times, The Oxford Times* and *MovieMail*. He edited *Mornings in the Dark: The Graham Greene Film Reader* and is the author of *The Bloomsbury Good Movie Guide, The Young Oxford Book of Cinema, Oxford at the Movies, The Rough Guide to Film Musicals, 100 Ideas That Changed Film,* and *History of Film*, which is now its second edition. His happy association with The Phoenix dates back to 1979 and he now programmes the monthly *Parky's Pic* slot.